Open Universities:
A British Tradition?

SRHE and Open University Press Imprint
General Editor: Heather Eggins

Michael Allen: *The Goals of Universities*
Sir Christopher Ball and Heather Eggins: *Higher Education into the 1990s*
Ronald Barnett: *Improving Higher Education*
Ronald Barnett: *Learning to Effect*
Ronald Barnett: *The Idea of Higher Education*
Tony Becher: *Academic Tribes and Territories*
Robert Bell and Malcolm Tight: *Open Universities: A British Tradition?*
Robert Berdahl *et al.*: *Quality and Access in Higher Education*
Hazel Bines and David Watson: *Developing Professional Education*
William Birch: *The Challenge to Higher Education*
David Boud *et al.*: *Teaching in Laboratories*
John Earwaker: *Helping and Supporting Students*
Heather Eggins: *Restructuring Higher Education*
Colin Evans: *Language People*
Gavin J. Fairbairn and Christopher Winch: *Reading, Writing and Reasoning: A Guide for Students*
Oliver Fulton: *Access and Institutional Change*
Derek Gardiner: *The Anatomy of Supervision*
Gunnar Handal and Per Lauvås: *Promoting Reflective Teaching*
Vivien Hodgson *et al.*: *Beyond Distance Teaching, Towards Open Learning*
Jill Johnes and Jim Taylor: *Performance Indicators in Higher Education*
Margaret Kinnell: *The Learning Experiences of Overseas Students*
Peter Linklater: *Education and the World of Work*
Ian McNay: *Visions of Post-compulsory Education*
Graeme Moodie: *Standards and Criteria in Higher Education*
John Pratt and Suzanne Silverman: *Responding to Constraint*
Kjell Raaheim *et al.*: *Helping Students to Learn*
John Radford and David Rose: *A Liberal Science*
Marjorie Reeves: *The Crisis in Higher Education*
John T. E. Richardson *et al.*: *Student Learning*
Derek Robbins: *The Rise of Independent Study*
Tom Schuller: *The Future of Higher Education*
Geoffrey Squires: *First Degree*
Ted Tapper and Brian Salter: *Oxford, Cambridge and the Changing Idea of the University*
Gordon Taylor *et al.*: *Literacy by Degrees*
Kim Thomas: *Gender and Subject in Higher Education*
Malcolm Tight: *Academic Freedom and Responsibility*
Malcolm Tight: *Higher Education: A Part-time Perspective*
David Warner and Charles Leonard: *The Income Generation Handbook*
Susan Warner Weil and Ian McGill: *Making Sense of Experiential Learning*
David Watson: *Managing the Modular Course*
Thomas G. Whiston and Roger L. Geiger: *Research and Higher Education*
Gareth Williams: *Changing Patterns of Finance in Higher Education*
Alan Woodley *et al.*: *Choosing to Learn*
Peter W. G. Wright: *Industry and Higher Education*
John Wyatt: *Commitment to Higher Education*

Open Universities:
A British Tradition?

Robert Bell and
Malcolm Tight

The Society for Research into Higher Education
& Open University Press

Published by SRHE and
Open University Press
Celtic Court
22 Ballmoor
Buckingham
MK18 1XW

and

1900 Frost Road, Suite 101
Bristol, PA 19007, USA

First Published 1993

A catalogue record of this book is available from the British Library

ISBN 0 335 19126 6 (hb)

Library of Congress Cataloging-in-Publication Data

Bell, Robert E., 1930–
    Open universities: a British tradition?/Robert Bell and Malcolm
    Tight.
        p.   cm.
    Includes bibliographical references and index.
    ISBN 0–335–19126–6
    1. Distance education – Great Britain – History.   2. University
extension – Great Britain – History.   3. Correspondence schools and
courses – Great Britain – History.   I. Tight, Malcolm.   II. Title.
LC5808.G7B45   1993
378′.03 – dc20   93–36208
                                                                     CIP

Typeset by Type Study, Scarborough
Printed in Great Britain by St Edmundsbury Press Ltd
Bury St Edmunds, Suffolk

For Joy and Marjatta

Contents

List of Abbreviations

APEL	assessment of prior experiential learning
APL	assessment of prior learning
BA	Bachelor of Arts
BComm	Bachelor of Commerce
BD	Bachelor of Divinity
BEd	Bachelor of Education
BMus	Bachelor of Music
BS	Bachelor of Surgery
BSc	Bachelor of Science
BSc(Econ)	Bachelor of Science (Economics)
CAT	college of advanced technology
CNAA	Council for National Academic Awards
DipHE	Diploma in Higher Education
DipTech	Diploma in Technology
DLitt	Doctor of Literature
DMus	Doctor of Music
DSc	Doctor of Science
LA/LLA	Licentiate in Arts
LLB	Bachelor of Laws
LLD	Doctor of Laws
MA	Master of Arts
MB	Bachelor of Medicine
MBA	Master of Business Administration
MD	Doctor of Medicine
MS	Master of Surgery
MSc	Master of Science
MSC	Manpower Services Commission
NALGO	National Association of Local Government Officers
NCTA	National Council for Technological Awards
NEC	National Extension College
PhD	Doctor of Philosophy
RUIC	Royal University of Ireland, *Calendar*

RUISCM	Royal University of Ireland, Standing Committee, *Minutes*
RUISM	Royal University of Ireland, Senate, *Minutes*
UCC	University Correspondence College
ULASESAR	University of London, Advisory Service for External Students, *Annual Report*
ULC	University of London, *Calendar*
ULCDBAR	University of London, Commerce Degree Bureau, *Annual Report*
ULCESM	University of London, Council (or Committee) for External Students, *Minutes*
ULSM	University of London, Senate, *Minutes*
USALECM	University of St Andrews, Local Examinations Committee, *Minutes*
USALLACM	University of St Andrews, LLA Committee, *Minutes*

Acknowledgements

We would particularly like to acknowledge the help we received from the archivists at London University, the National University of Ireland, and St Andrews University; and from the Secretary for External Students of the University of London.

Acknowledgements

1
Open-ness, Distance and Higher Education

The idea of an open university is commonly thought of, at least in Britain, as being a modern invention; an idea which, until very recently, has been of relatively marginal significance. Nothing could be further from the truth. A number of models of British 'open universities' have been extant during the last two centuries, and their provision has had an enormous impact, extending educational opportunities to hundreds of thousands of people who could not make use of more 'conventional' courses.

The most important British open university model during this period, from its foundation in 1836 as a distance examining system up until the present day, has been the University of London (see Chapters 3, 6 and 7). This is, of course, not the only function that the University of London has pursued, but it has been a particularly significant one. Hundreds of colleges, polytechnics and schools, as well as thousands of private students and tutors, both in Britain and overseas, have been associated at various times with the University. Dozens of these institutions have subsequently become universities in their own right, while the London model has in addition served as a pattern for a series of new university foundations.

Many other British higher education institutions have also functioned, at least in part, as open universities during the last two centuries. Both the Royal University of Ireland (see Chapter 4) and the University of St Andrews (Chapter 5) operated extensive distance examining systems – in the latter case specifically for women – in a somewhat similar fashion to the University of London. The university extension movement which galvanized English adult education in the late nineteenth century, and the more general open-ness of access practised by the mid-nineteenth century Scottish universities, offer two further models (see Chapter 2).

Much more recently, of course, the Open University and other providers of open learning have appeared on the scene (see Chapter 8). Viewed in their proper historical context, these latest examples can be seen as part of a continuing and developing pattern rather than as major innovations, as they have raised much the same concerns and faced much the same problems as their predecessors.

This, broadly, is our field of study: the history of open universities in

Britain during the last two centuries. Our aim in producing this book is not, however, to attempt to say the last word on the subject, but to offer a structure for further historical study in a neglected area.

It seems appropriate to begin by briefly exploring the meanings of a number of key terms, and by indicating the limits which we have set on the scope of this study. Taking the title of this chapter as a guide, there appear to be three main issues which require immediate discussion: the notion of open-ness, the nature of distance education, and the meaning of higher education.

Open-ness and open learning

While the practice of 'open-ness' – that is to say, the adoption of measures to encourage widespread access to and participation in education – by universities and other educational institutions is, contrary to received wisdom, of long standing, its encapsulation in a general philosophy of 'open learning' appears to be a relatively recent development. The reasons underlying the creation of this concept will be discussed further in Chapter 8. For present purposes we should, however, note that the meaning and application of the term is being fiercely debated (see, for example, Boot and Hodgson 1987; Rumble 1989; Lewis 1990).

Of the many attempted definitions of 'open learning' which have been put forward during the last decade, the following two are not untypical:

> 'Open learning' is a term used to describe courses flexibly designed to meet individual requirements. It is often applied to provision which tries to remove barriers that prevent attendances at more traditional courses, but it also suggests a learner-centred philosophy. Open-learning courses may be offered in a learning centre of some kind or most of the activity may be carried out away from such a centre (e.g. at home). In nearly every case specially prepared or adapted materials are necessary.
>
> (Lewis and Spencer 1986: 9–10)

> Open learning is merely one of the most recent manifestations of a gradual trend towards the democratisation of education. The use of the term 'open' admits that education and learning have traditionally been 'closed' by various barriers – entrance requirements, time constraints, financial demands, geographical distances, and, much more subtly, social and cultural barriers, as well as those of gender. An open learning institution is one dedicated to helping individuals overcome these barriers to their further education. Our primary interest here is in open universities, institutions which provide open admission to adult students and, through flexible policies and a variety of delivery mechanisms, notably distance education, provide access to

and success in university education to those previously denied such opportunity.

(Paul 1990: 42)

Both of the authors quoted fall into the common trap of seeing the practice (as distinct from the nomenclature) of open learning as a recent development, to be contrasted favourably with a 'traditional' and 'closed' approach. This is both a gross simplification and a myth; and one which this book seeks to demolish. The notions of open-ness and democratization have been around and practised in education (in different ways and in different contexts) since at least the time of ancient Greece, and probably ever since education as such existed. Lewis's definition may also be faulted for putting too much emphasis on specially prepared materials, which are not essential.

Both definitions characterize open learning as being about the removal of barriers. These barriers can be classified broadly into three groups:

1. Physical/temporal: those restricting the time, place and pace at which learning may be undertaken.
2. Individual/social: those to do with the characteristics of individual learners (such as age, sex, ethnicity, class and wealth).
3. Learning: those to do with the nature of the learning provided (such as content, structure, delivery, accreditation and flexibility).

By implication and contrast, open educational institutions are in the business not just of removing some or all of these barriers, but also of adopting and presenting positive, outgoing and involving attitudes, practices and images to the community at large.

It would be foolish, of course, to imagine that any one educational institution or provider could realistically attempt to be wholly open in all of these ways. Most of those who see themselves as being involved in open learning have focused their open-ness on a particular group or set of characteristics. In reality, therefore, we can see all educational providers as operating somewhere along a spectrum or continuum between 'open-ness' and 'closure', with their position determined by their response to the who, why, what, how, where and when questions of study (Lewis 1986).

The quotation from Paul is particularly apposite in the present context, since it specifically deals with the notion of 'open universities'. Paul sees the key characteristics of open universities, and here we would agree with him, as having to do with flexibility in admitting students and in delivering learning opportunities to them. He, like Lewis, emphasizes the important role played by distance education, in enabling open learning, through addressing the first of the three groups of barriers identified.

Though many of the institutional examples which are discussed in this book have employed elements of distance education – or, at least, of its precursor, correspondence education – to open up their provision, it is important not to overemphasize the role of distance education in an understanding of the idea of open universities. The British open universities examined in Chapters 3 to 8 have all made extensive use of distance learning techniques, and this has been critically important for their success. But they have also sought to be open in a variety of other ways: in their admissions practices, in the characteristics of the students recruited, in the content and structure of the courses offered. And these other approaches to open-ness have been pursued by other institutions, both historically (as discussed in Chapter 2) and more recently (see Chapter 8), without adopting distance teaching methods.

It is quite clear that the naming, and the recency of the establishment, of the British Open University has resulted in an understandable confusion between the two terms 'distance education' and 'open learning'. The latter is, however, a much more general and all-encompassing concept; while distance education represents only one way, though an important and prevalent way, of enabling greater open-ness.

Distance education

The last two decades have witnessed an international upsurge of research in distance education, in part encouraged by the creation of the Open University, with a concomitant development of both theoretical work (for example, Perraton 1987) and comparative analyses of alternative systems (for example, Kaye and Rumble 1981; Rumble and Harry 1982; Rumble 1986). As part of this process a number of authors – notably Bååth, Garrison, Holmberg, Keegan, Moore and Peters – have attempted to define distance education and suggest areas for further study within this field. Their definitions have built on practice and reflect the different backgrounds and experience of the researchers concerned.

Holmberg, for example, building on the notion of distance education as a guided didactic conversation (Holmberg 1983), has offered the following definition of the field:

> Distance education comprises one-way traffic by means of printed, broadcast and/or recorded presentations of learning matter and two-way traffic between students and their supporting organisation. The one-way presentation of learning matter occurs either through self-contained courses or through study guides to prescribed or recommended reading. Most of the two-way traffic usually occurs in writing, on the telephone or by other media and, usually only secondarily or as a supplement, face to face.
>
> (Holmberg 1986a: 2)

This seems to be a very precise definition, but it is also restrictive. It appears, in fact, to be based firmly on the contemporary practices of a limited number of institutions.

Keegan, another widely quoted authority, starts his analysis from an

explicit recognition of the range of different concepts and practices which
have been drawn together under the banner of distance education:

> 'Distance education' is a generic term that includes the range of
> teaching/learning strategies referred to as 'correspondence education'
> or 'correspondence study' at further education level in the United
> Kingdom; as 'home study' at further education level and 'independent
> study' at higher educational level in the United States; as 'external
> studies' in Australia; and as 'distance teaching' or 'teaching at a
> distance' by the Open University of the United Kingdom. In French
> it is referred to as 'télé-enseignement'; 'Fernstudium/Fernunterricht'
> in German'; 'educación a distancia' in Spanish and 'teleducacâo' in
> Portuguese.
>
> (Keegan 1986: 31)

Having reviewed the other research in this field, Keegan concludes by
defining distance education in terms of five characteristics and two
'socio-cultural determinants':

> Distance education is a form of education characterised by:
>
> - the quasi-permanent separation of teacher and learner throughout
>   the length of the learning process; this distinguishes it from
>   face-to-face education.
> - the influence of an educational organisation both in the planning
>   and preparation of learning materials and in the provision of
>   student support services; this distinguishes it from private study and
>   teach-yourself programmes.
> - the use of technical media; print, audio, video or computer, to unite
>   teacher and learner and carry the content of the course.
> - the provision of two-way communication so that the student may
>   benefit from or even initiate dialogue; this distinguishes it from
>   other uses of technology in education.
> - the quasi-permanent absence of the learning group throughout the
>   length of the learning process so that people are usually taught as
>   individuals and not in groups, with the possibility of occasional
>   meetings for both didactic and socialisation purposes.
>
> . . . In addition there are two socio-cultural determinants which are
> both necessary pre-conditions and necessary consequences of distance
> education. These are:
>
> - the presence of more industrialised features than in conventional
>   oral education.
> - the privatisation of institutional learning.
>
> (ibid.: 49–50)

Keegan's definition is more comprehensive than Holmberg's and it has
been the subject of widespread discussion, criticism and amendment
(Keegan 1980, 1989; Bååth 1981). Some have criticized Keegan's adoption

of Peters' ideas regarding distance education as an industrialized form of education (Peters 1965, 1983, 1989; Garrison and Shale 1990). Some have seen distance education as involving a more general reconstruction of the time–space relations linking educational institutions and learners (Evans and Nation 1992). Others have sought instead to identify within distance education key dimensions such as communication, dialogue, structure, autonomy, independence and control (Moore 1973, 1977, 1990; Garrison and Baynton 1989). Some, misguidedly in our view, have even gone so far as to assert that distance education has established itself as a separate academic discipline (Holmberg 1986b; Tight 1988a).

A few of the more perceptive writers in this field have attempted to inject a note of much needed realism into these debates by arguing that distance education is really 'education at a distance' (Garrison 1989); that is, just one form of education, sharing the same key characteristics as all other forms:

> All of what constitutes the process of education when teacher and student are able to meet face-to-face also constitutes the process of education when teacher and student are physically separated. All the necessary conditions for the educational process are inherent in face-to-face contact. They are not necessarily actualised, but the potential is always there. This is not the case when teacher and student are physically apart. The task of distance education is to find means by which to introduce these necessary conditions, or to simulate them so closely as to be acceptable proxies.
>
> (Shale 1990: 334)

For us, however, the most telling criticism of the great majority of the definitions of distance education (like those of open learning) that have been offered is their very idealization and unreality. There are few, if any, examples of institutions or courses which would meet in full the definitions of either Holmberg or Keegan. Thus, it does not seem realistic to imply, as in the first characteristic specified by Keegan, that teacher/learner separation *throughout* the length of the learning process is to be regarded as the norm in distance education. Some elements or stages in the educational process – for example, needs assessment, programme planning, implementation, evaluation – may be carried out at a distance, others face-to-face, others by a mixture of these means. Indeed, in some institutions, both distance and face-to-face forms of provision may be offered, with a great deal of interchange and convergence in practice (Smith and Kelly 1987).

Similarly, the second of Keegan's characteristics seems to overplay, as does Holmberg's definition, the role and influence of educational organizations, which might in many cases be confined to particular (but perhaps critical) stages. Elements of private or independent study may also be incorporated within or alongside distance study. In the case of the third and fourth characteristics identified by Keegan, further reservations are also called for. After all, the technical media and two-way communication

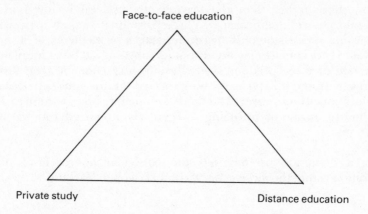

Figure 1.1   Poles of educational provision

employed in distance education may in practice be minimal, and possibly absent entirely.

The more flexible conception which these criticisms imply suggests that in reality there is a continuous spectrum between face-to-face and distance forms of education, the ends of which are never encountered in practice and along which there are no absolute dividing lines (Tight 1987a). Many providers of distance education include elements, sometimes optional, sometimes compulsory, of face-to-face tuition within their programmes (such as Open University tutorials and summer schools). These may play a crucial role in the educational process. And, perhaps more significantly, all providers of distance education – in common with all providers of face-to-face education – expect their students to engage in varying amounts of private or independent study on their own and away from the direct influence of the teacher or the course text.

In practice, therefore, we can think of forms of educational provision in terms of a triangular tension between three poles: face-to-face education, distance education and private study (Tight 1988b; see Figure 1.1). As in the case of 'open' and 'closed' forms of learning, no real example of practice is located on any of the three poles. All existing practice is somewhere in the body of the triangle, embodying varying elements of the three approaches identified. Distance education, practically defined, can then be seen as a form of education in which distance teaching techniques predominate, but not to the exclusion of other methods (Kaye 1988; Shale and Garrison 1990; Verduin and Clark 1991).

A more straightforward and general definition for this field of practice might then be:

'Distance education' refers to those forms of organized learning which are based on, and seek to overcome, the physical separation of learners and those (other than the learners themselves) involved in the organization of their learning. This separation may apply to the whole learning process or only to certain stages or elements of it. Some face-to-face contact may occur, but its function will be to supplement or reinforce the predominantly distant interaction. A good deal of private study will typically be expected of the student. Distance education offers one set of methods for opening up education to those who are unable or unwilling to regularly attend educational institutions.

Such a definition usefully sets the particular approach of distance education within the more general context of open learning.

Universities and higher education

The recent re-naming of the polytechnics and certain major colleges as universities has brought British nomenclature much more into line with international practice in higher education. Nevertheless, it remains difficult, perhaps impossible, to provide straightforward *and* meaningful definitions of either 'university' or 'higher education' which will be widely accepted and understood. Yet these are terms which both practitioners and members of the general public use without hesitation, and which they commonly believe have known and immutable meanings.

While there have been any number of attempts to define higher education in theoretical terms (for example, Newman 1859; Brubacher 1978; Barnett 1990), seeking to make distinctions, for example, between forms of learning which require different kinds of cognitive development or change, few if any of these analyses are widely known or understood. In practical terms, however, it could be argued that there is currently a common understanding of what is meant by higher education. To enter a university degree course, students normally have to have gained a given number of A-level certificates or their recognized equivalents. Higher education is, therefore, assumed to consist of post-A-level study and to take place in universities. Such a definition – like the international statements which explain 'tertiary' education as comprising post-secondary education – is close to being a truism.

There are a number of related, and largely unquestioned, assumptions bound up or associated with this understanding. Universities are expected to recruit their students direct from secondary school, selecting from among their applicants on the basis of academic performance. Students are expected to undertake a complete undergraduate course at one institution, preferably studying full-time and in residence. Universities are seen as organized by an academic elite for a social elite, with uniform and high standards of staff and provision. The university, in short, and particularly in Britain, is thought of as a relatively narrow and closed world, and stigmatized unfairly as an 'ivory tower'.

But this picture, though it portrays a recognizable institutional stereotype which has been influential at certain times and in certain places, is another myth. It is not true of British higher education as a whole today, and it has never been wholly (or even largely) true in the past. Degrees are not the only form of higher education. Other forms of provision – sub-degree, postgraduate, professional – have different entry expectations and make very different demands of their students. Mature students have always been present in higher education in large numbers alongside, or in different classes from, younger students. Part-time study has arguably always been more common than full-time study (Tight 1992). Institutions of higher education vary in the subjects they cover, and in the kinds of courses and facilities they provide.

At the present time, there is no common or absolute standard for higher education: it means different things to different people in different countries and institutions. And if this is the case today, then variations in meaning and practice are even more apparent in a historical study of the kind presented in this book. It should be constantly borne in mind that the nature of higher education has changed quite radically over time (Bell 1973).

For example, the curricula for degrees in the nineteenth century contain some elements which today would be studied at school or not at all. In other cases, whole new disciplines have become the subject of study. The entrance requirements and expectations of higher education used to be very different from those current now. In some towns and cities institutions of higher education were in competition with schools for students, rather than selecting their students from among those who had already completed school.

At times in the past the English higher education system has been much more overtly hierarchical than it is today, with some students taking degrees at the newer provincial universities in order to qualify or prepare themselves for entry to Oxford or Cambridge. This is, of course, similar to the current pattern in some other countries, such as the United States. It may well become the pattern again in Britain, partly as a result of the removal of the binary line, and partly because of the continuing escalation in qualification expectations.

All of these concerns and issues will be considered in more detail in the subsequent chapters of this book. The point to stress here is the need to maintain a flexible understanding of the nature of higher education, and thus of the changing means available by which institutions could open up their provision.

Geographical and historical focus

We have chosen to focus on the British Isles – that is to say, the present United Kingdom and the Republic of Ireland – rather than just the United

Kingdom or Great Britain. This area was, after all, a single political unit for the greater part of the period we are dealing with. During that time, the nineteenth and early twentieth centuries, much of the structure of the present higher education system in these islands was established. Many of the practices and links which were developed then have been retained in some form until the present day.

In focusing on the British Isles, it is also, however, our intention to say something about the development of open universities in the former British colonies (and even beyond). British educational practices and patterns were widely exported to the colonies, and then modified, with varying degrees of success and permanence. Given the far-flung nature of the former British empire, it should not be surprising to discover the continuing importance of distance forms of provision within the general pattern of education.

But where do we start? It is not uncommon, in general discussions of distance education, to come across references to, for example, St Paul's letters to the early Christian churches as an early expression of distance education. There is something in this argument, and there are undoubtedly other ancient or medieval examples which could be identified from various parts of the world. But these are hardly illuminating for our purposes.

Another common tendency is the presentation of a series of precise dates, with attendant places, names and brief biographies – and *exactly* the same examples are usually quoted – for the first known occurrence of correspondence education in particular countries. Thus, we hear of the Franco-German collaboration of Toussaint and Langenscheidt in language teaching from 1856, and of the establishment in 1873 by Anna Ticknor of Boston of the Society to Encourage Studies at Home (for example, Noffsinger 1926; Bittner and Mallory 1933; Erdos 1967; MacKenzie *et al.* 1968; Holmberg 1986a; Pittman 1990). The problem with this approach is that it presents these developments as somehow sudden and immutable, with an irreversible impact; whereas they seem to have been gradual, repetitive and heavily dependent upon other factors for their success.

In practical terms, the effective and widespread development of correspondence education was reliant upon the successful exploitation of a series of technological innovations. These were, most notably, the advent of modern printing techniques and the establishment of a publishing industry, the construction of fast and efficient transport and communication networks, and the creation of a cheap and reliable postal service. These were necessary but not sufficient conditions: the essential stimulus for development was then provided by the gradual buildup of demand for a highly educated workforce.

It was that demand, which grew in strength during the mid-nineteenth century in Britain, which encouraged the universities to open up their provision in other ways as well (albeit, in many cases, temporarily, as we shall see in later chapters). Distance education was, therefore, from the start just one aspect of a more general trend.

2
Alternative University Traditions: Open or Closed?

Observers of British higher education rightly see the 1980s and 1990s as a period of immense change. The number of institutions calling themselves universities has almost doubled. The enterprise culture has increasingly flourished in an academic context, encouraged by a government less willing than its immediate predecessors to pour money into higher education without asking questions about how it is spent. All kinds of new courses have been created especially for business people and managers, for new groups of professionals seeking training and for old groups of professionals needing updating. The whole organization of research and the measurement of its worth has been renovated, while the ending of tenure has shaken the previous security of academics themselves. Not surprisingly, amid such turmoil the universities and their supporters have sought out and clung to what they see as the unchallengeable and unchanging certainties of academic life.

Many of these 'certainties', however, can be all too easily challenged by the historian and form a very flimsy basis on which to defend current practice as a manifestation of traditions hallowed by the centuries. Many of them have been 'traditional' only in the twentieth century, even just the late twentieth century, and only in Britain. For example, as the Oxford professor Peterson put it:

> Those who [now] hold the view that the standards of undergraduates are going down are ... defending an untypical concept of the university. It may be none the worse for that, but it is important to realize that it is untypical and that it is peculiar to British universities since 1946. When they talk, for instance, about 'debasing the standard of the university degree' they are concerned only with people whose degrees were taken since this date.
>
> (Peterson 1961: 150)

We shall be defending the basis of Peterson's claim in this and subsequent chapters. In particular, we shall be re-examining the 'certainties' that until recently surrounded that staple task of the university, the education of undergraduates.

The late twentieth century introduction of an Open University with no entrance requirements has usually been seen as a remarkable, even astonishing, innovation, but an innovation designed to meet the needs of a very special group of students. Its abandonment of selection procedures was not seen as providing a new basis for the general organization of undergraduate studies (see Chapter 8). Rigorous selection procedures continue to be operated in the rest of the university world, and are seen as an unchanging necessity. The fact that entrance requirements, even of a less strict kind, were usually unknown in the universities of earlier centuries is a circumstance largely unknown. Indeed 'tradition' is often invoked as a justification for the defence of entry standards.

All too often the practice and conventions of our own day are influenced by a faulty view of the past. It is widely assumed, to give other examples, that universities have always been governed by an academic elite, maintaining and demanding universally high standards from both staff and students; that universities have always had serious, scientifically respectable research as the core of their activities; that entry to universities was until the mid-twentieth century largely reserved for a social elite, and that their doors were only finally opened to all the talents by a benevolent welfare state.

Yet none of this is true.

Oxford, Cambridge and the academic market

The belief in the universities' earlier social exclusiveness depends, in Britain, to a great extent upon common perceptions of Oxford and Cambridge. Life there has always been considerably influenced by the genuinely traditional role of those two universities as finishing schools for the children of a social elite. The recent success of television serials such as *Brideshead Revisited* and films such as *Chariots of Fire* have reinforced this image of the two ancient universities as being principally the haunt and playground of a social elite, of the aristocrat or the upper-middle-class gentleman attended by a manservant.

There is, of course, an element of truth in such a picture. There were many students of that kind in both universities during most of their history, and inevitably they provide colourful material for the media. Even so, there was never a general intention in either case to exclude people from colleges on social grounds. Indeed, any such ban would have considerably interfered with what was for many centuries Oxford and Cambridge's major academic function as training centres for the Church of England, a task that ensured a constant influx of poorer boys provided with patronage because of their choice of career. Until the mid-nineteenth century, these two universities practised a system of religious exclusion, with degrees being reserved for Anglicans, but that included some of the poorest of Anglicans as well as rich ones.

Rothblatt has suggested that some of the really idle rich students were regarded as a nuisance by the authorities; and that, if Cambridge in the nineteenth century did evolve a policy of exclusion, it was not based on wealth or social background but on the assumed cultural attitudes of potential students:

> One of the primary objectives . . . was to guarantee that Cambridge did not lose its traditional connexion with the professions and professional men, especially clergymen. . . . This did not mean that dons wished to definitely close the university to non-professional groups; merely that they had no intention of making Cambridge in any way attractive to students from non-professional families who might prefer a career in business, or were unprepared to accept Cambridge values and style.
>
> (Rothblatt 1968: 88)

The clear intention was actually to exclude the sons of the rich if their fathers had a faulty value system. While it is no doubt true that dons, used to the manners of the professional classes, might have been considerably disturbed by the sudden influx of large numbers of boys from humbler homes, their entry on a smaller scale was actively encouraged and there was quite a presence of such students even in the decades preceding 1914. A Royal Commission in 1919 noted that half of the scholarship holders were 'the sons of parents whose means were at any rate moderate' (Rothblatt 1968: 59). By then, some of the new local education authorities were already willing to spend money on sending promising school leavers to both male and female colleges.

Even the sons of professionals who were welcomed by the dons of an earlier period, particularly clergy children, were sometimes far from affluent. They, like many of the poorer candidates for ordination, found the financial challenges of residence very great. It was, in fact, their doctrinal insistence on residence rather than positive snobbery that made the two ancient English universities more difficult of access to poorer students than were the continental or Scottish universities, to which many poorer English students resorted. Nevertheless there were ways round the financial barriers of Oxbridge – to win a scholarship, to find a generous patron or to live a life of great frugality – and many of the universities' subsequently most distinguished academics did successfully embrace one of those ways, often to the great pleasure of the authorities.

But, even if they had become in both practice and appearance socially superior, the two ancient English universities were certainly never, until very recently, as academically elitist as their current reputation and entrance requirements might suggest. Before the 1950s and 1960s, they were not even much concerned with maintaining generally high standards. Excellent scholars were certainly to be found at Oxford and Cambridge, and the early development of the Mathematics Tripos at Cambridge during the late eighteenth century set a standard that proved difficult to emulate elsewhere. But it was not expected, until this century, that the majority of students would ever aim at more than a pass degree. Indeed, some dons were anxious for this situation to continue, in case a mass entry for the Honours Tripos posed a threat to its standards.

Even after the introduction of other Triposes alongside mathematics, entrants to such examinations were for long obliged to pass the mathematics one first, a regulation aimed not only at defending the vested interests of the powerful mathematics dons, but also at discouraging mediocre students from being too ambitious (Winstanley 1940). In the second half of the nineteenth century, expectations of undergraduates remained low. Between 1851 and 1906, one-quarter of all Cambridge undergraduates went down without earning any degree at all, and as late as 1902 only just over half the degrees awarded (53 per cent) went to honours men – women, of course, being still excluded from their degree system altogether (Rothblatt 1968: 185).

Nor were the standards demanded of the dons necessarily much higher. One Cambridge graduate, later a professor in Ireland, recalled the fellows of his own undergraduate college in the 1840s. They were, he said, 'mostly of the cobra kind. They swallowed their intellectual goat in early life and were passing through the years of inactivity requisite for digestion' (Attwater 1936: 117). As late as the 1940s and 1950s aged relics of the system of life fellowships, long since swept away, were still to be seen in the streets of Cambridge; academics still enjoying, on the basis of early examination success, guaranteed food, accommodation and income for the rest of their lives, whether they did any work or not.

They also recalled a world in which appointments to senior university posts were often far more influenced by ecclesiastical and college politics than by academic considerations. John Sparrow, in his study of the university reformer Mark Pattison (Sparrow 1967), recounts the story of the election of a Master of Lincoln College who was brought in from the country and chosen in order to keep out the candidate of some rival camp. His academic reputation, however, was of such dubiety that when he pinned a notice on the college board shortly after his election, this was reluctantly taken to be evidence that he could write but certainly not as evidence that he could read.

Almost a century later, in the 1920s, though things had without doubt much improved, an undergraduate at the same college, Osbert Lancaster, was to encounter a Reader in Spanish and Portuguese of whom, he says, 'few were convinced that his knowledge of Spanish was more than nominal, while his comparative knowledge of Portuguese was due rather to a childhood spent in Lisbon, where his father owned the municipal tramways, than to extensive research' (Lancaster 1967: 76).

These, of course, are extreme cases. Alongside such figures existed academic giants of great distinction, but the interesting thing is that the system could easily tolerate and reward those of no real distinction. It did not demand, even of the giants, any of the evidence of research and publications that would be commonplace nowadays. Until the 1960s, even conscientiously scholarly dons scoffed at the PhD as an American intrusion; and considered the MA degree, earned purely on undergraduate work, perfectly adequate even for holders of chairs and senior tutorial posts.

Why then did things change? Why, during the second half of the twentieth century, did the great majority of undergraduate places come to be reserved for those with a highly successful school career, and academic appointments for those with ever vaster and more impressive records of high-level publications and research? One of the most plausible explanations has to be that such changes were the inevitable result of just those market forces to which recent governments have naively assumed they were exposing the universities for the first time.

Until the final decades of the nineteenth century, there was in a sense no effective educational market at all. Most of the Oxford and Cambridge colleges themselves were well-endowed, and the fellows could lead a pleasant life without worrying themselves unduly about teaching. When, in the early nineteenth century, figures such as Newman were led by their religious beliefs to take the pastoral and intellectual care of undergraduates more seriously, and to welcome them in larger numbers, many of their fellow dons greeted their initiatives with apathy or even downright hostility. Most colleges were not particularly interested in attracting students. Some students arrived under the terms of close scholarships (only open to certain schools or categories of student), others were sent by their family or patrons, but there was little or no active recruitment and the teaching of undergraduates was rarely seen as a major task of most colleges.

The Irish professor quoted earlier also recalled his fellow undergraduates in the 1840s, who arrived at Pembroke College, Cambridge at the rate of less than nine a year:

A few were youths of pleasant gentlemanly ways; some able and unambitious; others, the majority, of moderate abilities and slender attainments . . . a small minority were illiterate beyond all redemption, but at the same time, were hearty, likable, hospitable fellows.

(Attwater 1936: 117)

Things there languished so much that in 1858 only one undergraduate was admitted and, Attwater suggests, possibly through loneliness, he left some months later for another college.

However, by the end of the nineteenth century both Oxford and Cambridge had developed a greater sense of purpose as trainers of professionals and, indeed, of the nation's leaders. The colleges, as a result, began to recruit more vigorously. The standards required of scholars and exhibitioners improved considerably, in line with the great curricular improvements in the public and grammar schools from which they were recruited, but admissions tutors still had little incentive to insist on high levels of scholarship from other entrants in what was still essentially a buyer's market. Colleges were more willing to seek out people of distinction in order to attract the attention of schools and parents but, in accordance with the feelings of the day, that distinction could be social or sporting as much as scholarly. But even if a potential student had no particular distinction, colleges were usually still willing to admit them so long as they had a parent or a patron who could pay.

As a result, the basic standards required of entrants remained low even as late as the 1930s. A distinguished Australian oarsman rowing in the Cambridge eight was rumoured to be still attempting to complete the Previous Exam (the basic entrance requirement at that time) during his third and final year of residence. Similarly, the actor, Michael Redgrave, later a successful schoolmaster, recounts how he found himself admitted to Magdalene College, Cambridge without even having passed the ordinary school certificate, let alone the higher, the equivalent of the later advanced (A) level (Redgrave 1983). A pass in the higher school certificate was not felt to be necessary for admission until after the Second World War.

In an academic sense, therefore, Oxford and Cambridge were, for most of their history, relatively open universities with minimal entrance requirements, even allowing those to be set aside or modified if a recruit had other characteristics to commend him. Peterson, defending his view quoted earlier, justifiably recalls that before the Second World War:

> a considerable proportion of Oxbridge undergraduates consisted of nice young men, sometimes known as hearties or not 'reading men'. They arrived with five school certificate credits at 18 and left with a pass degree. . . Today they are scattered all over the country as holders of Oxbridge BAs or MAs and no one is seriously concerned at the extent to which they debase the standard of the university degree.
>
> (Peterson 1961: 150)

This situation ended abruptly, as Peterson suggests, in the years following 1946. It was destroyed by the understandable, egalitarian demand that the country's two leading universities should be open to all the talents. Thus, Oxford and Cambridge became academically exclusive at a very late stage in their history. What had been a buyer's market suddenly turned into a seller's market, and the two ancient salesmen found themselves enjoying a monopoly trade in university places of unparalleled prestige, more coveted than ever before by both the parents and the teachers of budding undergraduates.

With the awarding of generous grants to ex-service men and women during the post-war demobilization, the number of students in receipt of state grants increased considerably. With the introduction in the 1950s of mandatory awards for everyone offered a place on a full-time degree course, the numbers seeking entry grew still further (Ministry of Education, Scottish Education Department 1960). Those seeking to enter Oxford and Cambridge now far exceeded the number of places available.

The post-war universities suddenly found themselves able for the first time to embark on the careful selection of their recruits, using academic and personality criteria that proved equally exacting for candidates from both poor and affluent homes. The fact that the secondary schools attended by the affluent found it easier to prepare people to meet those criteria nourished the misguided assumption that the ancient universities had traditionally been socially exclusive. At the same time, the new scholarly demands nourished the equally deceptive assumption that their general entrance requirements had always been high.

Oxbridge looks outwards

The myth that grew up in the post-war world of an age-old Oxbridge social and academic exclusivity dies hard, and has done much to obscure the realities of the two universities' rather more complex social development. It has also served to hide from view a remarkable educational venture when, in the second half of the nineteenth century, a great deal of energy was expended by a sizeable number of Oxford and Cambridge dons on work that was in no way self-seeking, was quite consciously egalitarian and specifically aimed at increasing accessibility to the kind of higher education the two universities set out to provide.

This group – which even included such distinguished figures as Jowett, the Master of Balliol College, Oxford – set about the deliberate task of extending the universities' intellectual influence and teaching to the industrial and commercial centres of England, and thus beyond the social classes from which their colleges then took most of their recruits. They wished to suggest the real possibility of a university education to those who had hitherto never considered it, but without necessarily requiring that they leave home and take up residence to achieve it. They knew that it was from among just such people that the leading teachers in the new state education system were being recruited, and that to influence them was a particularly fitting task for the two universities. This movement had a dual aim. As Marriott puts it:

> There was a democratising urge to provide teaching of the highest standard to localities deprived of intellectual nourishment; there was also an element of paternalism, a wish to keep the new bodies in the leading strings of the ancient universities and to make sure they walked along the ways of liberal education.
>
> (Marriott 1981: 5)

With these aims in mind, not only distinguished dons but also specially appointed 'extension' lecturers and organizers were from the 1870s onwards to travel the length of England, from Bristol and Devon to the Northumbrian coalfield, spreading their intellectual and cultural gospel. In doing so, they incidentally created local organizations that were, in many cases, to develop subsequently into conventional universities with, eventually, their own highly demanding entrance requirements and their own exclusivity.

However, until the end of the nineteenth century this movement and its aims remained more fluid. At Cambridge it owed its early inspiration to a natural scientist and fellow of Trinity, James Stuart. He was, significantly, both a feminist and a native of Scotland. He was thus both well acquainted with that country's non-residential and more democratically based universities, and in favour of opening the university world to that half of the British population still largely excluded from it. He propagated views of which many of his colleagues, brought up within a university based on all male, residential colleges, could hardly have approved. Even so, Stuart and his fellow enthusiasts did get official university backing. In both universities committees were set up to oversee the work, and these were eventually to organize the award of certificates and diplomas to those attending and completing the extension courses. As the *Journal of Education* noted in April 1892: 'private students in various parts of England are beginning to discover the great chance thus offered to those who have leisure but are for various reasons unable to leave home.' There can be no doubt that the work of both extension lecturers and students was taken seriously. The government recognized the value of the work as much as the universities. At the turn of the century, the extension students' summer schools at Oxford attracted visits and addresses in successive years from politicians as distinguished as Balfour and Asquith (*Journal of Education*, June 1900 and September 1901).

An early examiners' report (1876–7), anxious to quell the scepticism of those who opposed this new 'open' university, suggested that:

> The average level of the answers . . . is considerably higher than that of undergraduates who pass the university examinations. It would be absurd to compare it with the average of those who fail. Moreover several of the papers are definitely better than those of candidates for the Fellowship who are, I need not say, picked men.
>
> (*Educational Review*, March 1890)

Difficulties arose, of course, over deciding what the status of the awards to such students should be. There was general agreement that some of the work being done by extension students was of a very high standard indeed. There seemed a real possibility, therefore, of establishing out-stations of the two parent universities to run university examinations at a distance, distinguishing extension degrees from internal degrees by awarding a BA to the former and an immediate MA to the latter in the Scottish style (Marriott 1981).

Other enthusiasts saw even greater developments. The man whom Marriott regards as the greatest figure of the extension movement, the Welshman R. D. Roberts, in his most sanguine moments saw himself 'looking forward to the time when it will be considered as necessary to have in every town and district educated teachers of the people as it is now to have pastors to look after their religious education' (quoted in Marriott 1981: 36).

In fact, of course, the movement's achievements were to be less far-reaching. It was, no doubt, unreasonable to expect universities wedded to the idea of residence to abandon all their principles and to establish totally non-residential arrangements. This was particularly unlikely at a time when, as we shall see, it was becoming increasingly fashionable to cherish Newman's ideal of the university as a community. Sadler, himself a leading Oxford advocate of extension, continued to insist that some kind of residence was essential for the award of a 'real' degree. This insistence, he said, was based 'not [on] the protection of privilege, but the recognition of the fact that the benefit which the average man gets from his University life largely consists . . . in the social experience he gains' (quoted in Marriott 1981: 55). This belief was to bedevil all provision of non-residential education for a century or more.

As a result, neither university was willing to consider awarding degrees to students at a distance. They could be awarded a certificate for their achievements, and in later years such a certificate might provide some exemption from university entrance requirements. But the furthest Cambridge would go within their actual degree programme, as it then existed, was to award advanced standing to particularly successful extension candidates, allowing them to start their undergraduate course in the second year so long as they then came into residence.

Oxford made a similar offer, and was prepared to be even more generous if the local extension standards and enthusiasm seemed to justify it. Thus, it was eventually deemed that two years of study at the Reading centre, instead of the previously required three, was enough to count as one year at Oxford (*Journal of Education*, July 1898). But such offers, however magnanimous they seemed to the bodies making them, did not prove very attractive to the part-time students of Bristol or Nottingham who wished to continue in their jobs and to live at home.

Marriott estimates that at any one time there were rarely more than a hundred students in the whole country on their way to earning extension certificates – probably 2 per cent or less of the whole extension audience. Even so, they did provide evidence that the ancient universities' doors were not closed, and also gave early currency and respectability in Britain to the notion of advanced standing, now so often thought of as a late twentieth century idea. This idea was rapidly adopted by at least one of the newer universities, Leeds; for, in its annual report for 1904–5, Huddersfield Technical College noted that attendance at certain of its classes could be 'counted as equivalent to attendance on the corresponding courses at the University of Leeds and could shorten the degree course to two years' (Huddersfield Technical College 1905).

The fruits of extension

The extension movement did not produce, as some of its begetters had hoped, a series of branches of the ancient universities in the larger cities of England. Nor did it, as Marriott ruefully concludes, succeed in putting 'a genuine higher education within the reach of working men and women' (Marriott 1981: 86). But it did leave some interesting and enduring legacies. It led, as already noted, to the foundation of a number of cheaper teaching institutions that eventually blossomed into independent universities. Some of these began with particular interests in mind. At Bristol, for example, where Jowett himself played a particularly significant supportive role, there was a special commitment to developing higher education for women. Though some of these future universities were to serve half a century of apprenticeship, preparing people not for Oxbridge examinations but those of London University (see Chapter 7), others, like Bristol and Reading, achieved their independence more quickly.

But such institutions were not the only fruits of the extension movement. The students it recruited were not all interested in certification or graduation. Many of them had been attracted to the classes by the simple desire for a higher education without certification, and such people were not much distressed by the failure of Oxford and Cambridge to respond to the pleas of bodies, such as Nottingham City Council, which called for a more generous treatment of extension students in the examination regulations. They were natural recruits for a new and rival movement – the Workers' Educational Association of Albert Mansbridge, with its more flexible programmes and high degree of branch autonomy – which began to sweep the more formal arrangements of the extension workers aside.

Perhaps the main achievement of the extension movement was that it had successfully conjured up the vision of an ever more open system of higher education. This vision was also gaining popularity among Scottish educationalists, such as S. S. Laurie and Patrick Geddes, who foresaw the emergence of an ideal university in which everyone could pursue their own intellectual development in perpetual symposia, free of timetables and all examinations (Laurie 1901). Mansbridge's rhetoric reflected these attitudes perfectly:

> If the University spirit is a disinterested desire for knowledge, then there is much University spirit in many towns of England. The real University is mystical and invisible; it is to be found wherever scholars cooperate for the extension of the bounds of knowledge. It is not in one place, or in selected places. It is intangible, undiscernable, but none the less real and men know one another when they are of its sacred courts.
>
> (Mansbridge 1913: 37)

Mansbridge was an inspiring leader, whose development of the tutorial ideal in an adult education context was to be extremely influential internationally. It could, though, be argued that the uncertificated work of his movement, and of the non-graduating university extra-mural classes which shared its style, simply diverted well-motivated students away from a university world where they could have succeeded and which was never as closed as they sometimes believed. The subsequent chapters of this book will demonstrate just how numerous the opportunities were.

The vision of some of the extension leaders, as expressed in a document of 1884, was just as idealistic as that of Mansbridge. This accepted that universities were not simply educators, but also the engineers of certification, and pictured an open university that attempted to perform both functions. Access to degrees, it said, should 'be made the apex of an enlarged and systematised version of their own scheme', with its 'peripatetic lecture courses and associated paraphernalia of teaching and private study' (Marriott 1981: 15). By this means:

> The English people could be induced to sacrifice time and money to strenuous self-improvement if the universities would only recognise their efforts by throwing open, without regard to age, circumstances or class, the ultimate distinction . . . a part-time, nonresident teaching university operating a system of academic credits.
>
> (ibid.: 15)

Such a document provides yet further evidence that the minds of Victorian academics, in Oxford, Cambridge and elsewhere, were by no means all as closed or as elitist as we sometimes now assume.

Changes in the market

It is common, but over-simplistic, to interpret the gradual development of the other British universities, from the mid-nineteenth century onwards, as a reaction to the exclusiveness of Oxbridge. Such a view sees the creation of London, Manchester and the rest as part of a liberating process, opening the gates of the university world to students hitherto excluded on social grounds. In a purely financial sense, it did then become easier for people from poorer homes to attend universities that did not require residence as a condition of graduation. But we should be more cautious when we consider other barriers to access. We have already indicated the low demands made of Oxbridge entrants until very recently. As the twentieth century dawned, it became clear that it was some of the other British universities that were taking the lead in closing their doors to those who had not done well at school.

Throughout the nineteenth century, all the universities had remained in a buyer's market, and this had made the weaker of the new English institutions particularly aware of the need for marketing policies. The University of Durham, for example, having unsuccessfully established itself in the 1830s as a northern medieval substitute for Oxford and

Cambridge, was strongly aware of financial issues. It arose from an ecclesiastical attempt at tax avoidance, and it subsequently organized its college system to suit a variety of pockets and social groupings. It had even for a time, presumably in order to undercut its southern rivals, reduced the length of the BA course to two years (Whiting 1932). Similarly, Owen's College, the precursor of Manchester University, like some London colleges and other Victorian institutions of higher education (see Chapter 3), found it necessary to compete for students with the local schools (Charlton 1951).

With the new century, and the development of a state secondary school system, the smaller English universities moved into a quite different academic world. This was to provide them both with a ready supply of eighteen-year-old students, well able to afford the modest fees of a non-resident university, and with a new class of teacher in urgent need of university education. While this did not quite move them into the buoyant seller's market of half a century later, there were certainly more buyers around.

It seemed increasingly legitimate, therefore, to close a few doors and to be rather more demanding about entrance requirements. Some of the universities were all too willing to move some way up market, so as to satisfy the conditions of a government anxious to place its new grant-aided teacher trainees in the stimulating environment of the new University Day Training Colleges. This process continued after the First World War. At University College Nottingham, for example, the principal did not conceal his delight at being able to discontinue, despite local demand, two-year day training courses for teachers in the 1930s, replacing them with more academic four-year courses (Wood 1953: 112).

Ironically, Oxford and Cambridge were initially far less affected by the commercial attractions of the state school market, and therefore under less pressure for that reason to increase their entrance demands. The foundation of a Day Training College in Cambridge simply provided an opportunity to make a further demonstration of that same goodwill to the educationally deprived that had prompted the extension movement. The delicate business of introducing a group of teacher-trainees, including a handful from elementary schools, to college life seems to have been managed successfully by a fellow of King's, Oscar Browning, already noted for his 'open' educational views. But the new standards of teacher certification were of far more importance to the universities and university colleges of Scotland and the North of England, who used, and indeed soon became dependent on, the teacher training grants to build up Arts faculties that seemed unlikely to attract much in the way of gifts from local industry (Adams 1923).

The closing of Scottish doors

North of the border were four universities that were in no sense new, and that were indeed older than many Oxford and Cambridge colleges. The

Scottish universities had been the major model for the new English institutions and initially had shown them an example of open-ness never exceeded in British higher education. In the mid-nineteenth century not only was any man in Scotland free to matriculate regardless of previous academic experience, but he was also free to drop in on lectures whether he matriculated or not (Laurie 1901). The size of the Scottish professor's salary was entirely dependent on the number of students whom he could attract. Only the size of the lecture room imposed a limit on the number of students recruited. The fee was placed directly in the professor's hand by the student at the beginning of the session and, as Robert Louis Stevenson recalls, those with bulging pockets attracted even more custom because this was evidence to the newcomer of a particular professor's worth (McPherson 1973).

This was, therefore, very much a buyer's market into which the Scottish universities, unlike their ancient English counterparts, had shown a willingness to launch almost any new and relatively respectable subject that seemed likely to draw an audience. Until the 1850s the supreme governing body of Edinburgh University was a subcommittee of the town council, and always anxious to seize opportunities to reduce expenditure by more attractive marketing, while the professors themselves also regularly sought out patrons for new chairs and classes.

In the 1830s, for example, one professor despatched to a rich London patron a lively proposal for a chair of business studies that, it was hoped, would attract a wide and varied new student body of all ages from every part of town (Southey and Southey 1844). Alas, in this case the private sponsor remained unconvinced. It was, however, his legacy that 40 years later, in 1876, enabled Edinburgh and St Andrews to establish the first English-speaking university chairs in education, specifically to catch the market that they hoped would result from the creation of the new state school system by the Education Act of 1872 (Bell 1986).

Principal Grant of Edinburgh was even willing, in his address opening the autumn session of 1874, to draw attention to the continuing commercial concern that a university like his must show. Indeed, as he pointed out, such a concern was an inevitable consequence of the university's open-ness to the non-affluent student. For, whereas Oxford, Cambridge and Trinity College, Dublin could count on an annual income of £200 from each student, Edinburgh could count on only £12 (*The Scotsman*, 3 November 1874).

At the same time, it would be wrong to suggest that the absence of academic entrance requirements in Scotland was simply a function of a buyer's market. The reorganization of the three oldest universities – St Andrews, Glasgow and Aberdeen – at the time of the reformation, and the subsequent establishment of Edinburgh at the end of the sixteenth century, all formed part of a Lutheran-style plan to create a meritocratic common-wealth, providing a pathway by which any boy could reach the highest academic level if he chose to do so. An institutional pyramid was proposed, with the schools to be erected in every parish feeding into more centralized burgh schools and then into lavishly supplied university places that should be fully open to the talents (*The First Book of Discipline* 1560).

For economic reasons this ambitious system was never fully implemented. Some parishes remained for centuries without adequate schools, and not all boys of talent proceeded to a burgh school. But even in the remotest parts of Scotland as late as the 1870s, and especially in the north-east, it was still possible to find certain parish schools where talented schoolmasters prepared their students directly for the university course, often offering such a sophisticated curriculum that at least one English cabinet minister was appalled at the, to him, excessive intellectual riches being provided in what he assumed was an elementary school (Scottish Universities Commission 1893).

And for those not provided with such tuition in their own town or village, there were professors, especially in the large universities of Glasgow and Edinburgh, prepared to provide preliminary induction courses for young students. These not only brought those professors an extra salary, but placed them, like their Manchester colleagues, in competition with local schools, whose complaints were still being voiced in the press as late as 1900 (Bell 1973).

Attendance at such preparatory courses was not, however, obligatory, and the number of university places available per head of the population remained one of the highest in Europe, exceeded in 1880, it was claimed, only by Switzerland and far ahead of Germany let alone England (University College, Dundee 1883). Moreover, the principle of easy entry was widely seen as a national glory. The philosopher S. S. Laurie defended open access to the university as a civil right of the people of Scotland, who for long continued to place far more emphasis on their actual exposure to the higher education process than on the acquiring of traditional academic honours. Indeed, for most of the nineteenth century, a student rarely completed the full degree course and even more rarely submitted himself to the actual ceremony of graduation unless it was absolutely necessary for professional purposes (Bell 1973; Anderson 1983).

Eventually a number of factors was to produce change even in Scotland. First was the growing desire, on the part of the professors and the government, to see the Scottish universities bearing a closer resemblance to the socially and academically prestigious ancient universities of England. The introduction of at least rudimentary entrance requirements was clearly an essential ingredient of any such transformation. Even to the defenders of open access, the imposition of such requirements in the early 1890s seemed less oppressive than it might have done earlier, given that there had by then been a widespread development of adequate secondary schools in the most populous parts of Scotland.

Egalitarians were also reassured by the decision of the Scotch Education Department (as it was then called), during the 1870s, to finance the university attendance of 'suitable' male teacher-trainees for both elementary and secondary schools. The scheme was such a success, with an increasing number of students deemed to be 'suitable', that by the time of the First World War almost all male teachers in Scotland, both secondary and elementary, were already proceeding to graduation. In the 1920s it became finally possible for the government to make a successful university career mandatory for virtually every secondary teacher as well as every male elementary teacher.

These developments provided a guaranteed, government-financed audience, a market far more rewarding to the Scottish universities than the one in England. At the same time, it also ensured that the entrance standards now introduced were never too exacting, for many of the teacher-trainees had a relatively low school achievement and were usually aiming at no more than an ordinary degree (Cruickshank 1970; Bell 1986). The financial risks involved, in thus closing the doors a little, were made considerably less by the admission of women to the Scottish universities in the 1890s.

Perhaps the most potent element of all in the narrowing of access to the Scottish universities was, however, the introduction of a standard salary for professors. This clearly insulated them from the market for the first time so far as the size of their individual salary was concerned, though they might still have anxieties about the prosperity of the university as a whole, especially in the tiny and ever-threatened St Andrews (as we shall see in Chapter 5). They now had no need to worry about how the new entrance requirements would affect trade. Indeed, by removing the academic dross from their classes, their work would be made easier. Maintaining the traditional Scottish open-ness no longer brought them a financial advantage, but seemed a positive evil from the increasingly academic elitist point of view that so many of them were now adopting. It was, after all, very depressing to hear the English increasingly referring to their institutions as glorified secondary schools, even for example in such a prestigious journal as *Mind*, and to be reminded that when Scottish graduates proceeded to Oxford and Cambridge after winning highly demanding prizes they continued to be treated as undergraduates.

Significantly, the Scottish universities launched no major extension movement, either because they believed that Scotland already afforded enough higher education opportunities or because they were rejoicing in their new found exclusivity. As McPherson has noted, by the end of the nineteenth century the Scottish universities had become far more middle class in atmosphere as they absorbed the products of the new secondary schools. Even some of the teacher-trainees, from whom so much of the universities' new prosperity derived, began to feel socially ill at ease in institutions more and more dominated by the well-heeled denizens of their increasingly affluent medical faculties (McPherson 1973).

But the doctors and teachers were only two of the many professional groups that began to look to the universities for the conferring of prestige. The creation of elaborate training programmes, involving the taking of a degree, became an obligatory part in the planning of every profession attempting to increase its social standing (Reader 1966). This again helped to quicken the inexorable process that was pushing the universities towards a seller's market, with the imposition of ever more demanding entrance requirements and, eventually, the actual selection of students.

The gradual closing of the Scottish universities' doors did, of course, do a great deal to raise their academic standards. The rate of graduation increased and the number of students attempting honours gradually rose, but an educational price had to be paid. Inevitably, the universities moved away from the philosophy-based, generalist ordinary degree as the initial target of students, and introduced an honours programme. Though the latter remained generalist in its early stages, it soon lost its wide-ranging nature in its attempts to emulate the specialist degree system now increasingly normal in England (Davie 1961). The notion of an examination-free university conducted on Socratic lines, in which anyone could pursue knowledge and argument for their own sake, remained an ideal only for Laurie, Geddes and other academic dreamers. The Scottish universities were now highly organized mechanisms for supplying qualifications and were no longer places where people of any age could drop in when they felt like it.

The end of open-ness

Open-ness was continually eroded as the British universities made their way through the century from 1870 to 1970. A university career came to be seen more and more as suitable only for those who had been successful in secondary school. By the late twentieth century, the universities themselves seemed content to have replaced what they, rightly or wrongly, saw as their socially exclusive past with a new, academically exclusive present. True, many academics felt somewhat guilty, knowing that academic achievement might still be a function of the student's family's affluence and that selection systems might still be affected by the general inequalities of society, but then such things were the responsibility of society rather than of the university. In imposing strict entrance requirements they felt, mistakenly, that they were simply maintaining a centuries-old duty or tradition.

That they might, at the same time, be shutting the door on people quite capable of proving perfectly adequate, or even distinguished, students was a problem that no longer seemed to bother most academics. To the Oxbridge supporters of extension it had seemed eminently desirable that all adults should, if they wished, be able to sample the joys of academia, but such joys could, alas, only be fully appreciated through residence, an impossibility for most people. A later generation of academics would deny that universal higher education was even desirable and might even declare remorselessly that 'more means worse'. Open-ness came to be seen not merely as difficult to attain but as a nonsensical concept, destructive of academic values. The new seller's market that enabled the defenders of the British university to make such claims was a uniquely twentieth century phenomenon. Yet, by the 1980s, it had come to seem traditional, and as such helped to disguise the real traditions that had still been so obvious and influential as recently as Victorian times.

3

The Royal Road: The University of London in the Nineteenth Century

The University of London has, virtually throughout its history, provided opportunities for higher education to be pursued at a distance from its associated educational institutions. The provision of distance education has not been its only (or even necessarily its central) function, of course, and it has been offered in a particular way – that is to say, largely through its examination system – and in part indirectly. This function was, however, especially important and increasingly controversial during the second half of the nineteenth century.

Once the University had been clearly established as an examining and accrediting system, few restrictions were then placed by it either on the location, time or pace at which its students might study, or on who might study, or on the subjects which they could study. Indeed, towards the end of the century the institution opened itself up further by relaxing such restrictions as then existed, enabling women to enrol on an equal footing with men, permitting students to both study and sit examinations throughout the Empire (and beyond), and expanding the range of subjects, syllabuses and qualifications available.

Seen in this context, the University of London represents a major and early example of a British open university, an example which was much copied and highly influential.

The development of the University

The history of the University of London has, perhaps somewhat surprisingly, been the subject of relatively little serious study. This is undoubtedly due, in part, to the relative complexity of the institution; but it probably also has a good deal to do with the lack of identification with the University felt by many of those who have worked for or studied with it. Thus, while detailed studies of most of the main Colleges or Schools of the University are available (see, for example, Burns 1924; Bellot 1929; Hearnshaw 1929; Godwin 1939; Hayek 1946; Harte and North 1991), few have attempted a history of the University as a whole. Indeed, the most recent such history available, produced in 1986 for the University's sesquicentennial, is modestly subtitled 'an illustrated history' (Harte 1986; see also Bellot 1969; Thompson 1990a).

While the broad pattern of the University of London's history is quite well recorded, there is no substitute, therefore, in a study of this kind for direct consultation of the University's *Calendars, Minutes of Senate*, Committee Papers and other contemporary sources. It is not, of course, our purpose here to attempt anything like a comprehensive study of the University in the nineteenth century. Rather, the aim is to focus on those aspects of the University's history which are relevant to an appreciation of its significance as an open university. With this aim in mind, it will be adequate to give a brief sketch of the University's history, and then concentrate in more detail upon specific aspects of its development.

The so-called 'University of London' began its life in 1826 in the guise of a limited liability company with buildings in Gower Street, which was then on the outskirts of the city. This was the institution which subsequently became known as University College. Other institutions which later became part of the University proper, most notably many of the medical schools, had been established long before. King's College, chartered in 1829, was set up shortly afterwards as an Anglican rival to the original 'godless' foundation. Intervention by the government, acting in a mixed spirit of compromise and innovation, soon regularized the situation, and the University of London received its first charter in 1836 as a state examining body. University College, King's College and other approved institutions were permitted to prepare their students for its examinations. In short:

> The nineteenth-century University of London was, in modern terms, an amalgam of an Open University and a Council for National Academic Awards. It had neither the technology of the one, nor the system of inspection of the other, but its functions were perceived as a sort of cross between the two.
>
> (Harte 1986: 25)

Despite these contemporary references, the notion of a university as an examining body may seem rather strange to the modern reader. But this is not how it would have appeared in the nineteenth century:

> In the 1850s the idea of a university as a purely examining body would not have seemed out of place. For during the first half of the nineteenth century the universities of Oxford and Cambridge had not been much more than this.
>
> (Ashby and Anderson 1966: 25)

This model of the university as a federal examining body was subsequently adopted as the basis for universities not only in England (the Victoria University, based in Manchester, with member colleges in Leeds, Liverpool and Manchester), but in Ireland (see Chapter 4), Wales, Canada, India,

South Africa, Australia and New Zealand as well (Houle 1974; Rothblatt 1987).

These transplantations were not always successful. That in Australia was uprooted almost as soon as it had been made, while the Indian transplant was hampered by both its avowedly political purpose, the preparation of students for government employment, and its disregard, through offering an essentially English degree, of Indian religion and culture (Ashby and Anderson 1966: Chs 2 and 3). Nearer to home, both the Victoria University (Fiddes 1937; Charlton 1951) and the Royal University of Ireland barely survived into the twentieth century. Yet, on the other hand, both the Universities of New Zealand (Beaglehole 1937; Parton 1979) and South Africa were long-lasting and successful, while the University of Wales – like London itself – still exists as a federal examining body.

The latter part of the nineteenth century was also the period in which much of our current examination system first took shape (Montgomery 1965; Bryant 1986; Foden 1989). The University of London had a major influence on this process:

> The development of examinations for school students during most of the 19th century is inextricably linked with the spread of the University of London degree and pre-degree examinations through-out Britain and the developing British Empire.
>
> (Kingdon 1991: 33–4)

Given its nature, it is perhaps not surprising that the University did not regard itself as being 'an educating body' as such. It made its view of its own status clear in its submission to the Secretary of State in 1845, regarding the Medical Reform Bill which was then going through Parliament:

> The University of London differs from other graduating Medical Schools in not being an educating body – in being under the immediate control of the Government . . . and in its being supported chiefly by the public money.
>
> (University of London *Minutes of Senate* (ULSM) 9 April 1845: 45)

The University's records for the mid-nineteenth century contain in-creasingly long lists of 'institutions empowered to issue certificates to candidates for degrees in arts and laws'. These certificates enabled their students to enter the University's examinations. Other lists record the 'recognised medical institutions, schools and teachers' with whom medical students had to register for training. Significantly, while the former lists were compiled by the Home Office without consultation with the University, the University's recommendation was required in the case of the latter. Institutions in the colonies and in the territories of the East India Company were included in the lists of those recognized after 1849, when a supplemental Charter was obtained.

A much more radical widening of the University's role soon followed. In

1854, the University Senate received two lengthy memorials from the subscribers to the journal, *The Popular Educator*, arguing:

> That in consequence of the increasing demand for the diffusion of useful knowledge, the extension of the blessings of education, and the equitable distribution of the honours and rewards of learning, among all classes of the community, it would seem to be both wise and politic, on the part of a liberal and paternal Government, to throw open the Royal Road to the valuable and permanent distinctions which the University of London confers upon its members, to all the aspiring and self-taught Students of the British Empire, irrespective of their various conditions in life, or of the different places and ways in which they have acquired their learning.
>
> (ULSM 1 February 1854: 3)

The University's intention to do just that was signalled in a new draft Charter prepared in 1857. A torrent of objections were soon received – from University College, King's College, 16 other affiliated institutions, professors, lecturers, graduates, undergraduates and other established interests who wished to restrict access to the University's examinations.

However, the Senate (or, rather, the key members of it), secure in its belief in the values of free trade, self-help and examinations (Brook 1958), felt quite able to overrule these objections:

> the Senate claim to be released from those restrictions which have hitherto confined the Degree to the pupils of Colleges specially named. Repudiating all idea of multiplying new enlistments by degrading the standard of admissibility, they wish to invite diligent and accomplished students from all places of education and all tutors indiscriminately. It is for the University of London to proclaim the comprehensive principle, that while testing by strict examination the amount of acquired knowledge, and requiring reasonable evidence of antecedent continuous study, it will no more tie down the deserving student to a few privileged Colleges than to a particular religious creed.
>
> (ULSM 22 July 1857: 136)

The 'Royal Road' was thrown open by the new Charter adopted in 1858.

With hindsight, this action may be seen as one of the most significant developments in higher education policy in this country. From that date, the University's non-medical examinations, from matriculation level upwards, were open to all-comers anywhere in the world. Or, rather, at least until 1867, to all-male-comers who were prepared to pay the fees (which, from 1859, were £2 for matriculation, and £5 each for the first and pass degree examinations). The University was no longer concerned whether its students had pursued a course of study at a recognized institution, or studied with a recognized tutor, or had gained their knowledge purely by self-study. Henceforth, all were to be allowed to enter the examination system on equal terms.

As we have indicated, this development was not without its opponents, and it attracted considerable invective at the time. John Henry Newman, in a famous passage in his Dublin discourses on the nature of university education, was clearly referring to London when he said:

> I protest to you, gentlemen, that if I had to choose between a so-called University which dispensed with residence and tutorial superintendence, and gave its degrees to any person who passed an examination in a wide range of subjects, and a University which had no Professors or examinations at all, but merely brought a number of young men together for three or four years, and then sent them away as the University of Oxford is said to have done some sixty years since, if I were asked which of these two methods was the better discipline of the intellect . . . if I must determine which of the two courses was the more successful in training, moulding, enlarging the mind, which sent out men the more fitted for their secular duties, which produced better public men, men of the world, men whose names would descend to posterity, I have no hesitation in giving the preference to that University which did nothing, over that which exacted of its members an acquaintance with every science under the sun.
>
> (Newman 1859: 137–8)

Indeed, the last quarter of the nineteenth century was marked by continuing debate and controversy over the relative importance of the teaching (and pastoral) and examining roles within the University (Allchin 1905; Humberstone 1926; Dunsheath and Miller 1958; Harte 1986: Ch. 4). Karl Pearson, the famous statistician and a professor at University College, was among the University's most forthright critics:

> To term the body which examines at Burlington House [then the headquarters of the University of London] a university is a perversion of language, to which no charter or Act of Parliament can give a real sanction. . . . Examinations may be excellent, may even fulfil all that could be expected from them; but it is the teachers, not the examinations, the scholars, not the degrees, which constitute a university.
>
> (Pearson 1892: 7–9)

These debates (along with related medical concerns) substantially occupied two Royal Commissions: the Selborne Commission of 1888–9 and the Gresham (or Cowper) Commission of 1891–4. Neither was able to resolve the issues in a way which proved broadly acceptable to all of the main parties concerned, and the result was a messy compromise.

The Selborne Commission produced a fairly modest report, arguing that the teaching and examining functions should be combined within a reorganized University:

> It was no part of the original conception of the present London University, that it should be a mere examining body, without direct

connexion with any teaching institutions. . . . A mere examining body would not then have seemed to fulfil the true idea of a university, as a seat and centre for learning. . . . The teaching institutions of a University of London, in the proper sense of those words, ought, in our judgement, to be in or near London. For other parts of the kingdom (as for the Colonies), it is sufficient that there should be access, as heretofore, to examinations and degrees.

(University of London Commission 1889: viii, ix, xiii)

Nevertheless, a minority of the Commission members aligned themselves with the view that a separate teaching university should be established in London. A compromise reconstruction plan was then developed by the Senate, but vetoed by the Convocation, and in the resulting impasse support for a separate teaching University (to be called the 'Albert' or 'Gresham' University) grew.

The arguments were then reconsidered in a clearer and more thorough fashion by the Gresham Commission, though it reached much the same conclusions as its predecessor. Drawing on the existing example of the University of Dublin (see Chapter 4), it recommended that the teaching and examining functions of the University should be split between two separate operations within the one institution:

> The University will, according to our proposals, have power to admit to degrees as internal students persons who have fulfilled such conditions of examination and attendance as the University shall from time to time lay down; and it will retain its present function of examining candidates, and conferring upon them degrees, diplomas, and certificates without regard (except in the case of Medicine) to the place or institution in which they may have received their education.
>
> (Gresham University Commission 1894: xxxi)

The 'internal' teaching University was to be based on the Colleges in the London area, which were designated as Schools of the University. The 'external' examining University would take on the distance education role, and continue to serve students studying elsewhere or on their own.

It was not until 1898 that a University of London Act to implement these changes (from 1900 onwards) was passed by Parliament. And, even then, the arguments continued, exercising another Royal Commission in 1913, and reverberating right up until the present day (see Chapter 6).

The University's system of examinations

During the nineteenth century, the examinations offered by the University of London increased in number and gradually changed in character. By the latter part of this period, the London examination system had become very influential. Its curriculum was viewed as a standard by new university and college foundations, as well as by many schools. It even helped to bring about changes in practice in the old established institutions: Oxford, Cambridge and the public schools. At the same time, the London system – by virtue of its national status, convenience and availability – played a major role in establishing the acceptability of examinations as a means of assessment and advancement. This development both anticipated and underpinned the rise of the meritocracy in the later Victorian period:

> Rigorous examination by means of written papers in a wide range of subjects at entrance to the University and at the successive stages of the degree course was a deliberate and much cherished reform in academic habits and a novelty of the first importance. London matriculation won a place for itself as a school-leaving examination quite independently of its function as a test for university entrance, and, including, as it did, English history, geography, chemistry, and natural history, played a great part in the modernisation of the curriculum of the secondary schools.
>
> (Bellot 1969: 7)

At first, the range of examinations offered was rather limited. The matriculation examination controlled entry to the whole system, and could be followed by further examinations for the BA, LLB, MB, MA, LLD and MD qualifications, or by one of a number of scripture tests. The MB involved an intermediate examination and, together with the matriculation, BA and LLB qualifications, could be taken at pass or honours level.

Any apparent limitation in the range of these examinations was, however, compensated for by the breadth of study and knowledge expected of the candidates. In this, and a number of other respects, the London system betrayed the influence of contemporary Scottish university practices. In 1844, for example, the syllabus for the matriculation examination covered mathematics, classics and either chemistry or natural philosophy. Classics included not just the Greek and Latin languages, but also the English language and 'outlines' of history and geography. Natural philosophy required 'a popular knowledge' of mechanics, hydrostatics, hydraulics, pneumatics, acoustics and optics. This examination, which had, naturally enough, more candidates than all of the others put together, lasted for five consecutive days. Candidates had to be at least 16 years old, but there were no other entrance requirements.

The next most popular examination, for the BA pass qualification, required a minimum of a further two-years' registration. It had a similar scope, covering mathematics and natural philosophy, animal physiology, classics and logic and moral philosophy. Classics at this level also included the French and German languages (University of London, *Calendar* (ULC) 1844).

While the level of knowledge which was required to pass these examinations was undoubtedly rather less than what is required of candidates now (as was the case in other universities), the examinations were certainly demanding. Indeed, they were regularly criticized at the time for being far too demanding. The BA pass examination in 1844, for example, included questions such as:

- Explain the action of the air-pump;
- Is logic properly defined to be 'the art of right reasoning'?;
- How long did Edward I reign? What renders his reign one of the most important in our history?

The matriculation pass examination for that year included the following questions:

- Describe briefly the state of society under the Anglo-Norman kings;
- Define specific gravity;
- Explain the action (1) of the siphon, (2) of the air-pump.

(ULC 1845)

It is easy, of course, to see how such questions could (and did) encourage cramming by candidates, by placing more emphasis on memory than on understanding.

In time, further qualifications were added, while the curricula for the existing examinations were periodically revised and restructured. The BA was split into first and second examinations in 1859, and the minimum period of registration was increased to three years, to give further force to the Senate's wish that candidates should display 'reasonable evidence of antecedent continuous study'. From the same date the matriculation examinations – in response to growing demand and the lack of space in the University's examination halls – were set twice a year.

In 1860, BSc and DSc qualifications were introduced, the former also involving first and second examinations. The MB was extended to include a preliminary scientific examination, which shared much of its curriculum with the first BSc examination. The MS (Master of Surgery) qualification was introduced in 1863, and the BS in 1866; to be followed in 1868 by the DLitt, in 1878 by degrees in Music (BMus and DMus), and in 1882 by a postgraduate teaching diploma (The Art, Theory and History of Teaching).

The standards required to pass the examinations were also raised as time progressed, but not too far. Thus, in 1882, Senate instructed the Registrar:

> to inform all Examiners on their appointment that the Matriculation examination is primarily intended for students of 16 or 17 years of age; and to remind them that the Papers in each subject form a part only of the formidable ordeal of an examination lasting for five days; therefore, that while the knowledge required of each subject should be sound as far as it goes, the Examination in each should never be otherwise than of a simple elementary character within the limits of the syllabus, – more searching tests being reserved for later Examinations.

(ULSM 19 April 1882: 46)

By the end of the century, the London matriculation examination was established as a high quality, national, school-leaving examination. As a standard, it was comparable with practices in other European countries, and it provided a mechanism through which changing national policies could be introduced. At the turn of the century, the matriculation examination covered Latin, English, mathematics and general elementary science; plus one subject chosen from: Greek; French; German; Arabic; Sanskrit; mechanics; chemistry; sound, light and heat; magnetism and electricity; or botany. This curriculum subsequently became the basis for the school leaving certificate and, later on, the General Certificate of Education (see Chapter 6).

By this time, the final BA pass examination had developed to include Latin with Roman history, Greek with Grecian history, and two subjects chosen from: English; French, German, Italian, Arabic or Sanskrit; history; pure or mixed mathematics; mental and moral science; and political economy. The final BSc pass examination involved taking three subjects from: pure mathematics, mixed mathematics, experimental physics, chemistry, botany, zoology, animal physiology, and geology and physical geography (ULC 1897–8). An increasing number of candidates were, however, opting to take the honours examinations as well, specializing in a specific subject area.

The University's relationships with other institutions

During the nineteenth century, the University of London developed links – either directly or through its students – with an enormous array of educational institutions throughout the British Isles and overseas – schools, colleges and universities. At one level, it operated as a kind of finishing school or crammer for Oxbridge candidates:

> It rather looks as though the nineteenth-century market place directed a stream of able young men to the London colleges who required topping up before they were ready to go on to tackle Greats at Oxford or the moral science Tripos at Cambridge, and another stream of the less able or less wealthy who were content to stay the course and take a London BA. The high ability stream, it may be surmised, were those who were excluded from the conventional public-school route to Oxbridge, for a variety of financial, social, and religious reasons; for them Victorian London served as a kind of superior sixth-form college, an Oxbridge feeder that broadened and deepened the narrow and socially exclusive intake of Isis and Cam.
> (Thompson 1990b: 68)

But it is the University's developing relationships with institutions of rather lower status which is of key interest here, since these are indicative of its

Table 3.1 Numbers of institutions associated with the University of London 1841–1901, by location

	1841	1851	1861	1871	1881	1891	1901
'institutions empowered to issue certificates for degrees in arts and laws':							
London	4	4	5	5	5	–	–
England*	17	26	31	31	31	–	–
Scotland	–	4	5	5	5	–	–
Wales	–	1	3	3	3	–	–
Ireland	4	6	10	9	9	–	–
Overseas	–	–	2	2	2	–	–
Total	21	37	51	50	50	–	–
'recognized medical institutions, schools and teachers':							
London	16	13	17	19	20	21	27
England*	28	33	50	53	53	57	67
Scotland	8	7	9	9	9	9	12
Wales	–	–	–	–	–	–	2
Ireland	13	20	21	21	22	23	24
Overseas	3	4	6	6	7	10	11
Total	52	64	86	89	91	99	116

* the figures for England include those for London

Sources: ULC, ULSM, various dates

federal nature and of its role as a distance examining body. These relationships may be explored by using a number of complementary sources of evidence.

First, lists of 'institutions empowered to issue certificates to candidates for degrees in arts and laws' and of 'recognised medical institutions, schools and teachers' appear in the *Minutes of Senate* from 1839 onwards, and in the University *Calendar* from its first publication in 1844. The medical institutions are then listed for every year throughout the remainder of the century. In the former case, however, the lists were effectively made irrelevant by the 1858 Charter. Indeed, the opening up of the non-medical examinations to all-comers was partly intended to address the rather dubious standards of certification practised by some of the recognized institutions. Nevertheless, the lists of 'institutions empowered to issue certificates' were continued until 1883, when one of the members of Senate finally drew attention to the anomaly.

Second, from 1859 onwards it became possible to take some of the University's examinations at a number of provincial centres within the British Isles. And from 1865, as the University became more and more an imperial institution, it was possible to take some examinations overseas. Lists of the centres involved appear in both the *Minutes of Senate* and the University *Calendar*.

Table 3.2 'Institutions from which the University is empowered to receive Certificates for Degrees in Arts and Laws', 1851

The Universities of the United Kingdom [i.e. Cambridge, Durham, Oxford; Aberdeen, Edinburgh, Glasgow, St Andrews; Trinity College Dublin]

University College, London
King's College, London
St Cuthbert's College, Ushaw
Stonyhurst College
Royal Belfast Academical Institution
Manchester New College
St Mary's College, Oscott
St Patrick's College, Carlow
St Edmund's College, near Ware
Homerton Old College
Highbury College
Colleges of St Peter and St Paul, Prior Park, near Bath
Spring Hill College, Birmingham
Stepney College
College of St Gregory the Great, Downside, near Bath
Countess of Huntingdon's College at Cheshunt
The Baptist College at Bristol
Airedale College, Undercliffe, near Bradford
Protestant Dissenters College at Rotherham
Presbyterian College at Caermarthen
St Kyran's College, Kilkenny
Huddersfield College
Lancashire Independent College
Wesley College, near Sheffield
Queen's College, Birmingham
Wesleyan Colegiate Institution at Taunton
Western College, Plymouth
West of England Dissenters' Proprietary School, Taunton
St Patrick's College, Thurles

Source: ULC 1851: 75

Third, the University's growing relations with providers of secondary education may also be examined. Lists are provided from 1878 onwards of schools which had been successfully inspected and examined by the University.

Fourth, and finally, further evidence of other institutions' involvement in the preparation of candidates for the University's examinations is provided in the lists of successful students which were published each year. This evidence is considered in the next section of the chapter.

Table 3.1 gives details of the numbers of institutions associated with the University of London for both arts/laws and medicine over the period from 1841 to 1901. It illustrates a number of interesting trends.

Table 3.3 'Institutions from which the University is empowered to receive Certificates for Degrees in Medicine', 1851

Birmingham	Queen's College; Birmingham General Hospital
Bristol	Bristol Medical School; Bristol Infirmary; St Peter's Hospital
Haslar	Royal Naval Hospital
Hull	Hull and East Riding of Yorkshire School of Medicine and Anatomy
Leeds	Leeds School of Medicine; Leeds General Infirmary
Leicester	Leicester Infirmary
Liverpool	Liverpool Infirmary; Liverpool Fever Hospital and Infirmary
London	University College; King's College; Middlesex Hospital; School of Anatomy adjoining St George's Hospital; Charing Cross Hospital; St Thomas's Hospital; St Bartholomew's Hospital; Westminster Hospital; Guy's Hospital; St George's Hospital; the Physicians of the St Marylebone Infirmary; Royal College of Chemistry
Manchester	Royal Manchester School of Medicine and Surgery; Union Hospital; Royal Infirmary
Newcastle	School of Medicine and Surgery
Northampton	Northampton General Infirmary
Nottingham	General Hospital near Nottingham
Sheffield	Sheffield Medical Institution
York	York School of Medicine
Aberdeen	King's College and University
Edinburgh	University of Edinburgh; Minto House Dispensary; Royal Infirmary
Glasgow	Andersonian Institution; Royal Infirmary
Belfast	Royal Belfast Academical Institution
Cork	Cork Recognized School of Medicine; Cork North Infirmary and Cork South Infirmary (in conjunction)
Dublin	Original School of Anatomy, Medicine and Surgery, Peter Street; School of Physic in Ireland; Apothecaries' Hall of Ireland; School of Medicine, Park Street; Richmond Hospital School of Anatomy, Medicine and Surgery; Theatre of Anatomy and School of Surgery, 27 Peter Street; St Vincent's Hospital; Mercer's Hospital; Jervis-Street Hospital; Dublin School of Anatomy, Surgery and Medicine, Digges Street; Royal College of Surgeons in Ireland; Meath Hospital; City of Dublin Hospital; Coombe Lying-in Hospital; Dr Steeven's Hospital
Maryborough	Queen's County Infirmary
Malta	University of Malta
Ceylon	Military Hospital
Bengal	Medical College
Canada	University of M'Gill College, Montreal

Source: ULC 1851: 76–7

After the 1858 Charter was adopted, no new institutions were added to the list of those 'empowered to issue certificates to candidates for degrees in arts and laws'. The number recognized then stabilized at about 50, of which 15 were universities or university colleges. Though all the British universities, together with the Queen's Colleges in Ireland, were automatically included in this list, most of them seldom issued candidates with the appropriate certification.

The great majority of the institutions recognized in this way were located in either the English provinces or in Ireland:

> the institutions were, it has to be admitted, a pretty mixed bag. The line between secondary education and higher education, both as yet anachronistic terms, was still to be drawn, and alongside the varied catholic and nonconformist establishments were some institutions that were clearly schools.
>
> (Harte 1986: 96)

In 1851, for example, the list of recognized institutions includes – alongside University College and King's College – St Cuthbert's College Ushaw, Stonyhurst College, the Baptist College at Bristol and Queen's College Birmingham (see Table 3.2). Later additions to the list included the Working Men's College in London and Owens College in Manchester (later to become the core of Manchester University).

The 'recognised medical institutions, schools and teachers' were both more numerous and much more carefully regulated. From the 52 institutions recognized in 1841, the number more than doubled to 116 by 1901. Most were major teaching hospitals, and many were associated with universities or university colleges (see Table 3.3). About one-quarter were located in London itself, and were later to become part of the 'internal', teaching University. One-third were in major English provincial cities and towns, one-quarter in Ireland (mostly in Dublin) and one-tenth in Scotland, with a similar proportion located overseas in Australia, Canada, Ceylon, India, Malta or New Zealand. There were no associated medical institutions in Wales until the very end of the century.

Table 3.4 provides information on the second category of evidence noted: the numbers of provincial centres at which it was possible to sit University of London examinations. The table is confined to the period 1871–1901, and it should be interpreted with some care, as the available lists relate to the plans announced beforehand. It is not possible to say whether the institutions involved provided facilities only for their own students, though it does seem likely that this was the case for some, but not all, of them. The table shows that little advantage was taken of these arrangements at first. Only three provincial centres are mentioned in 1871, and only five in 1881. During this period, Owens College in Manchester stands out in hosting not just the matriculation examinations, but also the first BA, first BSc, preliminary scientific, final BA and final BSc examinations (the practical examinations for the science and medical degrees did, however, have to be taken in London). Indeed, the link with Owens College provided an early model for the University of London's subsequent relations with developing university colleges. This relationship also foreshadowed, in many ways, the structure of the Victoria

Table 3.4 Numbers of provincial centres for University of London Examinations 1871–1901

Examination	1871	1881	1891	1901
Matriculation	3	5	21	18
First/Intermediate BA	1	1	11	12
First/Intermediate BSc	1	1	10	12
Preliminary Scientific (MB)	1	1	11	12
Second/Final BA	1	1	6	9
Second/Final BSc	1	0	0	5
Total Centres	3	5	22	18

Sources: ULC, ULSM, various dates

University which was established in 1880 around the College itself (Fiddes 1937; Charlton 1951).

A continuing concentration by the provincial centres on the lower level examinations is apparent as the system expanded in later years. Thus, in 1891, of the 22 centres identified, 11 only hosted the matriculation examination, and just six offered examinations at final degree level (all for the BA).

The institutions which served as provincial centres were mainly – unlike those which had earlier been involved in the certification of students – actual or aspirant institutions of higher education. In 1891, the university colleges at Aberystwyth, Bangor, Bristol, Cardiff, Leeds, Liverpool, Manchester, Nottingham and Sheffield were all listed as centres. Five of them hosted the full range of examinations up to and including that for the final BA (see Table 3.5). These links were of major importance in enabling and encouraging the development of higher education throughout England and Wales.

There were, however, some institutions which acted as provincial centres which were not, or at least did not remain or subsequently become, institutions of higher education. In 1891, it was possible – providing you were female – to sit all of the examinations listed in Table 3.4, with the exception of the final BSc, at Cheltenham Ladies College. This college prepared whole classes of students for the London matriculation examination, as well as for the Oxford senior and Cambridge higher examinations. Many of its students then went on to study for a London degree within the College's 'university department':

> the College was fully accepted as a University College for women. It is mentioned on equal terms with the women's colleges in Oxford, Cambridge and London. For some years, in fact, Bedford [Bedford College in London] and Cheltenham were the only collegiate centres where women could be prepared for the London degree.
>
> (Clarke 1953: 78)

Table 3.5   Provincial examination centres, 1891

Institution	Examination				
	1	2	3	4	5
Aberystwyth, University College	*	*	*	*	
Bangor, University College	*	*	*	*	*
Bedford, Modern School	*				
Birmingham, Mason Science College		*	*	*	
Birmingham, Queen's College	*				
Bristol, University College	*	*	*	*	
Cardiff, University College	*	*	*	*	*
Cheltenham, Ladies' College	*	*	*	*	*
Downside, St Gregory's College	*				
Edinburgh, Heriot-Watt College	*				
Epsom, Royal Medical College	*			*	
Glasgow, Training College	*				
Leeds, Yorkshire College	*	*	*	*	*
Liverpool, University College	*	*	*	*	*
Manchester, Owens College	*	*	*	*	*
Newcastle, School of Science and Art	*	*	*	*	
Nottingham, University College	*				
Oswestry, High School	*				
Portsmouth, Grammar School	*				
Sheffield, Firth College	*				
Stonyhurst College	*				
Ushaw, St Cuthbert's College	*	*			

Note – the examinations are:
1 Matriculation
2 Intermediate Arts
3 Intermediate Science
4 Preliminary Scientific (for the MB)
5 Final BA
Source: ULC 1891: 30–1

The College's work in this area continued until the 1920s. The College was also closely involved in the preparation of candidates for the St Andrews LLA examinations (see Chapter 5).

Both the matriculation and the intermediate Arts examinations could be taken at St Cuthbert's College, Ushaw. Less surprisingly, a number of other schools, including Bedford Modern School, St Gregory's College Downside and Stonyhurst College, also hosted the matriculation examination. Some of these institutions, and others which prepared candidates to take the examinations elsewhere, were catering for both children and young adults. Sometimes – for example in the case of the North London Collegiate School for Girls (Scrimgeour 1950) – staff would also take the examinations alongside pupils (this was also the case with the Irish and Scottish examinations discussed in Chapters 4 and 5).

The arrangements made to allow candidates to sit University of London examinations overseas, at a time when most communications went by sea, clearly caused the authorities some problems. Nevertheless, between 1865, when the first colonial examinations were held in Mauritius, and 1899, University of London examinations were held in a total of 18 colonies spread right across the globe. A much more limited range of examinations was offered than at home, focusing on matriculation and on the arts and law degrees, and excluding science and medicine (Namie 1989: 428, 434).

The 1882 University *Calendar* mentions no less than 17 colonial centres at which the matriculation examinations could be taken: Bombay, Calcutta and Madras in India; Barbados, Demerara, Jamaica and Trinidad in the West Indies; Fredericton, Halifax, Kingston, Montreal, Ottawa, Quebec, St John's and Toronto in Canada; plus New Zealand and Tasmania. In most cases, the students concerned then came to Britain if they wanted to sit further examinations and complete a University of London degree. These facilities were cut back at the end of the century, in recognition of the establishment of independent universities in some of the colonies; though they were subsequently expanded in those colonies which did not have universities (see Chapter 7).

The third aspect of the University's relationship with other institutions – the examination and inspection of schools – began in 1878 (ULC 1878: 200–1). These procedures were apparently adopted in response to demand, and built upon the University's role as a national provider of school-leaving examinations. The procedures represented a more satisfactory version of the earlier provisions for empowering institutions to issue certificates to candidates. They also demonstrated a recognition of the University's growing responsibility for the maintenance of standards throughout an educational system which was becoming organised and stratified on more 'modern' lines.

Between 1878 and 1900 a total of 50 schools were examined and inspected on one or more occasions. Indeed, one school, Bedford Modern School, was inspected every year during this period: a total of 23 consecutive inspections! These examinations took the form of written questions, supplemented by visits undertaken with or without warning (ULSM 18 December 1901: 37–42). All of the schools examined were in England or Wales, with half in the London area alone. They cover a rich variety: boys' and girls' schools, public and private schools, small and large schools. Only a few of those which were inspected had earlier appeared in the lists of those empowered to issue certificates.

The examination records

The University of London has always published lists of the successful candidates in each of its examinations. Table 3.6 gives details of the numbers of candidates, and of the numbers of these who were successful,

Table 3.6   Numbers of candidates and passes, University of London examinations, 1841–1901

	1841	1851	1861	1871	1881	1891	1901
(A) Numbers of candidates:							
Matriculation	89	241	444	902	1,576	2,839	4,198
First/Intermediate BA	–	–	137	221	364	586	537
BA Pass	40	67	76	152	224	403	317
First/Intermediate BSc	–	–	24	41	76	227	681
BSc Pass	–	–	6	14	50	154	322
Preliminary MB	–	–	90	118	209	218	346
First/Intermediate MB	80	34	20	39	101	226	334
MB Pass	21	21	29	23	54	107	211
First/Intermediate LLB	–	–	–	39	49	68	107
LLB Pass	10	5	3	17	24	34	54
Total all examinations	248	379	855	1,600	2,816	5,049	7,335
(B) Numbers of passes:							
Matriculation	64	214	265	398	847	1,488	2,121
First/Intermediate BA	–	–	88	85	202	350	218
BA Pass	35	49	55	63	116	242	170
First/Intermediate BSc	–	–	10	17	37	96	425
BSc Pass	–	–	5	11	18	75	156
Preliminary MB	–	–	58	43	116	99	202
First/Intermediate MB	50	27	15	28	63	74	227
MB Pass	18	19	20	19	49	75	128
First/Intermediate LLB	–	–	–	23	22	35	65
LLB Pass	9	5	3	8	15	13	35
Total all examinations	184	324	543	721	1,545	2,685	3,880

Sources: ULC, ULSM, various dates

for each of the main examinations during the period 1841 to 1901. The numbers of candidates involved increased dramatically during this period, rising from 248 in 1841 to 7,335 in 1901, almost doubling every ten years. By the end of the century, the numbers involved were far in excess of those studying with any other university in the country. The numbers of those who passed the examinations also rose, but at a slower rate, increasing from 184 (74 per cent of those who entered) in 1841 to 3,880 (53 per cent) in 1901. Those taking the matriculation examination outnumbered all of the other candidates. The BA examinations remained the next most popular until the end of the century, when they were overtaken by the BSc examinations.

The increased failure rates evident in these statistics caused the University some disquiet at the time, and investigations were periodically instituted by Senate. The first of these took place in 1861, when it was noted

Table 3.7 Institutions and methods of study mentioned for successful candidates, University of London, 1861 and 1891

Examination	No. passes	Institutions mentioned	At/with an institution	Solely by: Private study	Solely by: Private tuition
1861					
Matriculation	265	104	203	12	50
First Arts	88	22	57	14	17
BA Pass	55	16	45	2	8
First Science	10	6	8	1	1
BSc Pass	5	4	4	–	1
Preliminary MB	58	18	58	–	–
First MB	15	7	15	–	–
MB Pass	20	8	20	–	–
1891					
Matriculation	1,488	550	998	235	145
Intermediate Arts	350	77	194	128	28
BA Pass	242	50	126	98	18
Intermed. Science	96	48	79	11	6
BSc Pass	75	36	58	11	6
Preliminary MB	99	34	92	3	4
Intermediate MB	74	16	74	–	–
MB Pass	75	20	75	–	–

Source: ULSM, various dates

that 76 per cent of the candidates aged 16 years old had passed the July matriculation examinations, compared with an overall proportion of 64 per cent (ULSM 31 July 1861: 56–7). Nothing was found to be at fault with the examinations, and this was again the verdict in 1872, when only 41 per cent of candidates passed the January matriculation (ibid. 21 February 1872: 21).

In 1877, when 47 per cent passed the June matriculation, above average failure rates were noted for the Latin paper and for candidates aged over 19 years old (ULSM 17 October 1877: 106–7). And in 1900, when just 37 per cent of candidates passed the January matriculation, with Latin again a major stumbling block, all examiners were circulated to see if they could offer any explanations. They were not particularly forthcoming, and it appeared that the main reason was a simple lack of adequate preparation (ibid. 25 April 1900: 85–99).

The examination records provide further and more detailed insights into the University of London's relationship with other institutions. The lists of successful candidates record the institution or institutions at which they studied, and also indicate whether they prepared themselves wholly or partly by private study or tuition. We cannot, of course, rely entirely on either the accuracy or comprehensiveness of these listings, since they derive from forms filled in by the candidates themselves (which were not checked by the University). Where candidates prepared themselves by a variety of means, or attended a range of institutions, over a number of years, this may not have been fully recorded. Similarly, the records do not tell us whether students were studying full-time or part-time. But they do provide a useful and suggestive source for our analyses. And they can also be compared in some instances with the records kept by the other institutions concerned.

Table 3.7 provides details of the numbers of institutions, and of the frequency of other methods of study, listed for successful candidates for the main examinations in two sample years, 1861 and 1891. It is clear from this table that the numbers of institutions involved in preparing students for the University of London's examinations increased steadily in the latter part of the century. The 104 institutions mentioned for successful matriculation students in 1861 had risen to 550 by 1891.

Only a minority of the institutions involved in preparing successful matriculation candidates were in London itself: 23 (22 per cent) in 1861 and 90 (16 per cent) in 1891. This confirms the increasingly national pattern of provision identified in Table 3.1. The institutions which prepared the largest numbers of successful matriculation students were, however, in London. In 1861, University College stood out with 22 successful candidates (8 per cent of the total), while King's College had 16.

By 1891, many more institutions were involved, and larger numbers of students were being prepared in non-university institutions (see Table 3.8). In that year, the North London Collegiate School for Girls recorded 30 successful candidates in the matriculation examinations (2 per cent of the total), as did King Edward's Grammar School in Birmingham. The Birkbeck Institution and St John's College Battersea each recorded 25. University College recorded just 10 successful candidates, King's College 8; but University College School had 22 and King's College School 12. A clearer separation between higher and secondary education was becoming apparent.

Naturally enough, fewer institutions were involved in preparing students for the higher level examinations, and these tended to be mainly universities or university colleges, or, in the case of the degrees in science and medicine, medical schools. In 1861, more than half of the institutions mentioned for successful BA pass candidates came into these categories, along with three-quarters of those mentioned for BSc pass students, and nearly all of those recorded for students passing the MB examinations. In that year, two-thirds of the institutions mentioned for successful BA pass candidates were in London. This was also the case for three-quarters of those mentioned for the BSc pass examination, and for four-fifths of those for the MB pass qualification.

Table 3.8 Institutions most commonly mentioned by successful students, matriculation, final BA, BSc and MB examinations, 1891

Institution	No. mentions
Matriculation	
1 King Edward's Grammar School, Birmingham	30
North London Collegiate School for Girls	30
3 Birkbeck Institution	25
St John's College, Battersea	25
5 St Mark's College, Chelsea	24
6 St Paul's School	23
7 University College School	22
8 Borough Road, New College	19
Epsom College	19
10 City of London School	15
11 University College, Aberystwyth	14
12 Wyggeston School, Leicester	13
13 King's College School	12
14 University College, Cardiff	10
Borough Road Training College	10
Merchant Taylor's School, Crosby	10
St Cuthbert's College, Ushaw	10
University College	10
Westminster Training College	10
20 Clifton College	9
Manchester Grammar School	9
Woodford Wells, Bancroft's School	9
23 Aske's Schools, Hatcham	8
Dulwich College	8
King's College	8
Mason College, Birmingham	8
Royal Holloway College	8
Westminster School	8
York, Friends' School	8
York, Mount School	8
Final BA	
1 University College, Aberystwyth	15
2 University Tutorial College	13
3 University College	12
4 Cheltenham Ladies' College	10
5 Royal Holloway College	9
6 Bedford College	6
University College, Cardiff	6
8 Mason College Birmingham	5
University College, Bangor	5
10 Flounders College	3
King Edward's Grammar School, Birmingham	3
St John's College, Battersea	3
Stonyhurst College	3

continued

Table 3.8—continued

Institution	No. mentions
Final BA	
14　Borough Road, New College	2
Headingly College	2
King's College	2
Kingswood School	2
Owens College, Manchester	2
Richmond Wesleyan College	2
St Gregory's College, Downside	2
University College, Jamaica	2
University College, Liverpool	2
Westfield College	2
Final BSc	
1　Birkbeck Institution	9
University College	9
3　Royal College of Science	8
4　University of Cambridge	5
5　University College Bangor	4
6　King Edward's Grammar School, Birmingham	3
King's College	3
Mason College Birmingham	3
St Thomas's Hospital Medical School	3
10　Bedford College	2
Pharmaceutical Society	2
St Bartholomew's Hospital Medical School	2
University College, Aberystwyth	2
University College, Bristol	2
University College, Cardiff	2
University College, Liverpool	2
University College, Nottingham	2
University of Oxford	2
University Tutorial College	2
Yorkshire College Leeds	2
Final MB	
1　University College	20
2　Guy's Hospital Medical School	12
3　St Bartholomew's Hospital Medical School	9
4　London School of Medicine for Women	6
Owens College, Manchester	6
6　Manchester Royal Institution	5
7　London Hospital Medical School	3
St Mary's Hospital Medical School	3
Yorkshire College, Leeds	3
10　Birmingham General Hospital	2
Liverpool Royal Institution	2
Queen's College, Birmingham	2
Royal Free Hospital Medical School	2

Source: ULSM 1891, various dates

An increasing number of institutions outside London became involved in the preparation of students for the degree examinations towards the end of the century. By 1891, in the case of the BA pass examination, nearly two-thirds of the institutions mentioned for successful candidates were outside London, a direct reversal of the position 30 years earlier. The Welsh university colleges at Aberystwyth (which had the best record for the BA examination that year: 15 passes, or 6 per cent of the total), Bangor and Cardiff show up particularly well in the 'league tables' included in Table 3.8.

This growing regional spread is confirmed by the records of the institutions concerned. These included, for example, Owens College in Manchester (see Fiddes 1937), University College Bristol (Cottle and Sherborne 1951), University College Nottingham (Wood 1953), Hartley College Southampton (Patterson 1962) and Yorkshire College in Leeds (Gosden and Taylor 1975). The students which these institutions prepared for the University of London examinations represented a small, but increasingly important, part of their total recruitment.

Not all of the institutions preparing successful degree candidates were actual or aspirant university colleges. Among the 23 leading institutions for the BA degree listed in Table 3.8 are to be found ten which were (or which became) schools or training colleges. Cheltenham Ladies College again stands out, with ten successful candidates in 1891 (4 per cent of the total), only two fewer than University College and five times as many as King's College! Another of those listed, the University Tutorial College, which is perhaps best described as a successful crammer, features in the table in an even higher position with 13 successful candidates (5 per cent of the total).

Relatively few of the institutions concerned were located outside the British Isles. Indeed, only one, University College Jamaica, with two successful BA students in 1891, features in Table 3.8. Yet, over the period between 1865 and 1899, some 1,682 candidates sat University of London examinations in the colonies, of whom 714 passed. Just over half of these candidates, though only 38 per cent of those who were successful, took their examinations in one small colony, Mauritius (Namie 1989: 434).

Returning to Table 3.7, perhaps its most interesting aspect, particularly when viewed from the perspectives of open-ness and distance education, is the number of students who apparently did not attend a conventional educational institution as part of their preparation for the examinations. They prepared themselves by private tuition or private study – which, so far as the University was concerned, included correspondence tuition as well as self study – or by a combination of both. Many more candidates mixed private study and/or tuition with limited institutional attendance.

In 1861, 50 (19 per cent) of the successful matriculation candidates stated that they had prepared themselves by private tuition alone. This was also the case for 17 (19 per cent) of those passing the intermediate arts examination, and for 8 (15 per cent) of those achieving the BA pass degree itself. In 1891, the respective figures were 145 (10 per cent), 28 (8 per cent) and 18 (7 per cent).

Numerous advertisements from private tutors appeared in the journals of the day (Elliott 1973), and some were included in the University *Calendar*. Thus, in 1871, we find that 'Messrs A. Bassett Hopkins, MA, and T. Smedley Oldfield, BA, receive at their chambers, 12 South Square, Gray's Inn, candidates for . . . matriculation, first BA and second BA examinations.' And, in 1878, another advertisement was offering 'country preparation for matriculation, first BA and other examinations. The Rev. Dr Lucas MA and LLD . . . receives Pupils into his house for all the necessary subjects.'

The numbers preparing themselves by private study only grew dramatically during the last part of the century. By 1891, 235 (16 per cent) of the successful candidates at matriculation level stated that they had prepared themselves solely by these means. A further 221 (15 per cent) indicated that they had prepared themselves partly by private study. The proportions for the BA degree are even more impressive. At intermediate level, 128 (37 per cent) of the successful candidates prepared themselves only by private study, with a further 53 (15 per cent) partly using this means. And at pass degree level, the respective figures were higher still: 98 (40 per cent) and 49 (20 per cent).

At this time, for these examinations, private study was clearly the normal method of preparation, and one used to some extent by the majority of successful candidates. Even in the case of the BSc pass degree, 11 (15 per cent) of the successful students in 1891 apparently prepared themselves for the examinations solely by this means.

Most of those preparing for their examinations by private study probably made at least some use of correspondence courses. Indeed, the main correspondence colleges had a far greater role in the preparation of candidates for the University of London's examinations at this time than any of the university colleges, colleges or schools listed in Table 3.8:

> in the year 1890 nearly 40% of successful Arts graduates had received their tuition, in whole or in part, from University Correspondence College. By the year 1899 the percentage figure was just over 60.
>
> (Elliott 1973: 80)

University Correspondence College had been founded in 1887 in Cambridge (it eventually became part of the National Extension College). Other correspondence colleges involved in preparing students for London examinations at this time included the similarly named University Correspondence Classes, founded in 1882, and the University Examinations Postal Institution, founded in 1891 (these two colleges amalgamated in 1894).

The University Correspondence College was so successful that it was able to take out a 30 page advertisement in the 1889–90 edition of the University of London *Calendar* (following which such advertisements were banned). Its advertisement detailed the comprehensive range of textbooks, model answers, tutorial classes, revision classes, tutors, library facilities and correspondence courses available. Full correspondence courses were organized on the basis of a 'general method of work':

> Each week the pupil receives a Scheme of Study, which consists of Selections from Text-books, Distinction of Important Points upon which stress is laid in his Examination, Hints, Notes on difficult and salient portions, etc., and Illustrative Examples with selected Text-book Exercises in Mathematical Subjects. After the first week, along with these, a Test Paper (compiled from previous Examination Papers) is given on the work of the preceding week, the answers to which must be posted to the Tutor on a day arranged. These are then examined and returned with corrections, hints and model answers in each subject, and solutions of all difficulties.
>
> (ULC 1889–90, advertisements: 41)

These courses were not, however, particularly cheap. That for the matriculation pass examination cost £6 6s 0d, but provided 18 lessons in each subject taken. The one-year intermediate arts course was slightly more expensive, at £9 9s 0d; with the one-year BA pass, intermediate science and BSc pass courses priced even higher at £12 12s 0d. Less expensive 'self-preparation' courses were also available, for half these prices or less, but these did not include any tutor contact.

An archetypal nineteenth century open university

Without doubt, the University of London was a major provider of distance education opportunities through its examination system in the latter half of the nineteenth century. More generally, it was also an outstanding example of an open university, in that it paid little regard to international borders, was unconcerned about the race or religion of its students, set only a minimum age limit, was in the vanguard in extending educational opportunities to women, and was little concerned with how its students prepared themselves for its examinations.

The importance of understanding the University's role in this way needs to be stressed, partly because its significance has not been adequately recognized by educational historians, and partly because it continues to have consequences (and lessons) for those involved in higher education today. Four aspects of the discussion in this chapter merit further emphasis in conclusion.

First, the adoption of the 1858 Charter by the University of London was a key moment in the expansion and democratization of higher education in this country. The opening up of the University's non-medical examinations to all candidates, regardless of their method of preparation, sanctioned and greatly stimulated higher level study outside formal educational institutions. Those undertaking such study were given the opportunity to gain credit and recognition for their knowledge and understanding. And this took place at a time when the possession of formal qualifications was becoming of increasing importance for career advancement.

Second, this development also enabled and encouraged the establishment and growth of institutions of higher education both in Britain and throughout the British Empire. The University of London provided nationally- and internationally-recognised syllabuses and examinations, allowing institutions gradually to build up their provision in different subjects in response to the spread of local demand. When this demand reached a certain level, institutions were able to host the University's examinations themselves. Later on, of course, many of them reached the point when they were able to function as fully autonomous universities.

Third – and, so far as the nineteenth century is concerned, more significantly – the opening up of the University's 'Royal Road' acted as a catalyst for the creation and rapid expansion of correspondence colleges to serve the needs of the private or distant student. It is indicative of the rudimentary state of higher education in most parts of the country at this time that these colleges enrolled many more students to prepare for the University of London's examinations than did any of the formal institutions which taught by face-to-face means.

Fourth, the University of London examination system had a major influence during this period in establishing more clearly the distinction between secondary and higher education. It did this by developing a carefully graded and structured, sequential series of syllabuses and examinations. By doing so, it effectively set the standards for both secondary and higher education sectors, making manifest their continuing mutual interdependence, while stimulating the demand for each.

One interesting consequence of this, which was to have deleterious effects for all those who subsequently sought a 'higher' education, was to be the creation of the notion of an entrance requirement, in the modern sense of that term (see Chapter 6).

4

Ireland's Temporary Open University: The Royal University of Ireland

The decision to establish the University of London (see Chapter 3), and the launching of extension programmes by Oxford, Cambridge and other universities (see Chapter 2), constituted deliberate attempts to extend the boundaries of British higher education and to provide learning opportunities for a whole new student body. The British government's motives in creating the Royal University of Ireland in 1879, however, were somewhat more mixed. Certainly the new institution was to provide graduation opportunities for a wide swathe of the Irish population hitherto denied them, but at the time the political advantages of the new settlement were probably of far more importance to Disraeli's government than its purely educational benefits.

Throughout the nineteenth century, a major theme of British policy in Ireland was the attempt to provide an educational system that would satisfy the needs and aspirations of the Catholic majority without offending Protestant susceptibilities, not just in Ireland but in the United Kingdom as a whole. In 1831 a general system of elementary education had been established in Ireland, some 40 years before any similar experiment in Great Britain itself. Intended to be run on non-denominational lines, it formed what eventually proved to be an abortive attempt at healing the religious divisions underlying Ireland's political problems (Akenson 1970). The difficulties of providing Irish Catholics with a university to equal in status the Protestant Trinity College in Dublin proved just as formidable.

The 1840s witnessed an attempt to develop a new state-sponsored institution in a way that would ease the path to higher education, particularly for those living in areas away from Dublin. A federal 'Queen's University', with constituent Queen's Colleges in Cork, Galway and Belfast, was then established to break the monopoly of Trinity College, Dublin. There were at first great hopes that the three colleges would develop on non-denominational lines, and act as a further balance to Trinity which was still firmly in Anglican hands. Such hopes were given a particular fillip in Galway, where the first college buildings were erected by a Protestant president on land made available to him by a Catholic priest. A denominational mix of students was also initially to be found, not only in Cork but also in Belfast, where the presence of numerous Catholics in a mainly Protestant college caused the more purist Presbyterians to withdraw and to set up their own college (Magee College) in Derry.

However, any hopes that the founding of the Queen's University in 1845 would solve the Irish University Question were inevitably dashed. Clearly, the biggest problem was that the new university did nothing to provide church-approved higher education for Catholics in what was by far the country's largest conurbation, Dublin. Although Trinity College was willing to admit Catholics, many parents were unwilling to send their sons to an Anglican institution, and indeed in some cases were forbidden to do so by their bishops.

But, even in the case of the officially interdenominational Queen's Colleges, there was considerable opposition from members of the Catholic hierarchy. Despite the access allowed to the colleges for the clergy of all the churches, the Catholic Archbishop of Tuam could still condemn them as 'Godless' establishments (an epithet also earned by University College in London). The government, for its part, rebuffed all the efforts of more conciliatory bishops who attempted to reach a compromise, involving the guarantee both of a Catholic presence on the colleges' staff and of a Catholic influence on their curriculum (Akenson 1970).

Catholic opposition to the whole scheme was given a considerable boost by the arrival on the scene of a new and powerful Catholic leader, Paul (later Cardinal) Cullen. First as an Irish representative in Rome, and then as an Archbishop in Ireland, he encouraged Irish Catholicism to adopt new ultramontane attitudes and to foster ever closer relationships with the Holy See. Cullen believed that such a policy made it impossible to participate in the British government's interdenominational education schemes and it was inevitable that under his aegis there should be a renewed outcry for a clearly Catholic set of schools crowned by a Catholic university (Bowen 1983).

In 1850 Cullen summoned the first Synod of the Irish Catholic church to have been held since the twelfth century. Meeting at Thurles, it enunciated unequivocally the official attitude of the Church on the university question. It described the three Queen's Colleges as:

> institutions which would have called forth our profound and lasting gratitude had they been framed in accordance with our religious tenets and principles [but] must now be considered evil of a most formidable kind against which it is our imperative duty to warn you with all the energy of our zeal and all the weight of our authority.
>
> (Irish Universities Commission 1902: 303)

A Catholic university?

Not unnaturally, this declaration was followed by an attempt to establish a purely Catholic university in Dublin under the Catholic hierarchy's auspices.

An invitation to head the new institution was issued to John Henry Newman, recently converted to the faith and a known veteran of university development. As a young Anglican don at Oxford, he had been a leader of the movement to revive those qualities of college teaching and pastoral care that had almost universally languished during the previous century, and he had continued to be a powerful influence in Oxford as Vicar of the University Church. His conversion was seen as a great victory for Roman Catholicism generally, and it was, no doubt, felt that in the Dublin post he could combine the religious zeal of the convert with that of a fervent educational reformer keen to emphasize the role of pastoral theology in the university.

Newman favoured a residential Oxford-style college system (see Newman 1859, as quoted in Chapter 3), a pattern that was likely also to appeal to many of the bishops even if not to the Catholic parents who would have to foot the bill. Trinity College, Dublin had for many years allowed a large number of non-resident students, who confined their appearance on its premises to examination times, to take part in what Foden suggests was a genuinely external examination system. By 1852, half of Trinity's undergraduates were non-resident, some of them living in England (McDowell and Webb 1982). These students were supplied with a syllabus, and each year there was a regular series of tests from which what would now be called credits were collected, without there being any final overall examination. Foden himself questions whether this 'complex but clearly defined process influenced developments at the London University' (Foden 1989: 17).

Nevertheless, Trinity College did still provide residence in the Oxbridge manner, especially for its most socially prestigious undergraduates. At its foundation in the sixteenth century, it had been deliberately modelled on Trinity College, Cambridge. Moreover, residence was usual in the many colleges throughout Ireland run by the religious orders. It was natural, therefore, that pastoral ideas should be given special emphasis by Newman in his celebrated Dublin lectures on 'The Idea of a University', delivered in 1852. These both defended the supreme place to be accorded to theology in the ideal university curriculum, and highlighted the face-to-face interaction of students and teachers in a mutually supportive academic community.

The qualities emphasized by Newman were clearly acceptable to a Catholic audience, though whether the personal liberalism which he had shown in his work at Oxford would necessarily be acceptable to the more authoritarian of the Catholic bishops and parents was another matter. However, he was never given the chance to prove himself. The Catholic 'University' was duly established, and a number of handsome small-scale buildings were provided in St Stephen's Green, but government money even on the meagre scale provided to the Queen's Colleges was unforthcoming.

The London government was well aware that a Protestant-dominated parliament at Westminster would be reluctant to agree to the provision of any public subsidy for a Catholic university institution. Controversy in the 1840s, surrounding an increase in the public grant to Maynooth, the main training centre for Catholic clergy, had made this abundantly clear (Akenson 1970). The most that could be tolerated was the financing of some interdenominational arrangement of the Queen's University type. Yet this was failing, and the idea of undermining it still further by supporting another university clearly dedicated to its destruction was totally out of the question.

As a result, in the absence of adequate funding and amid other mainly ecclesiastical controversies, the new Catholic University went into a youthful decline. The whole Irish university problem was then allowed to fester for two decades until, at the end of the 1870s, matters were brought to a head by a further event. This was the introduction into the Commons by the Nationalist MP, the O'Conor Don, of an actual Bill to establish a Catholic University for Ireland, using, in part, the funds relinquished by the disestablished Church of Ireland (Rice 1957). Although his attempt failed, it was likely to be followed by others, and at each moment of failure Irish feelings of frustration would be likely to increase, thus fuelling an already general political unrest.

At this point the government turned in desperation to a different model of university provision, one that might not be ideal but would satisfy at least some of the needs of all the denominations, without necessarily bringing them together in particular collegiate settings. The model, of course, was that of the University of London. It had already proved capable of providing a publicly subsidized degree system that could satisfy both secular and denominational institutions; not least in the capital itself, where the Anglican King's College and the secular University College shared examinations without noticeably reawakening recent religious controversies.

The London model was certainly not a perfect solution to the problems of the Catholics. It did nothing to encourage the pastoral ideals set forward by Newman, and denied all the denominations any real control over the shape and content of the university's curriculum. But it did have some virtues even in Catholic eyes. As Professor Patrick Semple later pointed out, it was the first official measure which recognized the grievances of Catholics in the matter of university education (Tierney 1954). It provided a basis on which all Irish people, both men and women, who were unwilling or unable to enter Trinity College, could meet. Moreover, Catholic willingness to accept the plan had, no doubt, been given a further boost by the increasing success achieved in the London examinations by a number of Irish religious houses, not least that of the Jesuits in Tullamore (Rice 1957). The new proposal provided even more opportunities for students to earn degrees in a larger number of purely Catholic establishments. Indeed, if new funds were ever forthcoming, the existence of a London-style university in Ireland would not actually rule out the establishment of a purely Catholic University in addition if the new experiment proved successful.

A new Royal University of Ireland, to be run on London lines, was therefore established by an Act of 1879. At last and at least, this made it possible, not just for Catholics but for anyone, to earn a university degree anywhere in Ireland, whether by attending an institution or by studying in private. The need for the government to make public provision for Catholic teaching was now obviated. The failed Queen's University was swept away, and though its three colleges still carried on an independent existence with a small state subsidy, their relationship to the new university was to be no closer than that of any other Irish institution. This was for the moment a neat, politically satisfying and relatively cheap, solution to a number of pressing parliamentary problems, though few people were under any illusion that it could provide a permanent solution. As Semple again noted:

> it was recognised from the beginning as an institution which by its very nature could not be permanent. Its faults were obvious and no effort was ever made to conceal or palliate them but like many threatened things it contrived to live for a long time.
>
> (Tierney 1954: 58)

The new university

Quite apart from its political merits, the new university had obvious and, in many ways, unexpected advantages for a large number of Irish students. Newman's plans, as well as the Act setting up the Queen's Colleges, had always envisaged bringing students to some fixed point to receive their instruction. Under the Royal University they need never leave home, except to sit the examinations, regardless of where they lived in the island.

Depending on their resources and geographical position, they could choose from a whole range of learning modes. They could be taught by a collegiate institution, such as a Queen's College, or by the Jesuit College that now called itself University College and had taken over the buildings of Newman's establishment. Equally, it was now possible to prepare for a degree in a whole range of seminaries, colleges and schools that might otherwise have been tempted to enter their students for London examinations (as some continued to do). Alternatively, students could patronize one of the many crammers that grew up to meet the new situation, especially in Dublin and Belfast. Or they could use the services of a correspondence college, including the one established at Halifax in Yorkshire that specialized in Royal University courses. Or they could study privately at home or in a local library.

The one exception to such freedom lay in the field of medicine. As was the case with London, budding doctors were naturally expected to undergo practical training in a recognized medical school. The list of such recognized schools was, however, a long one, including some hospitals outside Ireland, and tied no one to a rigid institutional structure. In fact,

Table 4.1   Royal University of Ireland, first and second medical examinations, successful candidates, 1884–1904

	1884	1894	1904
Queen's College, Belfast	68 (36%)	56 (34%)	67 (36%)
Queen's College, Galway	20 (19%)	15 (9%)	20 (10%)
Queen's College, Cork	52 (28%)	38 (23%)	53 (28%)
University College, Dublin	15 (8%)	26 (16%)	15 (8%)
Total of Fellowship Colleges*	155 (83%)	135 (81%)	155 (82%)
Others	32 (17%)	32 (19%)	33 (18%)
Total	187	167	188

* There were no medical students at the fifth fellowship college, Magee College in Derry

Source: RUIC various dates

most medical students studied in one of the four cities containing university colleges, and provided those ailing institutions with a basic income that helped them to resist the fierce competition for students that now arose in other fields (see Table 4.1).

As with the University of London, all that the Royal University required of those entering its degree programme was that they should first pass a matriculation examination. Despite many requests, the Senate persistently refused (perhaps learning another lesson from London), except in the case of medicine, to draw up any list of recommended colleges or tutors (Royal University of Ireland, Standing Committee, *Minutes* (RUISCM) 11 December 1888).

Membership of the Senate, the university's governing body, was in the gift of the government, but by an unwritten agreement there was always to be roughly equal representation for both of the main religious groupings. Unlike so many Irish institutions of the time, it was not to be dominated by Protestant interests. The Catholic hierarchy may have seen some promise of an eventual state subsidy for a purely Catholic university in the government's decision to finance, within the framework of the new university, a body of some 20 officially recognized and salaried teaching Fellows, who would perform their duties amid the staff of five selected colleges.

At first sight, the existence of such a university-wide teaching body appeared to be something of an anomaly in an avowedly non-teaching university, but the creation of the Fellows was probably a political necessity. Their presence certainly gave considerable reassurance to the Queen's Colleges, who now had to vie for business with so many new rivals; and there was a promise, again unwritten, that there would always be at least one such Fellow appointed to each college. Even more significantly in terms of Catholic hopes, a promise went to University College, Dublin that it would always be awarded Fellowships at least equivalent in number to the total of those awarded to all of the Queen's Colleges combined. In the interests of denominational equity, one Fellowship was also reserved for the as yet exclusively Presbyterian Magee College in Derry (Tierney 1954).

The Fellowships thus formed an essential ingredient in gaining goodwill and general acceptance for the new university plan among the main interested parties. It was, however, made absolutely clear that, while the presence of a Fellow in a college would no doubt bring it academic benefits and prestige, it would in no way increase its hold on university affairs. Fellows would enjoy no special privileges when it came to the choosing of members of examination boards or the making of curricular decisions, and they were specifically forbidden by the university to teach private students themselves.

These arrangements, along with the denominational balance of the Senate, did much to sweeten both Catholic and Protestant opinion. Indeed, the Royal University's operations became a model of interdenominational tolerance in an Ireland where such a thing was never to be taken for granted. Browne has noted how a typical examination board:

> consisted of . . . examiners nearly all from different colleges, trained in at least five different universities, representing all parties and faiths and unfaiths . . . evidently inspired by a common desire to make the examinations do everything that they could and should do for the advancement of learning in Ireland.
>
> (Teachers of the Society of Jesus 1930: 134)

When appropriate, Protestant academics began now to be regularly recruited by Catholic institutions, while Catholic and Protestant academics from the start worked amicably together in framing the new curriculum and staffing the new examination boards. This spirit of cooperation was perhaps most graphically illustrated in the case of the university's long-serving Secretary, himself a prominent Anglican, whose son became a most successful and distinguished graduate of the Royal University while studying at the Jesuit University College in Dublin.

The latter was not the only Catholic institution that was to develop considerably as a result of the new university arrangements. Many of the seminaries and colleges of the religious orders encouraged their students, often boys and girls from very poor homes, to take Royal University degrees. The establishment of the Holy Ghost Fathers at Blackrock in county Dublin actually began also, somewhat confusingly, to call itself a University College. In doing so, it challenged the right of the Jesuit College in central Dublin to see itself as the eventual Catholic University in embryo, and questioned whether it was really entitled to the full quota of Royal University Fellowships that were being allocated to aid the development of Catholic higher education.

Blackrock was only one of a number of Catholic colleges that seem to have felt entitled to battle for supremacy in the University's early days, and this was reflected in the high incidence of their students' names in the university pass lists. It was generally recognized that such, in many ways constructive, rivalries were only possible because of the open-ness of the Royal University system. This open-ness brought such considerable political and social advantages that the, often accidental, educational benefits of the Royal University were hardly noticed at the time. These have since been largely ignored because of more recent scorn for the idea of a university as an examination board.

One of the clearest of these benefits, and one that was readily acknowledged at the time, was the educational opportunity that the new university gave to Irish women. Female students were then still denied access to degree courses at Trinity College, and had never been admitted to the Queen's University. Under the Royal University arrangements all this changed, and in ways that were to prove acceptable even to those who mistrusted any coming together of the sexes in classrooms, or the admission of women to institutions seen as male preserves. Under the Royal University procedures there was no need for women to seek admission to any institution, let alone a male college, and admission to the university's courses was thus possible for everyone, even for nuns in enclosed orders.

Many Catholic women took immediate advantage of this new freedom, while Protestant women students, still barred from Trinity College, not only entered the new examinations enthusiastically but often scored well at honours level. This was particularly true of students at two institutions, Alexandra College in Dublin and Victoria College in Belfast. These had been established to encourage an ever higher standard of education for women, but had hitherto been restricted to secondary work or to university certification of a non-graduating kind (Jordan 1990). Significantly, entries for the Dublin University Examinations for Women, which offered no prospect of graduation, began to fall off immediately the Royal University began its operations (*Journal of Education*, April 1882).

It was probably wise to encourage separate tuition for women in such a socially conservative country. When Queen's College, Belfast attempted to recruit women in the early 1880s it occurred strong male disapproval, with the male students setting fire to pods of cayenne pepper on the arrival of the women in the lecture theatre (Jordan 1990). The idea of co-education was not a popular one at any level, and, as late as 1908, when a proposal came from Sligo to mix the sexes in the University's examination rooms there it was still rejected by the Senate, long after such arrangements had become acceptable in most other universities of the United Kingdom (RUISCM 13 May 1908).

The Senate's conservatism was possibly partly responsible also for the one failure on the part of the university to recognize women's rights. No woman could be appointed to a Fellowship, and no Fellow could open his lectures to women. However, judged against the opportunities with which women were presented, these seem relatively minor restrictions. It may be that government fears of parliamentary disapproval, from the graduates of universities (including Dublin) that still barred women from membership, may also have played a part in such decisions.

The fact that degrees were now available to students attending no institution, and living and studying anywhere in the island of Ireland, represented a revolutionary step forward. This was especially so as the Royal University's fees, intended to cover neither tuition nor residence, were exceptionally cheap when compared with those of other degree-granting institutions. As a result, *The University Correspondent* (15 April 1891) felt able to describe it as 'the cheapest university in the three kingdoms'.

The overall fee for a full degree was £6, £1 per year for registration plus examination fees. In the 1890s, fears were being expressed elsewhere in the United Kingdom that such a low price would entice more and more non-Irish students to enter its system, leaving the colleges geared to London University's examinations in great distress (*The University Correspondent*, 15 August 1892). Nor was it simply the university fees that were low. Many of the Catholic colleges had no need to pay salaries to teachers who were members of religious orders, and were thus able to offer cheap or even free tuition to those in need.

Given its general open-ness, one of the more surprising aspects of the university's development was its failure to follow the lead of London and (as we shall see in the next chapter) of St Andrews by making its facilities available to students outside Ireland. On occasions the Senate was asked to provide examination centres elsewhere, in Yorkshire and Scotland for example, but these suggestions were always voted down (RUISCM 20 October 1884: 17 July 1885). At first sight this refusal seems surprising, given the scale of Irish emigration, as well as the involvement of the Irish churches in missionary work and in the general development of the Empire. One would have thought that the idea of granting Dublin-based degrees to students in Irish-dominated denominational institutions outside Ireland would have had a great appeal. But the Senate appeared to see the institution as having been created to solve a purely Irish problem, and were perhaps nervous that any widespread activity outside Ireland could pose dangers for the always delicately balanced denominational arrangements concerning the distribution of Senate places and Fellowships.

The university's approach to the curriculum was equally cautious. Always generalist, the initial form of its degree programme was not dissimilar from that of its predecessor, the Queen's University, though its programme has been praised as representing a considerable step forward for its time (Ashby and Anderson 1966). In the Arts degree, classics very much held the place of honour and most of the special awards and prizes were reserved for Latin and Greek. While there were subsequent developments of the syllabus, these usually reflected the results of well-tried academic experiments elsewhere, rather than any attempt to adopt a fresh, let alone revolutionary, approach to specifically Irish needs. Even so, Hamilton, the last head of the Belfast Queen's College and an ardent advocate of the university's abolition, was prepared to concede that the development of its practical examinations in science had had a major effect, and that it was in the first rank of United Kingdom universities so far as science was concerned (Irish Universities Commission 1903).

The continual fear of disturbing the political settlement probably explains why it was not until 1900 that modern history found a place in the curriculum. Potential problems in philosophy had, however, been diplomatically overcome earlier by providing a Thomist alternative course for degree candidates studying in the Catholic scholastic tradition. Such was the tact deployed over these issues that the Senate minutes record little or no evidence of any disputes over claims of political or sectarian bias in the examination process. Indeed, the only details of any such dispute that are actually recorded concern the minor and relatively arcane topic of the role played by the Irish aristocracy in eighteenth century military history, hardly a key area of political or sectarian dispute in late nineteenth century Ireland (RUISCM 30 October 1907). Certainly this was not an issue as likely to inflame the Senate as Blackrock's rivalry with University College, Dublin over the allocation of Fellowships (reported in the Royal University of Ireland, Senate, *Minutes* (RUISM) between 30 January and 29 May 1884).

The University's public image

The Arts course followed by most students could be taken over three years. The first and second stage examinations took place at a wide variety of centres throughout Ireland, but at the end of the final year candidates had to travel to Dublin to face both a written and an oral examination at the University headquarters. These had, therefore, to be large enough to accommodate not only laboratories but also interview rooms and large halls which, during most of the year, were leased for concerts and other public events. When they thought of a university, the people of Dublin were likely to conjure up the image of Trinity College and its venerable student-filled range of halls and dwellings. They found it more difficult to accept the idea of a university as a collection of public halls open for continual hire to all and sundry.

Such a commercial attitude, largely unknown in Victorian times, did little to raise the University in public esteem. James Joyce, himself a not very respectful student of the Royal University, and his friend Oliver St John Gogarty of Trinity College, once confronted the porter at the University headquarters building in Earlsfort Terrace with the apparently naive question, 'Is this the Royal University?', to which the cautious porter, knowing the pair and not to be taken in, retorted, 'You know bloody well it is . . .', to which Gogarty crushingly replied, 'Oh! It was a flower show the last time I was here!' (O'Connor 1964: 65).

Nevertheless, such regular and large scale hirings considerably augmented the university's funding and helped it to keep down the examination fees. The authorities, as the guardians of public funds, were willing to risk their image in the process. As Cruise, a member of the Senate put it:

Other universities have all the advantages and the *eclat* of tradition. We have to make our way against the want of that in the Royal University. Therefore we must make our curriculum good and our examination stiff instead.

(quoted in Walsh 1897: 82)

The standing accorded to the Royal University's examinations was crucial for the university's reputation. The standards of any educational institution that does not insist on regular face-to-face contact with its students are always liable to be suspect in the eyes of outsiders. The Senate was not amused, therefore, when a whimsical Cork professor drew a pen-portrait of himself for a local newspaper, sitting in a small room in Earlsfort Terrace 'occupied in an impious attempt to fathom the depths of human ignorance – in other words examining pass candidates!' (RUISM 26 July 1894).

Some London periodicals, not least the *Journal of Education*, were always ready to pour scorn on such an Irish institution, implying that low fees must go hand in hand with low academic demands. Yet the reputation of the University's examinations remained high, even among those who would have preferred the Royal University to be replaced with a more conventional set of face-to-face colleges. As one professor of mathematics put it:

Whatever else was to be said . . . nothing could ever be said truthfully against its standards and the quality of its degrees. Its papers were carefully prepared . . . [and] no suspicion of bias could be charged against it. . . . It had to give place to another, better-endowed, free from government control, at liberty to expand without interference, better in every way. But we must not let 'better' crush 'good' under fire. The Royal University with all its faults was *good*.

(Tierney 1954: 60; original emphasis)

Occasionally there were hints that Fellows appointed as examiners might favour students from their own institution, but it would have been hard to sustain such a charge, given the degree of double and even treble marking that the University Secretary regularly insisted upon.

Even so, throughout the University's short life there were always many who were ready, like Joyce and Gogarty, to pour scorn on a university that was merely a government-organized examination board. Yet, interestingly enough, the Royal University's defenders had a convenient and useful precedent at hand. Trinity College, Dublin was certainly a prestigious face-to-face teaching institution. But the University of Dublin, which actually conferred the degrees on Trinity's students, was itself, like the nineteenth century universities of Oxford and Cambridge, also at that time largely a 'mere' examination board with no teaching function. The same could have been said, of course, of the Royal University's own predecessor, the Queen's University, which left all the teaching to its constituent colleges.

While it was true that the teachers at Trinity College and the Queen's Colleges had always had a say in the planning of the curriculum, and in examining their own students, the constitutional position remained the same. There was no reason to suppose that, as the Royal University's confidence grew, there might not be some new accommodation of the wishes of the college teachers based on a growing goodwill.

Bringing in the schools

One of the most striking characteristics of the Royal University to the modern eye is that, like London, it examined many candidates in institutions that were in essence secondary schools. Tierney, a later President of University College, Dublin, has seen in this not a weakness but a strength, given the then state of Irish education. He notes the fact that students from these institutions, having been carefully selected by their teachers, were often the most academically successful. In his study of Professor Eion MacNeill, the distinguished historian of ancient Ireland and cabinet minister in the Irish Free State, Tierney suggests that the degree preparation available to senior pupils in St Malachy's College for Boys in Belfast was almost certainly superior to that available in the local Queen's College (Tierney 1980). The latter eventually attracted far fewer students than the other Belfast crammers and colleges.

Eamonn de Valera, later university lecturer in Mathematics and President of Ireland, worked for his own degree as a student at Blackrock, a college of the Holy Ghost Fathers. In the continental style, no clear distinction was made between secondary and tertiary work, allowing senior boys and junior staff (often recent pupils themselves) to study for university examinations together (Dudley-Edwards 1987).

In Ireland, perhaps longer than elsewhere in the British Isles, it also remained possible for promising pupils to attempt university examinations at a very early age. On at least one occasion the Royal University Senate positively refused to establish a minimum age of 16 for those taking the matriculation examination. Irish schools were slower than those in England to develop the modern pattern of sixth form study, which in England eventually incorporated much of the old pass degree courses and left the universities free to concentrate on the honours degree. In Ireland the pass degree continued to remain important throughout the twentieth century, and it was natural, therefore, that academically ambitious Irish schools should seize the opportunity to prepare their 16- and 17-year-old pupils for Royal University graduation.

Naturally not everyone welcomed the strong involvement of schools in such work. One disgruntled and very interested party, President Sullivan of Queen's College, Cork, deplored the fact 'that there are no longer any grammar schools [in Ireland]; they are all become Colleges . . . combining all the functions of all the educational establishments from kindergarten to university . . . inclusive' (Rice 1957: 123). Yet in many ways these Irish attitudes reflected not merely the procedures of the continental religious orders, but also general British attitudes from earlier in the nineteenth century. Then Brougham, as one of the founders of University College, London, could view it at one stage not as an English version of Edinburgh University but as a London equivalent of Edinburgh's Royal High School, a school which remained in competition with the University for pupils as late as 1900 (Bellot 1929).

The beginning of the end

By the end of the nineteenth century it did, however, seem increasingly unlikely that a university that was purely an examination board, and which allowed 'schoolchildren' to take its degree examinations, could continue to enjoy respect. As one witness was to say to the Irish Universities (Robertson) Commission, whose report was to bring about the Royal University's demise:

> I boldly say that I regard the word 'university' as applied to an institution of such character as a misnomer. No person will ever induce me to say . . . that it should be regarded as a university at all.
> (Irish Universities Commission 1902: 126)

The British academic world was by then increasingly modelling itself on the college and graduate school system of North America, where face-to-face teaching, if not residence, was seen as an essential ingredient. The agitation for a teaching university in London (see Chapter 3) in itself posed a great challenge for the Royal University. If the original model upon which its foundation had been based was to be abandoned by the government, then the Irish institution did not seem likely to endure for long.

Moreover, Irish politics and expectations had themselves moved on, not least in Dublin. A lively generation of far more self-confident young Catholics now began to change and enliven the character of University College, Dublin. Meenan suggests that the decision to concentrate Catholic university education in this college helped to bring to it an access of variety and vitality (Meenan 1956). This led, in some cases, to the creation of a form of semi-Bohemian life, graphically portrayed in Joyce's *Portrait of the Artist as a Young Man* and *Ulysses* (Ellman 1959). This was largely new to Ireland and had little in common with the previous ethos of the Royal University colleges.

Inevitably, many nationalists saw the government-controlled Royal University as a pillar of British domination (Rice 1957). The Chancellor of the University had always been a leading member of the House of Lords. The Chancellor at the turn of the century, Lord Meath, a leader of the Empire Day movement and a convinced Unionist, unfortunately made heavy weather of dealing with a high-spirited student demonstration at what had hitherto been the routine and uneventful ritual of the annual graduation. He attempted to discipline the unruly students in the style of the proctors at Oxford and Cambridge, without realizing that he had absolutely no powers under the Royal University Act to do so, or indeed to control any aspect of a student's behaviour outside the examination room (*Journal of Education*, January 1906).

Such events did little for the University's image, especially in London, and gave great encouragement to those who felt that a new, and probably Catholic, collegiate university with greater pastoral and disciplinary powers was now needed in Ireland.

The work of the fellowship colleges

The Catholic hierarchy's main reason for accepting the Royal University arrangement in the first place had been the promise it gave of developing further the work of University College, Dublin. This had certainly been done. Indeed, the comparative success of that college was such that the other colleges involved in the fellowship scheme regularly complained of what they termed the 'destructive competitiveness' that University College, Dublin had brought to the University's operations (Moody 1958).

However, the success of University College, Dublin under the Royal University arrangements was still not spectacular, given the size of Dublin's population and the scale of the college's growth during its subsequent history. It may have been that not only the presence of Trinity College, where many Catholic professional families still sent their sons in defiance of the bishops, but also the activity of the other Catholic colleges provided too much local competition. Certainly University College, Dublin's success at this time was never as great as Moody has suggested. The College had affirmed its right to exist, but still needed to attract more students, especially in medicine (see Table 4.1).

This made it a particularly sensitive peruser of the Royal University's printed pass lists. Against each name these indicated, presumably on information given by the student, whether their study had been private or at a particular institution. University College, Dublin regularly complained that some of their students had been wrongly labelled (RUISCM 30 July 1890: 23 October 1894).

During the period of the Royal University's existence the three Queen's colleges, which in 1880 had enjoyed a monopoly of all Irish graduation outside Trinity College, suffered greatly from the more open competition. Only in medicine, as Table 4.1 indicates, did they manage to hold their own against all-comers, presumably because this was a subject in which crammers and private students found it difficult to operate, due to the specialized facilities and expert practical tuition required. Despite their location outside the Irish capital, the Queen's colleges managed to outstrip University College, Dublin, which faced competition from other Dublin

Table 4.2   Royal University of Ireland, first university examination, successful candidates from the Belfast area attending face-to-face institutions, 1884 and 1904

	1884	1904
Queen's College, Belfast	64 (75%)	28 (21%)
Schools	18 (21%)	50 (37%)
Coaching Establishments	3 (4%)	57 (42%)
Total	85	135

Source: RUIC various dates

medical institutions (see Chapter 3, especially Table 3.3) that chose to enter candidates for the Royal University examinations.

Queen's College, Belfast attracted more students overall than any other fellowship college, but it steadily failed to reach its potential in its own area of the country. The first-year university examination in Arts in 1884 produced 392 successful students, 64 of them from Queen's College, Belfast. These represented 75 per cent of the successful students attending institutions in the Belfast area (see Table 4.2). But 20 years later, only 28 out of the national total of 564 successful students for this examination had attended the college (representing only 21 per cent of local students), with schools and coaching establishments proving much more popular. The latter, in particular, posed a real threat to the Queen's College. Indeed, the Principal of Queen's College, Belfast admitted to the Irish Universities Commission that one single coaching establishment, Kelvin House, already had more students than his own college.

In fact, the five fellowship colleges' share of the market on the most populous course, the first Arts examination, remained small everywhere, while the numbers studying at other institutions steadily rose (see Table 4.3). The number of students studying privately remained fairly constant

Table 4.3   Royal University of Ireland, first university examination, origin of successful candidates, 1884–1904

	1884	1894	1904
Queen's College, Belfast	64 (16%)	19 (5%)	28 (5%)
Queen's College, Galway	13 (3%)	19 (5%)	19 (3%)
Queen's College, Cork	11 (3%)	4 (1%)	8 (1%)
University College, Dublin	39 (10%)	28 (8%)	39 (7%)
Magee College, Derry	12 (3%)	9 (2%)	16 (3%)
Total in Fellowship Colleges	139 (36%)	79 (21%)	110 (20%)
Schools, seminaries and religious houses	132 (34%)	160 (43%)	303 (54%)
Private study/tuition	121 (31%)	131 (35%)	151 (27%)
Total	392	370	564

Source: RUIC various dates

Table 4.4   Royal University of Ireland, second university examination, successful candidates, 1884–1904

	1884	1894	1904
Queen's College, Belfast	44 (20%)	29 (12%)	30 (11%)
Queen's College, Galway	10 (5%)	11 (5%)	7 (3%)
Queen's College, Cork	5 (2%)	5 (2%)	10 (4%)
University College, Dublin	20 (9%)	14 (6%)	24 (9%)
Magee College, Derry	5 (2%)	9 (4%)	8 (3%)
Total in Fellowship Colleges	84 (38%)	68 (29%)	79 (30%)
Schools, seminaries and religious houses	54 (25%)	73 (31%)	73 (27%)
Private study/tuition	82 (37%)	94 (40%)	116 (43%)
Total	220	235	268

Source: RUIC various dates

between 1884 and 1904, but exceeded that of the fellowship colleges by the end of the nineteenth century.

The fellowship colleges' loss of students was less dramatic at the more difficult second university examination level (see Table 4.4). Even so, more than two-thirds of students did not avail themselves of their services, while the proportion of students successfully studying privately increased to reach 43 per cent of the total in 1904.

It might have been expected that most of those studying privately or in 'lesser' institutions would have resorted to university colleges and Fellows' lectures in the final stages of their course. In fact the opposite was the case (see Table 4.5). The proportion of successful candidates attending such establishments in preparation for the BA pass degree examinations was

Table 4.5   Royal University of Ireland, BA pass examination, successful candidates, 1884–1904

	1884	1894	1904
Queen's College, Belfast	12 (20%)	16 (17%)	16 (9%)
Queen's College, Galway	3 (5%)	2 (2%)	9 (5%)
Queen's College, Cork	6 (10%)	2 (2%)	4 (2%)
University College, Dublin	–	2 (2%)	9 (5%)
Magee College, Derry	–	5 (5%)	3 (2%)
Total in Fellowship Colleges	21 (35%)	27 (28%)	41 (24%)
Schools, seminaries and religious houses	17 (28%)	30 (31%)	50 (29%)
Private study/tuition	22 (37%)	40 (41%)	83 (48%)
Total	60	97	174

Source: RUIC various dates

Table 4.6   Royal University of Ireland, BA honours examination, successful candidates, 1884–1904

	1884	1894	1904
Queen's College, Belfast	18 (35%)	11 (22%)	10 (29%)
Queen's College, Galway	3 (6%)	5 (10%)	5 (15%)
Queen's College, Cork	5 (10%)	1 (2%)	–
University College, Dublin	3 (6%)	11 (22%)	4 (12%)
Magee College, Derry	–	–	1 (3%)
Total in Fellowship Colleges	29 (56%)	28 (57%)	20 (56%)
Alexandra College, Dublin	3	2	2
Blackrock University College	4	1	1
Holy Cross College, Clonliffe	1	1	1
Lincoln College, Oxford	–	–	1
Maynooth College	1	–	–
Royal College of Science	3	1	–
Trinity College, Dublin	1	–	–
Ursuline Convent, Cork	–	1	2
Victoria College, Belfast	–	3	1
Total of schools, seminaries and religious houses	13 (25%)	9 (18%)	8 (24%)
Private study/tuition	10 (19%)	12 (25%)	6 (18%)
Total	52	49	34

Source: RUIC various dates

actually lower than for the second level examinations. An even higher proportion were preparing themselves as private students, rising to nearly half of the total, 48 per cent, in 1904.

It is only when we examine the relatively small, indeed declining, number of those gaining honours degrees that at least some of the fellowship colleges, particularly Belfast, begin to come into their own (see Table 4.6). Just over half of those in the honours list are shown to be students of the fellowship colleges, though the presence of so many other institutions, particularly the girls' schools, is also striking.

Despite their limited success in producing students of honours calibre, and their ability to hang on to their medical students, the overall number of students attracted by the fellowship colleges remained remarkably small. Their failure to attract first- and second-year Arts students, in particular, must have reduced their income and viability considerably. The Cork and Galway colleges especially faced a real crisis because of this, and it has been suggested that it was only the Royal University link that kept Galway safe from closure. On the other hand, Queen's College, Belfast felt that, by making a fresh start and emphasizing the increasingly fashionable virtues of face-to-face teaching, it could eventually wean northerners away from the Royal University system. Its President was even willing to contemplate a temporary fall in academic standards as the College struggled to establish a 'real' university in the northern city.

Somewhat surprisingly, when viewed through late twentieth century eyes, a large body of Belfast opinion opposed such a move. A number of leading figures, even in the Ulster Unionist party itself, felt that a purely local university would have none of that academic and social prestige that the Belfast college enjoyed, so long as it was linked to a national university based in what they saw as the far less provincial atmosphere of a Dublin then undergoing a powerful cultural revival (Moody and Beckett 1959).

The end of the Royal University

Given the University of London developments and the appearance of independent face-to-face universities in the largest cities of England, it was difficult for the government to ignore requests for a re-examination of the Irish university question. Anti-Catholic feeling in parliament, though still strong in certain quarters, was considerably less virulent than it had been a quarter of a century earlier. A whole generation of Irish Catholic academics had proved, within the Royal University framework, that they could work amicably with Protestant colleagues, and could avoid bringing to their work the bitter feelings that might well still motivate their private political allegiances. The government felt compelled, therefore, to appoint a Royal Commission to investigate the future of Irish university activity outside Trinity College.

At the outset of its hearings, the Irish Universities Commission heard a very long statement from the Catholic Bishop of Limerick. This brought to bear not only all the arguments for face-to-face relationships and teacher control that had led to the London changes, but also affirmed the right of Irish Catholics to have at last their own university, building on the progress already made at University College, Dublin. Much of the other evidence presented supported such views. Relatively little attention was paid to the needs of the isolated or private student, or to the advantages of spreading higher education opportunities as widely as possible throughout the island. When it was pointed out to the President of Queen's College, Galway, as he gave his evidence, that many in the south and west of the country would lose their chance of a degree if all higher education became centred in a few city institutions, his response was dismissive:

> That is true, but I do not think it would be a great loss to the country if they did not get a degree . . . I do not think the degree is of very much value unless the recipient has been taught at a college.
>
> (Irish Universities Commission 1902: 103)

Not surprisingly, in the face of that and similar evidence, the Commission committed itself wholeheartedly to the then fashionable notion of a 'real' university. They agreed that a purely examining body such as the Royal

University might well have helped to preserve and develop performance standards, but the system had also led inevitably to a decline in the real quality of academic life:

> A university helps to form a mental habit and attitude; it lays down the privileges of learning and unifies knowledge. To test results is an accident, an inseperable accident, perhaps, but not of the essence of a university.

(Irish Universities Commission 1903: 25)

A second commission was then set up to consider the position of Trinity College and the whole future shape of Irish higher education. It proposed that University College, Dublin should become an independent Catholic teaching university, while the Queen's Colleges should leave an abandoned Royal University and take their place in a newly expanded University of Dublin, in which Trinity would no longer be the single teaching college.

However, not only the well-endowed Trinity College, but also Queen's College, Belfast, refused to accept such an arrangement. Thus, in 1908, Cork and Galway were to range themselves alongside University College, Dublin in a new federal National University. This, ironically, though mainly Catholic in its student body, was deemed to be secular and avoided the teaching of theology, the subject that Newman, in his Dublin lectures, had seen as the keystone of all university study. These changes inevitably meant that it was now logical for Belfast to go it alone and to set up a new, separate, face-to-face teaching university very similar in atmosphere and form to the new civic universities of northern England (Moody and Beckett 1959).

In the light of contemporary academic beliefs, all this may seem to have been a great improvement. But amid these sweeping organizational changes, the idea of preserving or developing the opportunities that the Royal University had provided for the distance education of the isolated or poor individual completely disappeared from view. So did the Royal University's remarkable achievement in providing, through the upper forms of the seminaries and secondary schools, a comprehensive and widespread set of opportunities for acquiring a higher education.

It was true, as the *Journal of Education* regularly pointed out (for example in September 1899), that the Royal University's examinations produced many failures, and this was seen as a condemnation of the diffuse organization of its teaching. But, on the other hand, it could just as easily be seen as evidence of its exacting standards. Taking a second attempt at its examinations was very cheap, and it was perhaps better to allow unlimited numbers to make the attempt rather than to restrict access to a not necessarily carefully chosen few.

To have failed to complete a BA degree in nineteenth century Ireland, or indeed in Scotland or England, was not necessarily the personal calamity it would seem today. One had still exposed oneself to some degree of higher education, and had no doubt achieved some self-improvement. Until the

Second World War, it was still common for Irish family business people to despatch their more promising offspring to Trinity or some other college for one or two years, so as to achieve some smattering of culture and to make contact with at least some of the basic academic disciplines. Graduation was not an issue. No doubt that was the aim of many of those Royal University students who never got beyond the first or second examination stage.

Ironically, one minor element of the Royal University arrangements did linger on until the 1960s. Magee College in Derry, having lost its Fellowship and a great deal of its income following the university's collapse, was forced in the end to attach itself to another Irish university which confined itself to examining, the University of Dublin. This now took on the Royal University role of examining Magee's junior students at a distance. Nevertheless, in order to complete the remainder of the course, those wishing to graduate had to transfer themselves bodily to Trinity College. This relic of the Royal University system was swept away in 1970, when Magee was finally incorporated into the New University of Ulster. In this way Ireland's greatly undervalued and widely misunderstood experiment in providing higher education opportunities for students, excluded by distance or poverty from the normal centres of academic achievement, was finally brought to an end.

5

The Maddest Folly: Scotland, the Certification of Women and the St Andrews LLA

One of the most striking aspects of the development of the Royal University of Ireland was the increasing success of students in the new middle-class female establishments of Belfast and Dublin (see Chapter 4, especially Table 4.6). Victoria College and Alexandra College suggested by their very names that they aimed at more than secondary school achievements. By the time of the Royal University's demise their names figured in the lists of successful BA Honours candidates as regularly as those of the Queen's Colleges and University College, Dublin; just as Cheltenham Ladies' College did in the lists for London University examinations (see Chapter 3, especially Table 3.8).

At the same time, these colleges continued to provide what we would now see as a more normal curriculum for teenage girls. Their functioning at so many academic levels reflected the wide range of women's academic needs, which were still far from being generally satisfied in the late nineteenth century (Jordan 1990). While London University admitted women from 1867, and on fully equal terms from 1878, they were not admitted to Trinity College, Dublin until 1904. Even as late as 1907, the Royal University itself forbade the entry of women to the lectures of its Fellows and, as we noted in Chapter 4, to the same examination rooms as men.

The grudging admission of women into academic life was a general phenomenon. Despite the establishment of Girton College, Cambridge in 1870, and the eventual admission of its students to undergraduate lectures, that University was to deny women students actual graduation until after the Second World War. Nationally, for all too many people, the idea of female higher education remained hilarious, as the success of Gilbert and Sullivan's *Princess Ida* (first produced in 1884) demonstrated:

A Woman's College! maddest folly going!
What can girls learn within its walls worth knowing?

In the circumstances, it was not surprising that such 'girls' as saw some point in higher education placed an especial value on the opportunities for graduation provided by London and the Royal University; as well as on the special courses and certificates for women increasingly offered by those face-to-face universities that were anxious to encourage women's higher education without actually having to admit them to their degrees.

Cambridge University itself provided a popular higher level certificate, which was increasingly attempted by the staff and senior pupils of girls' schools. In Scotland there were also enough interested professors and dedicated women to stir all four universities into at least some sort of action. By the 1870s there was already considerable confidence that their doors would be opened to women, and in both Edinburgh and Glasgow influential committees were formed that eventually succeeded not only in establishing women's colleges, but also correspondence courses. These catered both for those unable or unwilling to attend local classes in person, and for those following the distance certificate courses of other universities (Bremner 1897). Most correspondence students, however, appear to have attempted the 'local' examinations of their nearest university, typically provided at a number of levels variously described as 'junior', 'senior' or 'higher'.

At this distance in time it is difficult to gauge the exact significance of such titles. The regulations, committee minutes and press reports all assume a familiarity with the then current standards and assumptions that we now find difficult to recapture. 'Higher' was not necessarily the equivalent of the English Higher School Certificate, and even less the equivalent of the Scottish Highers examination now attempted in the later stages of the secondary course. 'Higher' can, of course, mean something much more exalted, as in the current phrase 'higher education'. The problem is that all these certificates and 'local examinations' were being attempted by ambitious individuals and schools in a period when, as we have already noted, the boundaries between the secondary and tertiary curricula were less firmly fixed than they are nowadays; and schools that now behave like normal secondary establishments were quite willing to teach their students to honours degree level.

That the Glasgow higher examination was really intended to be at secondary level might well be inferred from the 1880 regulations, which allowed boys to enter if they were under the age of 18, and from a suggestion in the minutes of the University of Glasgow Correspondence Course Committee (8 February 1894), following the demise of the examination, that the London matriculation might be seen as a substitute. However, attendance at university by men aged under 18 was still extremely common in late nineteenth century Scotland, while the matriculation examination was often seen not as a preparatory stage but as an integral part of the new female higher education.

It seems likely that the organizers of such courses were themselves somewhat vague about equivalencies, and were only too happy when a woman of whatever age and academic experience embarked on something educationally worthwhile. Naively perhaps, they still saw the university as a place for personal development rather than as some kind of socio-economic sorting machine. They were simply anxious to provide an academic stimulus that stretched, and no doubt sometimes flattered their clientele.

It was only after Glasgow University announced that its undergraduate courses were finally to be opened to women, that the Correspondence Course Committee, in its report for 1889–90, began to publicize new and complex regulations for the granting of exemption from actual university classes on the basis of passes in the various 'local certificates'. By 1892, however, the correspondence and distance services provided for women by the enthusiasts of Edinburgh and Glasgow had virtually died out. In that year all ten of the successful candidates for the Glasgow higher certificate were attending Queen Margaret College, adjoining the University, or were pupils at secondary schools in the immediate vicinity.

The great St Andrews venture

However, the most unexpected and remarkable development in Scotland occurred not in the two major universities but at St Andrews. While this was the oldest university, it was also the smallest, the most traditional and the most financially ailing. Yet quite suddenly it was to establish, in 1877, a distance qualification for women that was expressly of university standard. It was to be successfully pursued for more than half a century by a wide clientele, not just in Scotland but in a hundred or more examination centres throughout the world, spreading its geographical coverage on the scale of the London degree. Yet, unlike the London system, it was never supported by any large-scale bureaucracy or by government grants. For most of its life this extraordinary initiative was managed on a part-time basis by one professor and a single clerk, proving a remarkable achievement for a tiny university almost always on the edge of bankruptcy.

As in the two large cities of Scotland, the movement to develop women's education had also met with the support of a number of St Andrews professors. But in such a small and isolated town, unlike in Edinburgh and Glasgow, the immediate local take-up for any women's classes that such enthusiasts could provide was likely to be far more limited. They had, therefore, to turn their attention also to the city of Dundee, some dozen miles away, where extension lecturers, like those from Oxford and Cambridge working in English cities, were amazed and greatly encouraged by the standard of the work they encountered from both male and female students.

Reporting to his Senate in April 1876, Principal Shairp of St Andrews noted that 'the first few papers would have stood high in any examination of university students', and claimed that the women in particular showed not only enthusiasm but real achievements. The chairman of the university committee organizing this Dundee venture was a man called Knight who, later in the same year, was appointed to the chair of moral philosophy. It was he who was to preside over the development and major successes of the new qualification designed expressly for women – the Licentiate in Arts – that was eventually to become available worldwide.

Until the 1890s the degrees and internal courses of the Scottish universities remained closed to female students, and this Licentiate was never a degree in the conventional sense. However, Knight was at pains to emphasize on numerous occasions that the standard required was that of the male first degree – the Master of Arts (MA) – and that the examiners, virtually all teachers in Scottish universities, were determined to maintain those standards (Knight 1887). There were precedents in the United Kingdom for such a procedure. The Presbyterian Church in Ireland, for example, had encouraged the development of university-style courses in the Royal Belfast Academical Institution, declaring them to be equivalent in standard to those of the Scottish MA, without ever pretending that that institution was claiming university status (Moody 1957). Victorians could be much more pragmatic about such issues than their twentieth century counterparts. A sincere hint that the St Andrews Licentiate endeavoured to meet the same standards as that of the MA seemed to satisfy Knight's early clients, even though its equivalence was never discussed or fully examined in any Senate debate.

But this new 'shadow degree' offered other benefits also. Unlike those competing for the Glasgow higher certificate or the many other similar qualifications then available, the St Andrews Licentiate was actually able to offer the candidate letters to put after her name: at first LA, but later changed to LLA for reasons we shall come to. The attraction of such a title, as well as its availability over such a wide area of the world, made it easily the most popular of the Scottish 'certificates', and it retained much of its vigour even after face-to-face university courses in Scotland became available to women (Lumsden 1911).

The origins of the qualification were not, however, quite as straight-forward as all this might suggest. At the first Senate meeting Knight attended, in December 1876, the immediate suggestion was not for an undergraduate level course, but for a female higher certificate like those offered elsewhere in Scotland. A course of that kind was actually being advertised in the press three months later. However, in February 1877, it was decided to give it the grander title of 'Licentiate in Arts', although the Senate continued for some time to refer to it as the Higher Certificate for Women, and it came under the control of the committee that organized examinations for schoolchildren. In June of the same year, Knight was appointed Convenor of this Local Examinations Committee, and from then on the fate of the LA began to take a different turn.

The launch of the Licentiate

It was widely believed at the time that the whole scheme was being launched not primarily for educational reasons, but as a money-spinner for a very hard-pressed institution. Even six years after the launch, a correspondent of the *Journal of Education* (June 1883) was still openly suggesting that St Andrews had 'embraced the scheme in order to avoid abolition'. But if it had been so motivated, the LA was initially a disappointment. In its first year of operation, 1878, the total income from its examinations, held in three Scottish centres, amounted to no more than £50, of which £43 1s 0d was swallowed up in payments to markers and invigilators, most of them St Andrews professors (University of St Andrews, Local Examinations Committee, *Minutes* (USALECM) 25 July 1878). It seems likely that any financial ambitions on the part of the Senate members who approved the scheme were personal rather than corporate. This was perfectly understandable at a time when the size of Scottish professors' salaries still largely depended on the number of students they were able to attract.

Later in the same year the scheme's further operations incurred a deficit, which the Senate had to make good (USALECM 10 December 1878), and this precarious financial situation continued for some years. It is difficult, therefore, to see how they could have persisted with such a scheme had they simply seen it as a means of corporate or personal gain. There were sufficient professors enthusiastic about women's education to see the scheme through hard times, and the disinterested approach of the university is further evidenced by the fact that the committee was allowed to bank rather than hand over the profits once the financial position improved. From the start, Knight had in mind other uses for this money (Lumsden 1911).

Initially, the concerns of the St Andrews Local Examinations Committee were confined to Scotland. Indeed, it was in relation to its certificates for children, rather than the LA, that the first talk arose of expansion outside that country. In response to a request from Weston-super-Mare, the Committee ruled that henceforth all of their examinations could be mounted in England so long as there were at least six candidates and that all the expenses were met in the locality (USALECM 18 September 1878). In fact the Weston scheme came to nought, but the Committee had established a principle, which was to apply to the Licentiate as well.

By the end of 1878, Knight had also persuaded his committee to make another change which, though ostensibly made merely to save money, did in fact do much to alter the public image of the LA. It was decided to move the examination date from June to April, the month in which the Scottish MA examinations were then held. This, as the Committee's minutes for 10 December 1878 record, not only reduced administrative costs but also enabled papers and examiners to be shared with the male degree course. At the same time, it finally removed the Licentiate from the world of the higher certificates, allowing Knight firmly to claim that the same standard was required for both LA and MA. This claim was, for the next half century, to place a great strain on the organizers' resources, because of the need to ensure parallel standards over the full range of what was from the beginning a very wide curriculum.

Expansion into England began, albeit on a very small scale, in 1879, when examination centres were recognized in London and Halifax. These two locations were sufficiently convenient to enable the St Andrews professors themselves to continue to act as invigilators, thus providing them not only with a welcome fee but with the basic subsistence and travel expenses for a holiday or business trip. In Halifax, not the most obvious site for initial development, there had been much preliminary work undertaken by 'a ladies' committee' (USALECM 10 April 1879), and for some years the university made the existence of a similar local committee a prerequisite for the establishment of further centres elsewhere in the United Kingdom.

Later in 1879 the LA scheme got a further fillip from its unconditional acceptance as a qualification for course entry (that is to say, the equivalent of graduation) by the Cambridge University Teacher Training Syndicate (USALECM 14 November 1879). As much of the interest in the Licentiate had come from women teachers, this was an important development. Much strengthened by this increasing recognition, Knight was able for the first time to suggest that students should have fulfilled at least one entrance requirement before registering for the LA, namely that they had passed their local 'junior certificate' examination. However, he was later at pains to emphasize that this was merely meant to help avoid embarrassment rather than to form a rigid entrance requirement (Knight 1887). Such a disclaimer was hardly surprising at the time, given that the Scottish universities still made no prior academic demands even on male students wishing to matriculate and study for the Arts degree.

Knight then established his own separate Licentiate committee, and the links with school examinations were finally broken. By 1882 the books had begun to balance and the scheme was further expanded to Ireland, where the Royal University had not yet got into its stride. At this point the short title LA was changed to LLA to avoid confusion, amid general Scottish proposals, later aborted, to introduce a two-year degree course (on lines similar to the Diploma of Higher Education that was to be developed on a small scale in England 80 years later). What the extra 'L' stood for was never quite clear. Many assumed it stood for 'ladies', as indeed Cant does in the standard history of the university (Cant 1970). Knight, however, denied this in terms that would have gladdened the hearts of feminists a century later, affirming that he recognized not 'ladies' but 'women' as his students (University of St Andrews, LLA Committee, *Minutes* (USALLACM) 12 December 1899). He showed those women further respect by having a badge designed for them to wear on occasions when actual (that is to say, male) graduates were expected to wear hoods and gowns.

Once the scheme reached beyond Scotland and the idea of hiring local invigilators had been accepted, there was no logical reason why it should be confined to the British Isles. In 1883, for reasons that are no longer apparent (was there a local committee in operation?), the first centre outside the United Kingdom was recognized in the Prussian city of Königsberg (USALLACM 3 January 1883). This was possibly because it was a city with many English-speaking governesses and teachers likely to find the LLA attractive. This was not the first Scottish foray into Germany, however, as the Glasgow Certificate Committee had opened a centre in Dresden two years earlier (University of Glasgow, Local Examinations Report 1881), though this was not the forerunner of expansion on the St Andrews scale.

Consolidation

While the overall number of candidates for the Licentiate initially remained relatively small (see Table 5.1), the widening circle of centres meant that the administrative tasks were growing. Knight estimated that by 1883 (USALLACM 16 May 1883) 4–5,000 postal items, including answers to enquiries, were annually passing across his desk. Ten years later, he was to make a further estimate that he personally wrote 4,500 LLA-related letters a year in longhand, and in German and French as well as English. He was able in 1883 to persuade the university to pay him £100 for his trouble, and to give him an assistant clerk.

In the same year, 1883, it was also decided that, without any remission of his duties as professor (at a time when such figures in Scotland taught all classes in their subject themselves), Knight should embark on an extensive tour of England to publicize the LLA programme. This led directly to the opening of five more centres, not just in large cities such as Liverpool and Nottingham, but also in Cheltenham, the haunt of many affluent families likely to employ governesses and also the site of new and prestigious girls' institutions employing women teachers in search of qualifications. This was a group of potential students of which, as we have noted in Chapter 3, the London authorities were also aware.

It was with the convenience of just such groups in mind that the scheme unhitched itself from the MA timetable, and began again to stage its

Table 5.1 University of St Andrews, LLA student numbers, 1877–1931

Years	Candidates entered	Passed in one or more subjects	Received the full diploma
1877–1881	379	320	84
1882–1891	4,752	3,964	928
1892–1901	9,044	6,946	1,189
1902–1911	10,398	8,072	1,166
1912–1921	7,305	5,409	1,024
1922–1931	4,130	2,971	727
Total	36,008	27,682	5,118

Source: Smart 1968

examinations in June and July, when governesses' young charges would have left for their holidays. Although this detachment from the main degree programme posed a risk to standards, or at least to the qualification's academic image, it proved a winner in terms of profits. These continued to evade the university's own coffers and were either invested (in 1884, for example, £500 went into the New Zealand Bank) or used to increase the fees paid to examiners. Knight was eventually even able to prove that, from a legal point of view, his was an enterprise not of the university in general but of his actual committee, which for the moment continued to enjoy the full disposal of the LLA's income (USALLACM 18 July 1884).

In 1885 the first candidate was examined outside Europe, in Barbados, where the presiding officer was a Church of Scotland minister. In the same year, further centres were established in half a dozen continental cities, where a prosperous Scottish presence was enough to support if not always an actual Kirk, as in Paris, then at least a resident Presbyterian chaplain as in Hildesheim or Eisenach (USALLACM 5 March 1885).

It is clear that one of the major attractions of the LLA, both at home and abroad, was the fact that the candidate could gradually collect credits over a number of years, in the style of the Scottish undergraduate course, and could add further credits even after graduation. This was not always the case on courses for women run by other British universities, which often demanded that a fully integrated course be followed in one place and within a set period of time. The collection of credits suited very well the needs of women continually on the move, and of teachers faced with a rapidly expanding school curriculum.

Further flexibility and commercial attraction was added in 1890, when for the first time non-English speakers were allowed to write all their papers in French or German (USALLACM 22 July 1890). Thus Knight attempted to attract not just the British expatriates of Königsberg, Paris and Geneva, but also the native women of continental Europe in places not likely to have a regular Scottish or English presence (as Table 5.2 shows).

Knight embarked on further English tours in 1889 and 1893, making speeches that were widely reported, not just in the local papers of the cities he visited but also in the national educational journals. The latter usually also reported enthusiastically each year's annual report on the LLA's development. By 1889 there had already been 1,887 registered examinees, and 808 had collected enough credits to earn the full diploma and title (USALLACM 24 July 1889). But Knight clearly saw himself not merely as a recruiting agent for his committee's scheme but as a general champion of the higher education of women, a cause to which he saw the committee's funds (showing a surplus of some £1,800 in 1890) being exclusively devoted.

He continually fought to preserve the LLA's good name. In evidence to the Scottish Universities Commission of 1889, which was to recommend the full admission of women to undergraduate courses, he spoke of the

Table 5.2   University of St Andrews, location of LLA examination centres, 1877–1931

Country	Number of centres
England	57
Germany	41
Scotland	37
France	33
South Africa	22
India	21
Canada	13
United States	12
Australia	9
Wales	8
Ireland	8
Belgium	6
British Caribbean	6
Italy	6
Switzerland	3
New Zealand	3

In addition, there were:
2 each in Poland, Russia, Romania, Ceylon, Turkey, Malta, Burma, Portugal and Austria;
1 each in Spain, Egypt, the Netherlands, Palestine, Kenya, Bermuda, China, Jersey, Guernsey and the Isle of Man.

16 other centres listed by Smart have names that cannot be identified.

Total number of examination centres throughout the world: 329

Source: Smart 1968

difficulties for holders of the qualification if its position were to be undermined by the new open-ness which he himself had advocated so assiduously (USALLACM 22 July 1890). The holders of the LLA now formed, he insisted, 'a large, intelligent, educated body, some of them headmistresses of important public schools, others of private ones, some assistant mistresses, many others women of leisure and culture' (ibid.). It was, he insisted, imperative that their qualification should continue to be accepted as a degree equivalent, for the sake of the many women who were unable to attend higher education classes. To increase its chances of acceptance, he expressed his willingness to impose a new system of subject grouping in order to strengthen the challenge of the putative degree.

The LLA threatened

However, the atmosphere of British academia was changing, and the open, hitherto non-elitist, attitudes of the Scottish universities in particular were being increasingly challenged. Despite the serious reputation they had acquired during the Enlightenment, and the part that they had played in the development of both the pure and applied sciences, by the end of the nineteenth century the traditional Scottish ways of doing things were subjected to more and more public scrutiny. Even the Scotch Education Department, as it was then known, made it clear that it was increasingly reluctant to recognize the LLA as a degree equivalent, on the simple grounds, as its notoriously elitist Secretary Craik indicated, that a 'real' degree must involve residence or, at the very least, face-to-face teaching (USALLACM 21 July 1891). Moreover, the Scottish attachment to the non-honours and generalist 'ordinary' degree, on which the LLA was modelled, became increasingly scorned by the leaders of opinion in the ancient English universities.

Oxford and Cambridge were to become increasingly prestigious models in Scotland (Davie 1961), especially at St Andrews, which could also boast medieval buildings and a 'traditional' Oxford-like atmosphere. As late as 1895, however, the voice of a more authentically Scottish tradition could still be heard, with Principal Donaldson of St Andrews asserting that the now fashionable emphasis on residence with its monastic rules and discipline was a mere relic of pre-Reformation times, that had thankfully died out in all of Protestant Europe save England (Donaldson 1911). But his impoverished colleagues were already seeking new ways to prosper in a changed academic world.

After the First World War they would, under Principal Irvine, begin to see great gain in exploiting their ancientness, as well as the town's unrivalled and socially prestigious golf connections (Young 1969; Cant 1970). More and more affluent parents would come to see in the small, attractive seaside town a very safe and healthy haven for the daughters that they were now willing to entrust to residential universities. Even before the First World War, St Andrews was to achieve a ratio of female to male students that many late twentieth century universities might envy. In October 1913, of the 300 or so undergraduates in residence, 130 were women, and men had already become a minority in an Arts Faculty that 20 years earlier had been an entirely male preserve (Cant 1970). It was no wonder, therefore, that there were increasing suggestions that the provision of the LLA was no longer necessary.

Knight himself in many ways welcomed the new situation. According to Lumsden, it had always been intended that the profits from the LLA would be accumulated in anticipation of the day when women would be admitted to full university membership (Lumsden 1911). Once that had happened, these funds were soon released in order to create Scotland's first hall of residence for women, at a time when even Scottish men had still not been accorded such a facility. Yet this new commitment to residential education did not mean that Knight wished to abandon the LLA. He continued enthusiastically his defence of the rights of those women who could not avail themselves of the new hall's facilities, though the struggle on their behalf was to become ever more difficult with the conversion of London into a teaching university, the disappearance of the Royal University of Ireland, and the general abandonment of the notion that a university could operate simply as the provider of a syllabus and a supervised examination.

Knight could, of course, legitimately claim that his own committee had been trying to provide more than just those things. Unlike London University and the Royal University of Ireland, he had not only actively sought cooperation with the correspondence colleges who were preparing LLA candidates, but had also provided advice for those groups arranging tutorials in United Kingdom examination centres (such as, for example, at University College, Nottingham). The teaching centre at Kelso had even seemed for a time to be the forerunner of a whole Scottish network (*Journal of Education*, September 1885).

Moreover, his committee had been known to commission special textbooks, when no appropriate one existed, thus following the normal procedure in Scotland whereby the Professor's own most recent book was usually the only set text on Ordinary Arts courses. One of these textbooks was an *Introduction to Old French*, modern languages being a subject which the LLA pioneered in the Scottish university sector. This particular book was to become a standard work throughout the university system (Roget 1887).

The LLA system was to continue for several decades after the admission of women to general undergraduate courses. Clearly, a real, if increasingly specialized, clientele continued to exist who appreciated the opportunities it could offer. Students were still to be found, for example, among British expatriate communities as well as in overseas homes and schools employing British governesses and teachers. At the turn of the century, the examination was being conducted in some 76 centres outside the United Kingdom (see Table 5.2), at a time when its official coaching centres in Aberdeen, Loughborough and Nottingham were on the point of closing down (USALLACM 12 July 1898, 12 December 1899).

By this time, after a quarter of a century of running the LLA virtually single-handed, Knight was beginning to feel the strain, especially in the committees of the University itself, where he felt the ground moving under him. In December 1899 he had felt it necessary to issue a detailed response to a Senate request for the adjustment of the whole scheme. He admitted it had become increasingly independent of the University as such, and that he had run his Senate subcommittee almost like a private concern. He was now willing to place its relationship to the University Court on a new footing, if only to expedite a more general recognition of the LLA in an increasingly bureaucratic educational world more and more obsessed with qualification recognition and equivalencies.

He also expressed his willingness to be more directive in his relations with students. He would, for example, 'draw up recommendations [though not rules] for candidates as to the order in which subjects should be taken and the best manner of study'. But he steadfastly opposed any regulations which might 'interfere with the autonomy of candidates', on the grounds that such rules would simply repel them, thus reasserting his belief in according students the maximum degree of freedom in framing their own study programme (USALLACM 4 December 1899).

Nevertheless, Knight was soon obliged to resign, and neither his new proposals nor his old view of the qualification's status and essential nature were to survive his vacating the chair. The first meeting to be held without him, early in 1900, immediately turned the clock back to the very earliest days. The old title of 'Higher Local Examination' was revived as a descriptive sub-title on the grounds that 'this would obviate the confusion between the LL.A. and a university degree' (USALLACM 12 December 1899). For Knight there had never been any such confusion. He really had seen them as equal, and would hardly have supported the committee's further attempts to lay down prerequisites for the study of certain subjects. Thus, geography could now only be attempted after a pass in geology or history, while, unlike undergraduates in the university proper, candidates for the LLA were strongly recommended only to take subjects they had done at school. For Knight all such rules and directions were patronizing and elitist in their assumptions about distant students.

He saw the subtitle 'Higher Local Examination' as being particularly degrading, smacking too much of the school work that he had long expected students to put behind them before embarking on his course. He also poured scorn on later attempts to introduce a 'universal' practical examination in certain subjects, on the eminently practical ground that he and his clerk had found it difficult enough to hire, world-wide, sufficient rooms for a great variety of written papers, without the added burden of employing local laboratory assistants, as well as hiring and insuring premises with drains and tables suitable for modern scientific procedures (USALLACM 12 December 1899).

What Knight saw as the process of degradation continued. His successor, Harkless, seemed quite happy to admit to the English Board of Education that the LLA was not and could not be seen as a degree, though Knight and his followers gained some comfort from the new and somewhat ironical recognition by the government that, though the LLA could not be seen as the equivalent of the newly reformed Scottish Ordinary degree, it might well be regarded as the equal of the more lowly pass degree at Oxford and Cambridge. There, unlike in Scotland, the possession of the highest level of school-leaving certificate was not yet necessary for admission to under-graduate courses (USALLACM 25 November 1902). Even so, the English Board of Education in giving that judgement could not forebear to ask why St Andrews persisted with the LLA, now that face-to-face undergraduate courses were generally open to women.

The obvious answer, of course, remained that it was still very popular overseas. As late as 1908 new centres were being requested in Brooklyn, Vienna and Constantinople. Moreover, while it was not, of course, mentioned in official documents, the existence of the LLA was still affording those St Andrews professors willing to invigilate or examine an acceptable extra income. Thus despite Harkless's lack of personal enthusiasm, the university allowed the examinations to continue.

The death of the LLA

In February 1910, however, there was another major upheaval when the Court, as the supreme governing body, decided to take over ultimate responsibility for the LLA, and demanded that its proceeds should now be paid into the University's General Fund rather than into the Trust established by Knight (USALLACM 28 February 1910). But any thought of major profit was soon swept away by the war. This not only hopelessly dislocated the overseas operation, but also produced social changes that swept away much of the privileged world that had employed thousands of governesses plus, no doubt, numerous examples of 'the many other women of leisure and culture' that Knight had seen (USALLACM 12 July 1890) as potential clients.

The pre-war profits melted away like snow, with the annual statement for 1923 recording an operational deficit of £47 19s 0d. Moreover, the intellectual and practical demands now being made of teachers seeking professional qualification seemed likely to present other, quite new, organizational difficulties (USALLACM 14 December 1923). This was especially true at St Andrews, which was intent on abolishing its chair of education (Bell 1986).

In 1924, the committee began desperately to look in quite new directions. Perhaps the future lay no longer, they surmised, in the provision of what now seemed a discredited degree equivalent qualification offered at a distance. Instead, it might lie in the field of general adult education, and in those less demanding intellectual activities suitable for middle class women with time on their hands. The committee decided that 'linking up with continuation classes should be carefully and sympathetically considered' (USALLACM 14 November 1924).

Nevertheless, the financial losses increased in 1925 and 1926, and in December 1927 it was decided to call a halt to the whole scheme at the end of 1931, when most of the current body of students would have left the system. A more sympathetic committee might, with imagination and without great organizational difficulty, have turned the LLA into a permanently useful means of helping part-time distant students, anticipating perhaps some of the eventual tasks of the Open University. But a committee displaying so many of the elitist attitudes then current in St Andrews, under the academically ambitious Principal Irvine, were unlikely to envisage such possibilities.

In the committee members' eyes the LLA had clearly outlived its usefulness if, indeed, it had ever been anything but an embarrassment. It belonged to the now lost world that had preceded the opening of the universities to women, and the establishment of the new regional universities in England. Stumbling on an overseas market had been a pure accident, and even that outlet seemed unlikely to revive in the future now that unqualified British women no longer sallied forth in such great numbers to educate the children of the rich. Those that still remained seemed increasingly less interested in paper qualifications. An attempt to establish a professional register of governesses and private teachers earlier in the century had proved abortive, and such women seemed to rely more and more for positions on personal recommendations rather than academic certificates. In any case, Principal Irvine, intent on attracting the rich daughters of England and America was hardly likely to be keen on catering for a class of student still often regarded as domestic servants.

From a modern viewpoint, it is perhaps strange that no one in St Andrews seemed to have considered enlarging the post-First World War take-up by admitting men to the Licentiate. Perhaps, given the traditional open-ness of the Scottish universities to all aspiring males, and the fact that in the early 1920s even the humblest male candidate for an elementary teaching job was guaranteed a state-financed university education, this was considered a non-starter. The St Andrews professors appear to have assumed that the LLA was terminally ill.

Yet, as Smart claims, in the fullest available account of the LLA, in its time it 'was widely recognised as an academic test of a genuinely high standard, and it met the needs of a wide cross-section of women' (Smart 1968: 27). Unlike the newly opened face-to-face courses that spelt its end, it catered for a really wide age range, and, given its part-time nature, for those many unmarried women who in the economic conditions then prevailing did not dare to leave their employment even temporarily in search of general learning. Far from catering merely for the intellectually inferior as some of its critics suspected, it is probable that it was also widely used as a preparatory course by those intending to embark on face-to-face undergraduate courses. Certainly, colonial governments set great store by it. Thus, the education authorities in Natal had seen it as a possible basis for the whole of their teacher-training programme, though their approaches had to be refused in the name of university autonomy (USALLACM 25 November 1902). Even in the LLA's dying years, the government of India was exploring a number of further possible uses for the qualification.

The important role played by the LLA in the general expansion of women's education cannot be ignored. The first two women school inspectors in England were both LLAs, as was the first woman president of the Educational Institute of Scotland. Marion Gilchrist, the first woman to gain a medical degree in a Scottish university, had first gained the LLA, as had an early editor of the *International Women's Suffrage News*. Quite apart from such individuals, the large number of headteachers, members of school boards and early women politicians who had also taken advantage of Knight's creation guaranteed it a considerable influence throughout Britain and overseas. Over its half century of life it attracted over 11,000 students, and over 5,000 collected enough credits to earn the full diploma and title (see Table 5.1). It touched far more people than the Royal University of Ireland.

No doubt, even in its heyday, the standards of the LLA were never quite as high as twentieth century academic orthodoxy came to demand. But then, neither were those of most other British university courses, both face-to-face and at a distance. The real opposition to the LLA was based on the same prejudices as the opposition to the old London University arrangements and those of the Royal University of Ireland. If it really was a swindle, it is difficult to see why so many able women persevered with it when the London alternative existed, and why a clearly devoted and academically distinguished figure like Knight spent so much time and staked so much of his reputation on it. That it made headway from such an unpromising base as the almost ruined St Andrews of the 1870s is a tribute to his imagination and effort and to the open attitudes of the Scottish university world of that time.

6

A Guidance by Test: The External Role of the University of London in the Twentieth Century

The passing of the University of London Act in 1898, and its implementation from 1900 onwards, provides both a significant and a convenient breakpoint for our analysis. Before the passing of the Act, as described in Chapter 3, the University of London, by its very nature as a state examining body and nothing more, was a major provider of opportunities for studying at a distance. It was also, in a more general sense, an archetypal open university, enabling increasing numbers of students to study a growing range of subjects at a higher level in their own time, regardless of their age, sex, class, race, religion, location or previous education.

From 1900 onwards, the nature of the University changed as it adopted two separate roles: an internal, collegiate, teaching (and research) role and an external, examining, distance education role. By mid-century, as the division between secondary and higher education became fixed in the 'modern' pattern, the University had also become less open. Subsequently, more and more restrictions were placed on those who could enrol as external students, and the range of subjects offered was reduced; though both of these trends have been reversed to some extent in the last few years.

The internal role came increasingly to be seen as the more important as the century wore on, and it is what most people nowadays would associate with the University. But the external role, if less obvious, also remained of major importance, and it has continued up until the present day. It is this latter role which is the concern of the present chapter, in which we will describe the context within which the external role developed and examine its changing nature.

Internal and external roles: the continuing debate

As noted in Chapter 3, the status of the University of London as a state examining body attracted increasing attention and criticism towards the end of the nineteenth century:

> Except to a large number of schools who found in the Matriculation Examination an excellent and cheaply conducted 'Learning

Examination' for their pupils, the majority of whom never intended to proceed further in a University course, the examinations either failed to supply the degree that was reasonably required as was the case with the medical faculty, or so hampered the teaching in Arts and Science as to drive the students to crammers to the detriment of all advanced instruction or of the cultivation of knowledge for its own sake, and the stifling of the higher development of the student's capabilities.

(Allchin 1905, Vol. 1: 62)

The split between the internal and external sides of the University, instituted from 1900 onwards, was intended to address these (and other) perceived problems. The changes which were introduced affected the whole structure and government of the University. An expanded Senate received reports from the Academic Council, which was concerned with the internal side, the Council for External Students, and the Board to Promote the Extension of University Teaching, which dealt with the extra-mural work. Boards of Studies were established to oversee the work of the University in no less than 32 different subject areas.

Involvement in the internal side of the University was restricted to selected institutions based within 30 miles of Charing Cross (though an exception was immediately made for the South-Eastern Agricultural College at Wye in Kent). University College and King's College were admitted (and later incorporated) as Schools of the University in six faculties. Twenty-one other institutions were admitted in one or more of the eight Faculties of Arts, Economics, Engineering, Law, Medicine, Music, Science and Theology. Other institutions – including polytechnics, technical institutes, training colleges and music colleges – were associated with the University through having 'recognised teachers' of university standing.

The early years of the century saw a succession of other institutions admitted to the University – Westfield College in 1902, the London School of Tropical Medicine in 1905, East London College in 1907, Imperial College (created through the amalgamation of a number of existing institutions) in 1908 and the London Day Training College (later to become the Institute of Education) in 1910 (Harte 1986: 173, 182). By then, as Table 6.1 shows, the University consisted of three incorporated colleges, three other institutions belonging to the University, 29 schools and 30 institutions having recognized teachers.

The internal University was then a federal mix of multi-faculty colleges, among which University College and King's College were dominant, single-faculty colleges (mainly in medicine and theology), research institutions and associated bodies. Some of the institutions referred to in Table 6.1 will already be familiar from the tables included in Chapter 3. Conversely, many others, especially those outside the 30 mile limit, are no longer listed. Subsequently, other institutions were admitted as Schools: the School of Oriental and African Studies in 1916, Birkbeck College in 1920, the School of Pharmacy in 1925, the School of Slavonic and East European

Table 6.1 'Institutions for instruction and research' University of London, 1911

Institution	Faculties							
	1	2	3	4	5	6	7	8
'Colleges incorporated in the University':								
University College	*	*	*	*	*		*	
King's College	*	*	*	*	*		*	
King's College for Women	*						*	
'Other Institutions belonging to the University':[†]								
Brown Animal Sanatory Institution								
Physiological Laboratory								
Francis Galton Laboratory for Eugenics								
'Schools of the University':								
Imperial College of Science and Technology			*				*	
Royal Holloway College	*						*	
Bedford College for Women	*						*	
East London College	*		*				*	
London School of Economics		*						
S.E. Agricultural College, Wye							*	
Westfield College	*							
London Day Training College	*							
New College, Hampstead								*
Hackney College, Hampstead								*
Regent's Park College								*
King's College: Theological Department								*
Wesleyan College, Richmond								*
St John's Hall, Highbury								*
St Bartholomew's Hospital Medical School						*		
St Thomas's Hospital Medical School						*		
Westminster Hospital Medical School						*		
Guy's Hospital Medical School						*		
St George's Hospital Medical School						*		
London Hospital Medical College						*		
Middlesex Hospital Medical School						*		
Charing Cross Hospital Medical School						*		
London School of Medicine for Women						*		
University College Hospital Medical School						*		
King's College Hospital Medical School						*		
St Mary's Hospital Medical School						*		
London School of Tropical Medicine						*		
Lister Institute of Preventive Medicine						*		
Royal Army Medical College						*		
'Institutions having recognized teachers':								
Goldsmiths' College	*						*	
Battersea Polytechnic			*			*	*	
Birkbeck College	*	*					*	

Table 6.1—continued

Institution	Faculties							
	1	2	3	4	5	6	7	8
City of London College								
Finsbury Technical College								
Jews' College	*							
Northampton Polytechnic Institute			*				*	
Northern Polytechnic Institute	*		*				*	
Royal Veterinary College							*	
Sir John Cass Technical Institute							*	
South-Western Polytechnic Institute	*		*				*	
West Ham Municipal Technical Institute	*		*				*	
Woolwich Polytechnic			*				*	
Maria Grey Training College	*							
St Mary's College, Paddington	*							
Mary Datchelor Training College	*							
Borough Road College, Isleworth								
St John's College, Battersea								
St Mark's College, Chelsea								
Royal Academy of Music						*		
Royal College of Music								
Trinity College of Music						*		
Bethlem Royal Hospital								
Brompton Hospital for Consumption								
Hospital for Sick Children								
London School of Dental Surgery								
National Dental College								
National Hospital for the Paralysed								
Royal London Ophthalmic Hospital								
School of Pharmacy								

Note – the Faculties are:
1 Arts
2 Economics
3 Engineering
4 Law
5 Medicine
6 Music
7 Science
8 Theology

† The 'other institutions belonging to the University' were research institutions which were not recognized for faculty teaching purposes

Source: ULC 1911–12: 313, 314, 462–82

Studies in 1932, the Royal Veterinary College in 1944 and the British Postgraduate Medical Federation in 1945.

Yet the debates over the teaching and examining roles of the University did not cease with the establishment of this internal structure. They were to form one of the key themes of a further Royal Commission on University Education in London, the Haldane Commission, which had been set up chiefly to resolve the organisational problems posed by the creation of Imperial College. This was the third such Commission to sit in 25 years, beginning its work in 1909 and reporting in 1913.

The Council for External Students strongly argued the case for the external degree system in a report submitted to the Royal Commission:

> One of the main contributions which the External side offers to the service of Education generally is the principle of guidance by test . . . the student is led from his Matriculation to his Doctorate along a closely systematised and strictly continuous course of study. . . The far-reaching and Imperial character of the work at present conducted by the External Side of the University of London, the wide range of subjects in which at present the University conducts examinations, and the high standards required for the Honours and higher degrees, constitute it a national necessity which cannot be replaced by any other educational system.
>
> (University of London, Council for External Students 1910: 4, 9)

The Council also showed a certain resistance to cooperating with the Royal Commission in its work. It was, for example, unable to reach agreement with the Commission on the format of a form to collect information from its examination candidates on their occupation and method of preparation. The Royal Commission in turn, in its final report, was highly critical of the working of the University:

> The evidence shows that the Academic and External Councils are dominated by incompatible ideals. The one side believes that training in a university under university teachers is an essential and by far the most important factor in a university education, while the other side believes that examinations based upon a syllabus afford 'a guidance by test', which is an adequate means of ascertaining that a candidate has attained a standard of knowledge entitling him to a university degree.
>
> (Royal Commission on University Education in London 1913: 12)

The Royal Commission came down heavily against the University's examination system, as it affected both external and internal students:

> We are convinced that both a detailed syllabus and an external examination are inconsistent with the true interests of university education, injurious to the students, degrading to the teachers, and ineffective for the attainment of the ends they are supposed to promote. The insistence on a system of external examinations is always based upon want of faith in the teachers. Even the so-called Internal examinations of the University of London are practically external, because of the large number of institutions involved, and the demands

of the common syllabus; and the syllabus is a device to maintain a standard among institutions which are not all of university rank.

(ibid.: 36)

The Commission's real ire was, however, reserved for the external degree, which was seen as placing a heavy and inappropriate burden upon its students, many of whom were working as, or training to be, teachers:

> we think there can be no doubt that in the broader national interests the sooner the demand for External degrees can be reduced to a point at which the degrees themselves can be abolished without hardship the better it will be for our schools and our teachers. . . We do not think, however, that it would be possible in the present state of public opinion for the University to abandon the granting of degrees on the results of examination alone. The best hope of advance lies in the direction of avoiding as far as may be individual hardship and injustice, and at the same time making the better kind of education easier of access.
>
> (ibid.: 178)

The Commission recommended dropping the distinction between internal and external students, excluding external candidates from the examinations in medicine and engineering, and limiting the examinations to the United Kingdom. It also recommended that the University's inspections of secondary schools should cease.

Discussion of the implementation of the Commission's report was interrupted by the start of the First World War, and its recommendations were not revived or acted upon when peace returned. It was then left to a Departmental Committee of the Board of Education (the Hilton Young Committee) to pick up the issues raised. In its memorandum to this Committee, the Council for External Students was able to demonstrate a continuing and growing demand for external study:

> The Council for External Students in their Report for Transmission to the Royal Commission [that is in 1910], pointed out that in the six years prior to 1901 the average entry of all candidates for Intermediate Examinations was 1447. In 1912, the total number of External candidates for Intermediate Examinations was 2067; and in 1923 this had grown to 4084. In the case of Degree Examinations, the total number of candidates in 1900 was 1001, which included all candidates whatsoever, as there was then no Internal side. In 1912, the number of External candidates for degree examinations was 985, and in 1923 it was 1499. This remarkable growth has occurred without in any way impairing the growth of the Internal side of the University. The growth of Overseas Examinations during the same period has been equally notable.
>
> (University of London, Council for External Students, *Minutes* (ULCESM) 4 February 1925: 2–3)

A very slim report was duly published by the Departmental Committee in

1926. This noted the past controversies, but also drew attention to the greater harmony which apparently then existed between the different factions within the University, stating that 'no member of the Committee contemplated the abolition of degree examinations for external students . . . no responsible body desired to give evidence in that sense' (Board of Education 1926: 8). And so no restrictions on the external examinations were recommended. The report was accepted by the government of the day, despite some resistance from the University, and quickly passed into law. A new body, the Court, was created to oversee the University's finances. This body, set alongside a smaller Senate made more representative of the constituent Schools, was to significantly strengthen the central University organization.

Post-War external policy changes

While the debates over the internal and external roles of the University, and the conflicts between them, did not disappear with the acceptance of the Hilton Young Report, they did noticeably quieten down. Seen from the perspective of the 1990s, the 1930s, 1940s and the first half of the 1950s appear as a time of relative structural stability so far as the University of London was concerned, during which its internal and external roles both continued to develop along essentially parallel tracks.

After the Second World War, and particularly from the 1960s onwards, the pressures for change began to build up again, largely in response to the rapid growth and diversification of the British higher education system (Lowe 1988; Stewart 1989). The effects of these pressures upon the University of London's external role were mostly determined by British government policy, mediated through the deliberations and recommendations of a range of external and internal commissions or committees. In the changed post-war world, there no longer appeared to be any powerful defenders of the external system left within the University of London itself. By then, the University's priorities were overwhelmingly with its internal role.

The first of these policy decisions led to a significant expansion, albeit temporarily, in the University's external work. During the latter part of the Second World War, when reconstruction issues were coming under consideration, a series of government commissions were set up to review the development of higher education in the British colonies. They recommended that existing or newly established colleges in the main African and West Indian colonies should be rapidly built up to university status, in anticipation of the coming independence of the countries concerned. This was achieved during the period between 1946 and 1970, with the London external degree system being employed in a way analogous to the role it had performed, during both the nineteenth and twentieth centuries, with respect to university colleges within the United

Kingdom (Maxwell 1980; Pattison 1984). These relationships are discussed in more detail, along with other institutional linkages, in the next chapter.

Subsequent policy decisions, by contrast, resulted in successive curtailments and restrictions being placed upon the University's external role. The remaining English university colleges were gradually accorded independent university status during the late 1940s and 1950s, at which point they ceased to prepare their students for London external degrees. The establishment of a National Council for Technological Awards (NCTA) in 1955 to recognize new course developments in the technical colleges, and the creation of the Diploma in Technology (Dip Tech) as a degree equivalent qualification, began to formalise an alternative route through advanced further education. This then inevitably drew students away from the London external engineering degree (Ministry of Education 1956; Burgess and Pratt 1970; Venables 1978; Silver 1990).

The report of the Robbins Committee on higher education (Committee on Higher Education 1963) was to have an even greater impact. In its written and oral evidence to this committee, the University of London outlined the history and recent development of its external degree system. It noted the problems which resulted from the syllabuses not being in the hands of those responsible for the teaching, and recognized that there were difficulties with student preparation and pass rates, but stressed the high standards of the qualifications obtained. The University made it clear that it was not seeking to expand its external role:

> The capacity of the University to deal adequately with increases in the number of External students cannot be indefinitely enlarged and the University therefore is not seeking to expand its activities on the External side.
>
> (ibid.: Evidence 1239)

The main concern of the Robbins Committee was with how best to achieve an orderly expansion of the British higher education system as a whole. It made no specific recommendations regarding the University of London's external system, being more concerned with its internal side and with the effective management of the federal university structure. The University's response was to establish immediately an internal Robbins Report Steering Committee, followed swiftly by the Saunders Committee on Academic Organization, producing a final report in 1966 (University of London 1966).

A series of reforms to the federal structure followed. The main colleges, or Schools, of the University were given greater autonomy, including the freedom to put forward their own course syllabuses. On the external side, the standard and equivalence of the external degree was once again stressed, and mechanisms for ensuring this where internal and external syllabuses differed were proposed. It was also accepted that there was no objection to the introduction of separate entrance requirements for internal and external students.

One of the main recommendations of the Robbins Committee, the establishment of a Council for National Academic Awards (CNAA), was to have a decisive effect upon the external system. The CNAA's role was to validate degree courses in the rapidly developing advanced further education sector (later to be called the 'public' or 'polytechnics and colleges' sector), absorbing and extending the functions of the NCTA. The University of London accepted the creation of the CNAA with some relief, although it came to regret the lack of collaboration between the two bodies, and began to seek a revised role for its continuing external work:

> The University of London is thereby relieved of the responsibility which it has carried for so long of being the sole channel through which students not in attendance at university institutions can obtain degrees. An opportunity is thus provided of reconsidering the University's proper role in this field with particular reference to the desirability of establishing a situation in which the Internal side of the University has no grounds for feeling that its legitimate academic aims are hampered by the existence of the External degree system . . . the Charter of the Council for National Academic Awards empowers it to grant degrees only to students who have followed courses of instruction at educational establishments. The External degree system of the University of London will remain the only means whereby the student who prepares himself by private study can obtain a degree. The University should therefore continue to regard the External degree system as an integral part of its activities.
>
> (ibid.: 48)

From its establishment in 1964, the CNAA pursued a policy of rapid expansion, focusing at first on the science and technology areas. The result was a steady decline in the numbers of home students, both full-time and part-time, registered with the University of London external system (Duke 1967; Lane 1975; Silver 1990).

The relationship between the CNAA and the polytechnics and colleges was different from the University of London's general practice. Whereas, at least in most subjects, any institution or individual could prepare students for the syllabuses and examinations set by the University, the CNAA invited colleges to devise and submit their own course proposals for consideration. These proposals, and the resources available to implement them, were then subjected to a very thorough and recurrent scrutiny, with many being rejected at first.

The CNAA's approach was more akin to the special relationships which were entered into by the University, particularly after the Second World War, with university colleges at home and overseas. It was compared favourably with the rather less demanding methods being applied at this time by the growing number of universities that had become involved in the validation of their local colleges, chiefly for the BEd degree and related qualifications (Committee of Enquiry into the Academic Validation of

Degree Courses in Public Sector Higher Education 1985). The CNAA's work was to lead to the establishment of a confident and mature public sector of higher education, which would come to rival the universities in terms of teaching provision, and result in most of the institutions concerned gaining university status in their own right.

A rather more radical innovation, the Open University – chartered in 1969 and admitting its first students in 1971 (see Chapter 8) – followed soon after the establishment of the CNAA, and was to have a similarly significant effect on the University of London external system. Once again, the University betrayed some pique over the lack of consultation:

> The Government is now fully committed to the establishment of the University of the Air, or the Open University as it is now called, and a Planning Committee has been set up to act as a midwife for the birth. . . I think it should be recorded that at no stage whatsoever were the views of the University of London on the matter sought, despite the fact that we have long experience in this field.
>
> (Principal's Report, ULC 1968–9: 142–3)

The University was, however, realistic, and resolved to give careful consideration to the implications of this development for the external system:

> With the establishment of the Open University the University of London is no longer the only university offering opportunities for a degree to the private student. In addition many universities offer limited opportunities to undergraduate and on a greater scale to graduate students attending part-time. . . The CNAA has stated its desire to encourage the provision of courses on a part-time basis leading to its degrees. The Council therefore considers that the problems of private and part-time study for degrees, and the place of part-time higher education in the national system should be the subject of study by a high-level commission.
>
> (ULCESM 7 January 1970, App.: 2)

The Council for External Students had already produced a report on 'University Development in the 1970s', which suggested that consideration should be given to establishing an 'External College', to further developing the advisory service (see Chapter 7), to possibly withdrawing all of the first degree syllabuses, and to reviewing the entrance requirements. A Review Committee was duly appointed, and in 1971 it recommended:

> a fundamental change in the role of the External system – that registration of students in public educational institutions should cease, with five year's notice being given, and that thereafter the External system should cater solely for private students; the Council supports this recommendation.
>
> (ibid. 30 June 1971: 6)

This recommendation was endorsed by the Murray Committee, which reported in 1972 (Committee of Enquiry into the Governance of the University of London 1972). The decision was finally taken in March 1972, when the University Senate resolved that the registration of full-time (but *not* part-time) students in British polytechnics and colleges as external students should cease from September 1977.

Then, two years later, in March 1974, a circular was sent to 'all overseas authorities', informing them that:

> On and after 1 September 1977 external registration will cease to be generally available overseas. For those registered before that date examinations will be held under existing arrangements for a few more years. . . Thereafter [that is, by 1985] the system of permanent overseas authorities will come to an end, and the University will itself make special arrangements, normally in consultation with the British Council, for individual candidates such as United Kingdom citizens temporarily resident abroad and other persons whom it has agreed in exceptional circumstances to register.
>
> (ULCESM 22 May 1974: App.)

It seemed that the University of London was about to turn its back on more than a century of educational service world-wide, relinquishing its role as an international open university. A rump external system would be left to focus its attention on the limited British market for private study in subjects (most notably law, economics and languages) not offered by the new national, and much better resourced, Open University.

Almost as soon as these decisions were agreed and acted upon, however, the authorities began to have second thoughts. The last ten years have witnessed a succession of attempts to redevelop the external system in a cost-effective, and hopefully cost-recovering, fashion which would not place an undue burden upon existing staff. A discussion paper by the then vice-chancellor, Randolph Quirk, got this process underway in 1982. He began by succinctly setting the scene:

> In the mid-[nineteen]seventies it seemed reasonable to suppose that London's External system could be allowed to decline. We had long since seen the external degree at university colleges replaced by degrees of independent universities. The growth of universities in the developing countries made it reasonable to expect that higher education overseas would no longer need the support of the London external provision. In Britain, the establishment of the CNAA within the non-university sector replaced our machinery for students work-ing in such colleges for a London degree. The advent of the Open University offered degree work for the private, home-based student. Finally, in the post-Saunders era [that is, post 1966], with a rapidly growing divergence between the syllabuses available for external students and those taught in the Schools of the University, Boards of

Studies came to find it increasingly unrewarding to maintain syllabuses solely for students whom they never saw and with whom they could have little contact. But more recent events and current circumstances have made us think again about the actual and potential value of our external system.

(University of London 1982: 1)

The paper went on to point to the considerable unsatisfied demand for higher education, both in many developing countries and in the United Kingdom itself. It argued that many part-time mature students were seeking provision rather more specialized, and perhaps individualized, than that offered by the Open University. The growing interest in continuing education was noted, along with the development – and application to distance education – of new communications technologies.

A Working Party was duly established to advise on the development of the external system. Another paper followed in 1983 setting out the University's policy for the external system (University of London 1983). This argued for the increased inter-availability of syllabuses between internal and external studies, for procedures to allow external and internal students to switch their status if desired, for the use of course unit-based degrees for external students, and for the further development of teaching and other forms of academic support for home-based students. It also suggested that the possibility of creating closer links between the external system and the Open University, university departments of extra-mural studies and the independent colleges should be explored. After a gap of five years, external registration again became possible overseas.

Within two years, the Secretary for External Students was able to report on an impressive range of small-scale developments and plans in these areas (ULCESM 27 February 1985: App. EC3). During the 1987–8 academic year, the first ever strategic development plan for the University's external work was produced, to be subsequently updated each year. This set out the external system's mission statement in the following words: 'The goal of the External System is to increase educational opportunity and interchange nationally and worldwide'. A list of objectives, priorities for development, and action plans for 15 subject areas and other concerns was also detailed (University of London, Committee for External Students, 1988).

Examinations and regulations

The examination system which had been built up by the University during the nineteenth century (see Chapter 3) continued to develop during the twentieth century. Minor additions and amendments to regulations were introduced from time to time in the light of changing national and institutional practices.

With the introduction of the new faculty structure in 1900, examinations in divinity were introduced (BD etc.), and separate BSc examinations were begun for agriculture, economics, engineering and veterinary science. It also became possible to complete a BSc degree by research, though this route soon fell into disuse, and was effectively superseded by the introduction of the MSc in 1914, and (belatedly, by international standards) of the PhD degree in 1919 (Simpson 1983: 90–2).

Soon after the end of the First World War, new syllabuses and examinations were introduced in estate management, commerce (to be absorbed within the revised BSc(Econ) degree in the early 1950s), pharmacy and dental surgery. It was not until 1966, though, that separate degree examinations in education (BEd etc.) were recognized, supplanting the earlier examinations in pedagogy which had become part of the arts syllabus.

A new structure for the honours degree was introduced from 1903. Before then all students sat the pass degree examinations in a broad range of subjects, and could then opt to sit further examinations for honours in one or more of those subjects. Subsequently, the student could choose to take either the pass or the honours examinations, thus enabling them to specialize earlier and cutting down the number of examinations involved. Honours examinations were still available at the intermediate level until 1924, having effectively been abolished at matriculation level in 1861.

For the first half of the twentieth century, except in the case of medical subjects, London external students could study and prepare themselves for any of the examinations available where and how they wished. From 1950 onwards, however, largely in response to continuing concerns about standards, external students in engineering and pharmacy had to study at institutions which were recognized for that purpose by the University, usually for a period of five years at a time. This practice was, somewhat curiously, extended to cover sociology in 1966, lasting until that subject was phased out in the 1970s (it has recently returned as part of the revamped BSc(Econ) degree).

All registrations for the BA general degree were ended in 1976, partly because of a wish to improve standards, and partly because of a desire to encourage specialization. In the same year, a Working Party on the future availability of subjects in the external BSc degree presented its report:

> It was unanimously agreed to recommend that the examinations at Standards I, II and III should be discontinued as soon as possible. Since these examinations had been specifically designed to meet the needs of External students when the Internal course-unit degree was introduced, their discontinuation would mean in effect the discontinuation of the BSc degree for External Students. Members of the Working Party recognised that many External students had successfully obtained the BSc degree in the past when it had served a very real purpose. The numbers registering for the degree have however fallen off considerably as polytechnics have transferred to CNAA degrees. . . It is not practicable however to prepare privately for the examinations

in experimental science subjects as adequate guidance in the laboratory work is essential, and the number of External students registering for the BSc degree will therefore soon be very low indeed. Furthermore, apart from the CNAA courses, there are now also Open University degree courses in science and mathematical subjects which offer opportunities for the mature student.

(ULCESM 27 October 1976, App.: 1)

Registration for all BSc degrees, except for the BSc(Econ), was discontinued in 1981.

From the beginning of the century, when the internal and external sides of the University were first separated, it has been a major concern of the University authorities to maintain the equivalence of standards between internal and external study, both generally and on a subject-by-subject basis. For much of the century, this equivalence was relatively easy to monitor and maintain, since internal and external students followed essentially the same syllabuses. There were some differences in detail, and a few syllabuses and qualifications were available only to internal or external students. In some subjects separate examinations were organized, while in others internal and external students (at least those in London) sat the same papers at the same time in the same examination hall. Each year all of the examiners responsible were required to submit reports, paying particular attention to the equivalence of standards between the two sides of the University, and these reports were then carefully considered and acted upon by the Council for External Studies.

After the Second World War, the differences between internal and external syllabuses began to multiply. With the acceptance by the University of the Saunders Committee report in 1966, a much greater divergence in practice took place as the main colleges or Schools of the University introduced their own syllabuses for internal students. The principle of the equivalence of standards between internal and external qualifications remained paramount, however, as it does to this day.

Variations were also introduced with regard to entrance requirements. In some subjects these became less strict for external students. From 1980 the Special Entrance Board was allowed to consider rather more flexibly the cases of mature age external applicants who lacked the standard entrance qualifications.

The twin issues of comparability and standards cropped up in other contexts as well. The University was increasingly willing, for example, to recognize other universities' qualifications – both British and overseas – as equivalent to its own. This was of most importance at the matriculation or entry level, and more problematic for degree and higher level examinations. It is only in the last few years that the restrictions on graduates of other universities registering for external Masters degrees of the University of London have finally been lifted. It is still the case, however, that only London graduates can register as external research students.

At matriculation level it is possible to trace a steady move away from the nineteenth century position, where matriculation was an immediate and internal concern of the University, to the modern position, where such lower level, generalist provision has become the business of the secondary schools. The University of London's matriculation and school leaving examinations were made the responsibility of the Registrar for External Students in 1903, when the inspection of schools, along with extra-mural work, became the business of the Board to Promote the Extension of University Teaching. In 1929 all of this work became the concern of a separate Matriculation and School Examination Council.

From 1904 onwards, a direct equation was made between the University's matriculation and school leaving examinations (it also then became possible to substitute a modern language in place of Latin in the syllabus). From 1917 the linkage between the two examinations was made even closer, with success in one exempting the student from the need to take the other. Other school examining bodies were recognized from 1936 onwards for the purposes of matriculation, and joint attention was then increasingly given to the raising of standards.

The University of London's school leaving examinations were, at this time, only held in those schools which had been recently and successfully inspected by the University. These examinations were offered at three, later two, levels: the Junior School Certificate, designed for 15-year-olds (discontinued after 1932); the (Senior) School Certificate, designed for 16- or 17-year-olds, and equivalent in standard and breadth to the matriculation examination; and the Higher School Certificate, requiring at least one further year's study, and equivalent to the intermediate degree examination. Students who successfully passed the higher school certificate could, under certain conditions, obtain exemption from the intermediate examinations and thus complete their degree studies in a further two years. However, because the regulations specified a three-year registration period, they had to wait a further year before they were actually awarded their degree.

The nineteenth century overlap between secondary and higher education is still apparent in these arrangements, which lasted until the 1950s. The matriculation/school certificate examinations were then supplanted by the national General Certificate of Education (Ordinary Level) examinations, with the intermediate/higher school certificate being replaced by the Advanced Level. In this way the lower levels of the University of London examination system provided the precursor and model for the present English and Welsh school examination system (Kingdon 1991), as well as being highly influential overseas. The matriculation examination was phased out, and from then on all intending University students had to provide evidence, through their previous qualifications, of their ability to study at degree level:

Matriculation now means first registration either as an Internal Student or as an External Student and since 30 April 1951 the

University has ceased to issue Matriculation Certificates. An intending matriculant must first satisfy minimum entrance conditions and then register as an Internal or External Student. With the abolition of the Matriculation Examination, the Examination for the General Certificate of Education has become the normal method by which minimum entrance conditions can be satisfied. Furthermore, the University has raised its qualifications for entrance, and Advanced Level passes as well as Ordinary Level passes are required at the General Certificate of Education Examination for those registering after 30 April 1951. In this comprehensive review of its entrance conditions, the University has taken the opportunity of making special provision for older students. For the first time it has become possible for approved professional qualifications to be regarded as satisfying minimum entrance conditions.

(Principal's Report, ULC 1952–3: 169)

Entrance requirements, in the modern sense, had arrived. With what formerly had been the intermediate examination also becoming the province of the secondary schools, the degree course, maintained at three years, was effectively extended, becoming more specialized in the process. The modern division between secondary and higher education had been established:

The new scheme is based on the premise that responsibility for general education should rest with the schools and should be accepted by them without reservation. Henceforth the University of London will not seek to achieve this end by remote control.

(ibid. 1955–6: 105)

The growth and decline of external student numbers

While a wealth of statistical information is available on the numbers of external students studying for University of London qualifications, on what they were studying and how, the data are not always consistent from year to year or from source to source.

It was only in 1931 that external students were first required to register with the University, and this applied initially only to students resident in the United Kingdom. Prior to that date the information available relates to those students who presented themselves as candidates at examinations. After 1931 the system was steadily tightened up. By 1939 external students following courses at British teaching institutions had to produce a certificate to show that the course was satisfactory. From 1950 all engineering and pharmacy students had to study at recognized institutions. From 1951 all new students had to obtain a statement of eligibility. And, from 1971, registration for external students was restricted to a

Table 6.2   Internal and external candidates, University of London examinations, 1901–38

Examination	1901	1911		1921		1931		1938	
		Int.	Ext.	Int.	Ext.	Int.	Ext.	Int.	Ext.
Matriculation/School Certificate	4,198	6,193		15,822		23,952			
First/Intermediate BA	537	297	924	504	1,022	504	1,783	505	998
Final BA	317	223	395	433	295	833	639	801	554
First/Intermediate BSc	681	455	856	1,104	1,497	1,024	2,533	1,358	2,290
Final BSc	322	320	426	867	483	942	868	1,539	1,223
Preliminary/First MB	346	166	121	370	301	342	358	570	498
Intermediate/Second MB	334	358	107	847	216	643	75	1,441	72
Final MB	211	153	51	256	44	420	25	672	30
First/Intermediate LLB	107	19	41	32	72	142	130	181	222
Final LLB	54	16	34	14	42	44	74	104	154
Total (excluding matriculation)	3,137	5,583		9,913		14,119		15,193	
Total	7,335	11,696		25,735		38,071			

Source: ULC various dates

period of eight years, whereas before it had been without time limit. All of these, and many other more detailed, changes are reflected in the statistics.

Table 6.2 details the numbers of candidates presenting themselves for University of London examinations at selected dates between 1901 and 1938 (compare with Table 3.6). As in the nineteenth century, a continuing and rapid growth is evident overall. The numbers of matriculation and school certificate candidates increased nearly sixfold in the 30 years between 1901 and 1931, from 4,198 to 23,952; while the numbers taking all other examinations rose by four and a half times, from 3,137 to 14,119, over the same period.

At post-matriculation level a fairly even split is apparent in the overall numbers of candidates studying internally and externally. At this level examination pass rates averaged between 56 per cent and 60 per cent overall for the years quoted, whereas at matriculation level they fell from 51 per cent to 37 per cent between 1901 and 1931. Pass rates were generally better, as might be expected, the higher the level of the examination, and for internal rather than external candidates. In 1931, for example, the pass rates for the post-matriculation examinations indicated varied between 45 per cent and 89 per cent for internal students, and between 39 per cent and 79 per cent for external students.

Table 6.3 provides figures for the numbers of registered external students from 1933 until 1990. Registrations remained steady during the 1930s, declining only a little during the Second World War (when, as during the First World War, the University went to great lengths to keep

Table 6.3   Registered external students, University of
London, 1933–90

Year ending	Number of students
1933	11,296
1936	10,943
1941	8,902
1946	19,257
1951	27,780
1956	24,957
1961	26,953
1966	29,524
1971	33,359
1976	27,470
1981	20,353
1986	24,498
1990	c. 24,000

Source: ULC, ULCESM, ULASESAR, various dates

the external study system going, not least for those in prisoner-of-war
camps). In its evidence to the Robbins Committee, the University itself
identified three phases in the subsequent post-war expansion: a rapid
growth between 1945 and 1952, from 11,000 to 29,000 students, in
response to the immediate postwar demand; a slight decline between 1953
and 1957, caused by the introduction of higher entry standards, the demise
of the intermediate examination, and the independence of the remaining
English university colleges; and an upward trend thereafter, though with
rising failure rates (Committee on Higher Education 1963: Evidence
1237).

It was not, in fact, until the 1960s that the number of internal students
registered by the University of London began consistently to overtake the
number of external registrations (Harte 1986: 241, 269). The peak year for
external registrations was 1969–70, with 35,198 registered. The last 20
years have witnessed a slow decline in the number of registrations, though
the 1990 figure of approximately 24,000 is still substantial. The great
majority of external students were registered as studying for a first degree,
with usually less than 10 per cent studying at a higher level (see Table 6.4;
compare with Table 6.2).

Throughout the twentieth century, the University has maintained a keen
interest in how its external students were preparing themselves for their
examinations. In its 1910 Report to the then Royal Commission, the
Council for External Students produced figures to show that, out of 10,215
external candidates for intermediate examinations in the six-year period
from 1904 to 1909, 3 per cent studied in Schools of the University, 10 per
cent in Institutions Having Recognised Teachers, 8 per cent in other
universities, 51 per cent in other institutions and 28 per cent by private

Table 6.4   University of London, registered external students by level of study, 1933–66

Year ending	Preliminary/ intermediate	Degree/ diploma	Higher degree	Overseas special relationship	Total
1933	6,130	4,100	1,066	–	11,296
1936	5,388	4,416	1,139	–	10,943
1942	5,270	4,266	1,263	–	10,799
1946	9,584	8,028	1,645	–	19,257
1951	10,658	15,790	1,332	–	27,780
1956	10,079	12,325	1,595	958	24,957
1961	6,882	14,821	1,669	3,581	26,953
1966	5,651	20,934	2,136	803	29,524

Sources: ULC ULASESAR, various dates

study. For the final degree examinations, out of 4,634 candidates, the respective proportions were 15 per cent, 12 per cent, 14 per cent, 31 per cent and 29 per cent (University of London, Council for External Students 1910: Tables A and B).

For a long time these proportions varied relatively little from year to year. Thus, in 1926 the Advisory Service for External Students concluded 'it seems . . . to be established that about 20 per cent of External Students study in London; about 40 per cent at Provincial Institutions; and that about 40 per cent carry out their studies privately' (University of London, Advisory Service for External Students, *Annual Report* (ULASESAR) 1926: para. 5). Private and/or correspondence study were to retain the position they had attained in the latter part of the nineteenth century (see Chapter 3), as important methods of preparing for the University's examinations, for the whole of the twentieth century.

Table 6.5 gathers together some more recent statistics, and shows the changes in external study patterns which have taken place since the 1950s. The numbers of external students studying at other British universities rapidly tailed off after the Second World War, while the numbers studying overseas began to increase substantially. A large minority continued to pursue their studies privately or by correspondence. From the mid-1960s onwards, the numbers studying at other British institutions also began to decline, so that by 1976 the great majority of external students were either resident overseas (39 per cent) or studying in Britain privately or by correspondence (37 per cent).

Over the same period changes also took place in the subjects studied by external students (see Table 6.6; compare with Table 6.2). In 1933, 29 per cent of registered external students were studying science, 24 per cent arts, 18 per cent economics, 12 per cent engineering and 17 per cent other subjects: in short, they were spread across the full range of university

Table 6.5 University of London, external candidates by method of preparation, 1926–76

(A) Year ending	London colleges	Provincial colleges	Other universities	Overseas colleges	Corresp. tuition	Private study	Total
1926	1,549	2,056	364	242	976	1,352	6,539
1931	1,302	2,304	181	276	1,430	1,020	6,513
1936	1,265	2,513	149	433	1,607	812	6,779
1941	700	2,001	141	750	897	527	5,016
1946	1,376	3,585	141	614	2,478	1,350	9,544
1951	2,765	6,233	273	836	4,560	1,790	16,457

(B)	Technical colleges	University colleges	Other institutions	Overseas	Correspondence	Private study	Total
1951	5,882	2,480	1,275	876	3,580	2,154	16,247
1956	3,933	484	1,561	2,033	2,839	1,475	12,325
1961	4,843	–	1,411	3,622	3,432	1,513	14,821
1966	9,319	–	2,421	2,774	4,150	2,270	20,934

(C)	Polytechnics	Other institutions	Resident overseas	Correspondence/private study	Total
1976	3,472	2,758	10,245	9,562	26,037

Sources:
(A) ULASESAR (post-matriculation candidates)
(B) ULC, Principal's Report (post-intermediate candidates)
(C) ULCESM (registered first degree/diploma students)

Table 6.6 University of London, registered external students by faculty, 1933–86

Year	Theology	Arts	Laws	Medicine	Science	Engineering	Economics	Total
(A)								
1933	162	2,747	539	586	3,221	1,328	2,057	11,296
1936	231	2,846	745	544	3,066	1,145	1,950	10,943
1941	280	2,093	367	629	2,587	1,208	1,388	8,902
1946	524	4,086	907	914	5,555	2,892	3,658	19,257
1951	764	4,977	1,509	612	10,824	2,786	5,429	27,780
(B)								
1956	273	1,194	799	107	1,704	581	592	5,276
1961	429	1,305	1,325	171	1,275	404	1,816	6,725
1971	224	2,012	2,124	–	1,198	86	1,734	7,378
1976	165	883	2,687	–	447	–	418	4,600
1981	103	364	1,074	–	–	–	114	1,655
1986	82	301	2,418	–	–	–	257	3,058

Sources:
(A) ULC, ULASESAR (all registered students)
(B) ULCESM (first degree new registrations)

subjects in much the same way as internal students. The pattern in 1951 was broadly similar, but with 39 per cent now registered in science, 20 per cent in economics, 18 per cent in arts, 10 per cent in engineering and 13 per cent in other subjects. Subsequently the balance began to change dramatically, as first the medical, then the science, and then the engineering syllabuses were cut back and then dropped altogether for external students.

By 1961, 27 per cent of the new external registrations for first degrees were in economics, 20 per cent in laws, 19 per cent in arts, 19 per cent in science and 15 per cent in other subjects. By 1986 the subject split had become much more highly skewed, with 79 per cent of all new external registrations in just one subject, laws. This was partly a reflection of the growth of alternative study opportunities in Britain resulting from the work of the CNAA and the Open University (indeed, if the latter had decided to offer a law degree, the University of London external system might not have survived). It was also in part a consequence of the increasing attraction of the London law degree, especially to overseas students.

7

External Student Support and Institutional Linkages in the Twentieth Century University of London

Much more attention was paid by the University of London during the twentieth century to the support given to its students studying at a distance than had been the case in the nineteenth century. This increased interest was partly due to the split between the internal and external sides of the University, and partly to the continuing concern of the latter with the quality of tuition and preparation which some external students were receiving.

At the same time, the University's relationships with other educational institutions in the British Isles and overseas became more widespread and more complex. During much of the nineteenth century, the University had had few direct dealings with the multitude of institutions involved in preparing students for its examinations, and its links with what would now be thought of as secondary schools appear to have been much better developed then than those with proto-higher education institutions. The twentieth century saw the development, often encouraged by the government, of a series of closer relationships with institutions in the process of becoming independent universities.

This chapter seeks to build on the general context provided by Chapter 6, by examining in some detail these two related aspects – external student support and institutional linkages – of the University of London's role as a twentieth century open university.

External student support

During this century, the University of London's growing concern with the preparation of its external students has led to three main practical developments (see also Elliott 1989: ch. 11):

1. The establishment of the Commerce Degree Bureau after the First World War.

2. The creation soon afterwards of a more general Advisory Service for External Students.
3. The recent development of an Independent Guided Study system.

These developments will now be considered in turn.

The Commerce Degree Bureau

The Commerce Degree Bureau was established under a Declaration of Trust accepted by the University in 1920, though it only began its work in 1922. It was endowed initially by a number of City of London businesses, and its primary function related to the newly created Commerce degrees at bachelor and master level:

> To guide, advise, and assist in matters of commercial studies and training, External Students of the University, whether residing in London or elsewhere, who are preparing for or intend to prepare for the Commerce Degree Examinations.
>
> (ULC 1939–40: 459)

The Bureau's other associated functions were to provide a reference library, to act as an employment agency, and generally to promote the interests of the degrees and their students. When the commerce degrees were absorbed into new BSc and MSc degrees in economics in the early 1950s, the functions of the Bureau were transferred to those degrees.

The mainstay of the Bureau's work was the provision of postal courses of study for first degree students who were unable to attend classes on a regular basis. The statistics provided in its annual reports clearly show that the Bureau had many customers (see Table 7.1), with the total number of students registered with it peaking at 940 in 1970. In that year the Bureau employed 60 part-time tutors, chiefly from among the University's academic staff, to correct 5,605 scripts, and 2,597 books were borrowed from its library. Courses of study were provided for all of the compulsory papers in the BSc(Econ) degree, and for many of the optional papers.

As Table 7.1 shows, however, the numbers of these students who proceeded to sit the degree examinations, and the numbers who successfully passed them, remained a relatively small proportion of the total registered. Indeed, it represented a decreasing proportion. This was partly because of the use of the Bureau's provision by an increasing number of overseas students, who came to Britain to study, were unable to secure a place on a course and turned to the Bureau as a last resort.

The Bureau was, nevertheless, confident of the value of its methods, at least for the right kind of student, while remaining disparaging of the 'spoon-feeding' approach adopted by many correspondence colleges (with whom it favourably compared its students' examination results – see Table 7.3):

Table 7.1 Students studying with the University of London Commerce Degree Bureau, 1938–76

Year	Numbers registered*		Numbers examined		Numbers passing	
	Intermediate	Final	Intermediate	Final	Intermediate	Final
1938	82	88	59	48	42	31
1941	122	68	36	27	24	22
1951	250	146	83	54	54	37
1961	595	97	47	40	31	34
1971	632	261	68	51	53	47
1976	398	170	26	35	17	32

* The BComm intermediate and final examinations were supplanted by the BSc(Econ) Part I and Part II examinations in the early 1950s.

Source: ULCDBAR, various dates.

Not all External Students find it easy to adapt themselves to the Bureau's method of tuition. This is based upon the Study Notes, issued for each subject, containing reading lists, advice on the scope of the subject, and guidance on the method of study. The reading lists are comprehensive and alternative titles are quoted wherever possible. Question papers are set in each subject and these are designed to give the student adequate practice in expressing *in his own words* the knowledge which he has acquired during his studies. Each paper is marked by an experienced University tutor and is returned to the student with the tutor's comments and suggestions. No provision is made of 'model answers'. Guidance is given to the student by dealing individually with his difficulties as these are recorded in his written work."

> (University of London, Commerce Degree Bureau, *Annual Report* (ULCDBAR) for the year ended 31 July 1960; original emphasis)

The Bureau, which, after an initial period of profitability, had been suffering financial difficulties, was integrated with the External Advisory Service in 1982.

The Advisory Service for external students

The Advisory Service was approved by Senate in 1924 and became fully operational the following year. It had a much more general responsibility than the Commerce Degree Bureau, being available to all external students, but was only able to offer a limited range of services. Its establishment followed on from a report by a subcommittee of the Council for External Students, which had been set up to advise on academic assistance for students:

> The field of work is considerable. Every town, every village, outside the thirty mile radius of London and outside a ten mile radius of the other Universities and University Colleges contains potential External Students. The administrative and educational services of the Colonies and Dominions include many persons, often already graduates, who wish to read for a London External Degree. There is evidence in the University to show that professional men – Clergymen, Teachers in Elementary and Secondary Schools, members of County and Municipal Administrations, Engineers and technical men in private enterprise and in public services – are looking in increasing numbers to the University of London as affording the opportunity to complete somewhat late in life the educational process that circumstances prevented their completing earlier. If the University itself were to assume the responsibility of offering to direct their reading, the number of External students would probably be sensibly increased. Much work could be done for students in Theology, Arts, Laws, Science, Engineering and Economics.
>
> (ULCESM 16 January 1924: 5)

Much of the work of the Advisory Service was on a fairly general level, involving the giving of advice on:

> the selection of the Degrees, the subjects of study, and the ways and means of carrying out the selected studies. . . . The Service continues to maintain a body of information relating to all places where teaching for the External Examinations of the University is to be obtained.
>
> (ULASESAR 1929: para. 3)

Most enquiries, in fact, related to the availability of library facilities, teaching institutions and correspondence courses. The other main aspect of the Service's work was the provision of written study schemes to those external students who were unable to avail themselves of regular tuition. These study schemes were prepared and regularly revised by University teachers:

> The experience in the conduct of the Service during the [first] five years has led to the development of a fuller conception of the study schemes. Originally these were quite short, consisting of an introductory note, a list of essential books, a supplementary reading list, and a note on method of study, the whole scheme being stencilled on one, or two, pages of foolscap. The schemes have now been amplified and, in addition to the original basic sections, now give commentaries on the books; while a beginning has been made with the inclusion of special introductory notes coordinating all the subjects necessary for any particular examination. The study schemes have also been considerably amplified so that, for example, the complete study scheme for an

Intermediate Examination will frequently run to 10 typescript fool-
scap pages, a Pass Degree to 15, while an Honours Degree study
scheme may well extend to 20 pages of condensed expert guidance.

(ibid.: para. 4)

In addition, in 1929 the Senate authorized the Advisory Service to organize
reading parties and vacation courses, and these were subsequently offered
with varying success from year to year.

As Table 7.2 indicates, increasingly large numbers of students used the
Advisory Service and a great number of study schemes were available. One
rise in the figures, during the early 1930s, was due to the introduction of
registration for external students. Another, in the 1940s, was linked to the
arrangement by which the Advisory Service's facilities were made available
freely to armed service personnel. Most of these students were studying for
degrees in the Faculties of Arts, Science or Economics, a reflection both of
the relative popularity of subjects and of the availability of tuition
elsewhere.

Table 7.2   University of London Advisory Service for External Students, numbers
of students advised, 1925–57

	1925	1931	1941	1951	1957
Total number advised	100	1,235	1,892	4,073	3,227
of which:					
Theology	5	40	81	128	191
Arts	37	471	568	1,345	1,375
Laws	10	99	134	294	274
Science	29	277	299	861	608
Engineering	4	145	100	165	81
Economics	15	130	350	871	381
Number given expert advice	n.a.	266	299	1,208	1,065
Number interviewed	n.a.	279	n.a.	289	n.a.
Study schemes available	n.a.	445	699	1,008	1,225

Source: ULASESAR various dates.

The Advisory Service attracted its greatest number of customers at the
end of the Second World War in 1945. In that year 5,755 students were
advised, with 2,670 receiving more focused 'expert' advice from a specialist
academic, and 429 being interviewed. Separate fees were charged, where
applicable, for anything beyond initial general advice.

Yet, as Table 7.3 shows, the numbers of external students who restricted
their study support to what the Advisory Service – or, for that matter, the
Commerce Degree Bureau – could provide, and who persisted to the
examination stage, were relatively small. In 1938, for example, these
services accounted for only 77 and 86 respectively out of a total of 2,214

Table 7.3   Success rates of correspondence and private study students, University of London, 1938

	Passes	Failures	% passing
Students studying by/with:			
private study	401	394	50
Advisory Service	39	38	51
Commerce Degree Bureau	55	31	64
University Correspondence College	221	262	46
Wolsey Hall	166	197	46
Metropolitan Correspondence College	126	86	59
Other correspondence colleges	113	85	57
Total	1,121	1,093	51

Source: ULASESAR

students studying by correspondence or private study who sat examinations. Many students were, no doubt, using the Advisory Service's facilities *and* studying with a correspondence college as well. The success rate of the Advisory Service's students in that year was only average at 51 per cent, not much different from that for those preparing by private study alone and well below the figures achieved by some correspondence colleges. The Commerce Degree Bureau, with a success rate of 64 per cent, stands out by contrast.

In 1948 study schemes were made available free of charge to all registered external students who were not attending teaching institutions. After the peak years of the 1940s and 1950s, the use made of the Advisory Service steadily declined, and its work was focused more on the needs of those studying privately. The same limited range of services continued to be offered, though the scope of the study schemes available was reduced, and fees were eventually dropped for all undergraduates.

In the late 1960s, three assistants were employed by the Service to give advice, one covering arts, theology and music, another law and economics, and a third science and engineering. A limited range of vacation courses continued to be offered in subjects where an element of oral tuition was thought to be desirable. In 1967–8, for example, two such courses were provided in French language and literature, four in geography and three in psychology; though a wider range of similar courses in the more popular subjects was offered by a number of university extra-mural departments (Glatter *et al.* 1971: 19–21). Thus, in 1980, 29 vacation courses were offered by university extra-mural departments in Bristol, Cambridge, Cardiff, Durham, Keele, Leeds and London for the degrees in divinity, economics, English, French, geography, history, law, music and philosophy (ULCESM 1979–80).

In the early 1980s, the Advisory Service was, together with the Commerce Degree Bureau, revamped and incorporated within the Independent Guided Study scheme.

Independent guided study

The early 1980s was, as has already been indicated in Chapter 6, a period when the positive development and expansion of the external system came back onto the University's agenda after two decades of steady disengagement. The question of facilities for the part-time teaching and support of external students was at the forefront of this debate. By 1982, a number of options – evening classes, a correspondence teaching unit, cooperation with the Open University, the use of university extra-mural departments as regional centres, the application of new technology – were being actively considered.

And, in the following year, the Committee for External Students resolved:

> That the University should as a general aim provide for External undergraduate students academic guidance where it is possible to do so, but without undertaking an obligation to provide guidance in all circumstances or imposing on undergraduate students a requirement that they seek guidance. In addition the University should seek to develop facilities for the instruction of External Students *by traditional and by distance learning techniques.*
>
> (ULCESM 23 February 1983: 6)

The result of these deliberations was the development of the independent guided study scheme.

This scheme was introduced from October 1987, and is intended to offer a flexible and optional student support system in the more popular subject areas (University of London, Committee for External Students 1987). Students are now able to subscribe to a coordinated programme of correspondence and audiovisual materials, study courses and informal tutorial assessment. The scheme does not operate on the same kind of level as the Open University's provision, but allows students to combine parts of the programme in different ways and to pace their studies as they choose. The major responsibility for planning remains with the individual student.

The system is intended to operate at three levels:

- at Level I, each student receives on registration, at no additional cost, relevant reading lists, a book on 'How to Study', and details of the correspondence and short courses available in their subject area.
- at Level II, all students may obtain for a fee:
  subject guides (*c.* £5–7 each), with up to four needed for part of an examination [these are now provided at no extra cost];
  past examination papers;

access to evening courses organised by the External System at
various locations (c. £60 a term for two evening sessions a week);
access to an adviser (*c.* £50 for two or three hours);
marking of a 'mock' examination paper.

● at Level III, students may obtain all Level II services for an all-in fee
(hopefully under £300 for part of an examination), and may submit
scripts relating to subject guides for marking and comment.

(Tight 1987b: 50–1)

It remains to be seen how successful this scheme will be, particularly at
undergraduate level.

Institutional linkages

Throughout the twentieth century, the University of London has been
linked, both directly and indirectly, by virtue of its external role with a wide
variety of educational institutions in the United Kingdom and overseas. As
in the nineteenth century, these institutional linkages included hundreds
with secondary schools, developed through the University's system of
school inspection, and sealed through the schools' involvement in the
University's matriculation and school certificate examinations. These links,
as indicated in Chapter 6, underwent a fundamental change in the early
1950s, when the modern division between secondary and higher education
was established. Though the University of London remains a major
provider of school examinations, it no longer has links with individual
schools.

The remainder of this section will examine the external University's
changing relationships with four other kinds of institution: British
university colleges; polytechnics and technical colleges; correspondence
colleges; and overseas institutions.

British university colleges

The nineteenth century pattern whereby newly established university
colleges began by preparing students for the degree examinations of the
University of London continued right up until the 1960s. Most of these
institutions acted during their apprenticeships as provincial examination
centres (see Table 7.4).

The establishment of the external London degree was one of the most
momentous steps ever taken in the history of the English universities.
It solved, at a stroke a baffling problem that had hitherto confronted
all new foundations. Henceforward, there need be no problem at all: a
provincial college could concentrate on the work of teaching, of
preparing students for examination. The examination itself would be

managed by London – and London's degrees were already recognised as stiff tests of academic competence.

(Simmons 1958: 21–2)

The older English civic university colleges – Manchester, Sheffield, Liverpool and Leeds; the last two initially as part of the federal Victoria University based on Manchester – and those in Wales, achieved university status towards the end of the nineteenth century. They then largely, but not entirely, ceased to prepare students for the London examinations. Other English universities were chartered and began to award their own degrees early in the twentieth century: Birmingham in 1900, Bristol in 1909, Reading in 1926 (Armytage 1955; Jones 1988).

The newer English civic universities had to wait until after the Second World War to achieve independent status – Nottingham first in 1948, Southampton in 1952, Hull in 1954, Exeter in 1955, and finally Leicester in 1957 (Shinn 1986). Prior to then, all five offered a range of courses leading to London external degrees. In the case of the last four named, independence was gained after a short but intensive period of 'partnership' with the University of London, during which they were given more and more control over student registration, course syllabuses, teaching methods and examination practices. By the end of this period, each of these nascent universities had a base of several hundred students on which to build.

After Leicester gained its charter, no similar partnership arrangements were entered into between the University of London external system and other British higher education institutions. Keele, the first university college to be set up after the Second World War, served its apprenticeship under the joint tutelage of Birmingham and Oxford universities. The universities which were established in the 1960s, following the Robbins Report, were either created from scratch as fully fledged universities (for example, Essex, Sussex and Warwick), or were developed from existing 'colleges of advanced technology' (CATs, for example, Aston, Brunel and Loughborough). Most of the latter had a long history, in earlier guises, of preparing students for London external examinations in science and technology.

Polytechnics and colleges

Apart from the university colleges, a great many other British educational institutions also offered courses in preparation for the external degree examinations of the University of London. Many of these institutions would nowadays be regarded as being involved, at least in part, in higher education, and these have mostly since become bona fide higher education institutions. This group includes the London polytechnics established in the nineteenth century, as well as technical colleges and teacher training colleges. Some of the institutions involved also functioned as secondary

Table 7.4   University of London, provincial examination centres, 1912 and 1939

(A) 1912
For the Intermediate Arts and Science, the First Medical and the BA examinations:

Birmingham
Bristol (Intermediate and First Medical only)
Epsom (First Medical only)
Exeter (Intermediate and First Medical only)
Leeds (Intermediate and First Medical only)
Liverpool
Newcastle upon Tyne
Nottingham
Sheffield (Intermediate and First Medical only)
Southampton

(B) 1939
For the Intermediate and First Medical, BD, BA, BSc and Diploma in Public Administration examinations:

Birmingham University
Bradford Technical College
Brighton Technical College
Cardiff Technical College
Cardiff University College
Dundee School of Economics
Epsom College (First Medical only)
Exeter, Washington Singer Laboratories
Glasgow Royal Technical College
Huddersfield Technical College
Hull University College
Liverpool Royal Institution
Manchester, Victoria University
Middlesbrough, Constantine Technical College (BSc only)
Newcastle, Rutherford Technical College
Nottingham University College
Plymouth Technical College
Portsmouth Metropolitan College
Rugby, St Peter's Hall (Intermediate and BSc(Eng) only)
Southampton University College
Wigan Mining and Technical College

Sources:
(A) ULC 1911–12: 297 (precise locations not given)
(B) ULCESM 1938–39: App

schools. Thus, Cheltenham Ladies' College, mentioned in Chapter 3, only ceased teaching for the London external degree in 1924, after which it focused on its present role as a girls' public school (Clarke 1953).

Many of the provincial institutions which were linked to the University in this way regularly acted as examination centres, as Table 7.4 indicates (compare with Table 3.5). By this means, the influence of the University throughout England and, to a lesser extent, Scotland and Wales, was maintained and extended during the first half of the century.

These linkages were particularly strong, though still to some extent kept at arm's length, for those institutions which were located in London and which, under the new regulations adopted in 1900, enjoyed the status within the University of institutions having recognized teachers (see Table 6.1). These institutions could enrol some of their students as internal students of the University:

> In spite of the prevailing view that technical instruction and the polytechnics should provide trade classes and elementary instruction, there was a strong pressure from the large student body in London for more advanced studies in both day and evening, including university work. By 1904, six polytechnics were providing complete degree courses, fifty of their teachers were recognised teachers, instructing 500 undergraduates. By 1908–9, this had increased to 100 recognised teachers, and 836 matriculated students, four-fifths of whom were evening students. Webb considered that: 'Even the new provincial universities, with all the dignity of charters and chancellors, diplomas and degrees, often do less work of university grade than a London Polytechnic'. This growth of an 'evening class university' met the growing demand by the lower middle classes and working classes for an advanced university education which had not previously been accessible to them.
>
> (Cotgrove 1958: 64–5; see also Webb 1904)

The importance of the London degree to the development of these institutions is evident in their individual histories – for example, Northampton Polytechnic (Laws 1946), Regent Street Polytechnic (Wood 1965), Woolwich Polytechnic (Locke 1978). However, at least one London polytechnic, Borough (Evans 1969), resisted making provision for the University of London's examinations for a long time on the grounds that they were academic rather than practical. Other London institutions, including teacher training colleges like Borough Road (Bartle 1976), and technical colleges like Acton (Faherty 1976), also developed a close dependence upon the London examination system, thereby raising their educational status.

These relationships began to alter, like much else, after the Second World War, as the University steadily tightened up its degree regulations. There was some, albeit limited, consultation with the major colleges involved. The revisions had a particular impact upon engineering and part-time study. So far as the University was concerned, the issue was primarily one of standards:

> The larger courses of preparation and the more comprehensive syllabuses which are now considered to be essential for adequate preparation for a first degree of the University in all branches of

science and engineering tend to discourage part-time students in technical colleges from attempting to read for an External Degree.

(ULCESM 18 April 1956: 8)

From the point of view of the participating colleges, however, the effect was to hamper their work:

The demand for opportunities for part-time study for degrees continued, although diminishing in volume and under increasing difficulty as the University of London raised the standards of its final examinations. In particular the London engineering degree, after a revision of regulations in the mid-[nineteen]fifties, became almost impossible by purely leisure-time study.

(Robinson 1968: 17)

Nevertheless, demand for the London degree remained strong throughout the advanced further education sector during the 1950s:

In 1957, 37 per cent of the [University of London internal and external] degrees in science, and 56 per cent in technology, were obtained by students attending technical colleges. Moreover, 35 per cent of all internal degrees in technology were awarded to technical college students, mainly at the London polytechnics. Altogether, over 1,000 London University first degrees in science and technology were obtained by technical college students, accounting for 44 per cent of the total.

(Cotgrove 1958: 145–6)

The creation of alternative national validation agencies – the NCTA in 1955, succeeded by the CNAA in 1964 (Silver 1990) – and the transference of the CATs from the advanced further education sector to the university sector in the mid 1960s (Burgess and Pratt 1970; Venables 1978) gradually shifted this demand away from the London external degree (see Table 6.5). The University of London recognized, and to a large extent welcomed, these developments, feeling that the expansion of the external system was in danger of getting out of control. The University ceased to register as external students those studying full-time in British polytechnics and colleges in 1977. A few part-time courses continued to be offered by some institutions, though these have now all also been discontinued.

Correspondence colleges

Correspondence study continued to assist a great many students in preparing for the external examinations of the University of London throughout the twentieth century. The statistics given in Table 6.5 indicate that between 15 per cent and 30 per cent of all London external students used correspondence study as their main or only method of preparation in any one year. Three correspondence colleges were particularly prominent during this period, achieving some grudging respect from the University authorities – the University Correspondence College, Wolsey Hall and the Metropolitan Correspondence College:

> an analysis has been kept for some years past of the candidatures of students from the several correspondence colleges and other miscellaneous institutions from which External Students obtain assistance in carrying out their studies. This analysis shows that the Advisory Service and the Commerce Degree Bureau offer satisfactory assistance, that the three proprietary correspondence colleges apparently discharge adequately their responsibilities to their students; that three professional bodies provide satisfactory correspondence courses for their several specialised studies; but that not a few corrrespondence colleges, while making in their advertisements a great, and often misleading display of facilities for preparation for the University's External Examinations, in reality have very few University students and so far, therefore, as the University is concerned, might as well not be in existence.
>
> (ULASESAR 1933: para. 7; see also Table 7.3)

The 'three proprietary correspondence colleges' referred to were only identified cryptically in the report as A, B and C; but fortunately the former owner of the copy of the report which is now in the University of London's archives had annotated it to indicate their true identities.

Of the three, the University Correspondence College (UCC) has had a particularly proud history in assisting London external students, and it could justly claim to have produced more graduates than many conventional university colleges. At the College's Jubilee dinner in 1937, the University's Member of Parliament:

> referred to the academic success of UCC students during the previous year – 407 London Matriculation, 245 Intermediate, and 237 Degree examinations, adding that this latter figure constituted nearly a third of the whole number who took degrees.
>
> (Elliott 1989: 289–90)

The University Correspondence College was taken over by the National Extension College (NEC) in 1963 (Jenkins and Perraton 1980). In this guise it has continued to offer support to London external students in selected subjects, typically by linking individual students with experienced subject tutors.

Other correspondence colleges have been more specialized in their role. The work of the University of London's own Commerce Degree Bureau in providing correspondence tuition in commerce, and later in economics, has already been described. The College of Estate Management, established in 1919 by the brother of the then vice-chancellor of the University of London, has had a similar function: to provide tuition, in this case both face-to-face and by correspondence, for the new estate management degrees that had been instituted in 1918 (Laurance 1969). The College was granted a royal charter in 1922, and offered courses both for professional (initially much the more popular) and degree examinations. In 1921–2, 810 students were enrolled, of whom 615 were studying by post. By 1939–40, enrolment had risen to 4,612 (3,774 postal) students, and by 1945–6, in the immediate post-war boom, to 8,405 (8,185 postal) students (ibid.: 7, 16–17, 27).

Since then the College has placed more and more emphasis on its full-time residential provision. This policy eventually led it to leave London, and to obtain university status as part of the University of Reading in 1967. It continues to offer a correspondence course for the University of Reading's BSc degree in estate management.

The recent massive expansion in the numbers studying for the London external law degree (see Table 6.6) has stimulated a growth in specialist correspondence provision. Much of this growth in demand has come from overseas, whether the students remain resident in other countries or come to study in Britain. In addition to the provision made by the National Extension College and Wolsey Hall, there are currently three other major specialist providers of correspondence tuition for this degree: Holborn College and the Rapid Results College, both based in London, and the Institute of Legal Executives' College in Bedford. Significantly, a number of other providers, such as Wolverhampton University (formerly Polytechnic) have now begun to offer law degrees by distance study.

Overseas institutions

The minutes of the Council for External Studies contain regular references to the difficulties involved in holding examinations for London degrees overseas, which contrast with the apparent ease with which a similar operation was conducted by St Andrews University (see Chapter 5). There was concern about the standards of the students and their preparation, about examination practices and security, and about the sheer bureaucracy involved. Many of these problems appear to have been caused by the University's close connections with the state, and by the consequent involvement of civil servants in its overseas activities.

For example, in 1912 sending examination papers to centres in Canada was not a simple matter of the University contacting the college involved, but rather a major diplomatic operation involving government at all levels. The papers went first to the Colonial Office, then on to the Governor General, the Colonial Secretary of State, the Lieutenant Governor, the Provincial Secretary and, finally, to the Examination Superintendent: the completed papers then followed an exactly reversed route back to the University for marking. Rather less complicated arrangements were later adopted with respect to the 'white' dominions, but the close involvement of the Colonial Office was retained in other areas.

It is little wonder, then, that consideration was given by the University at the beginning of the century to curtailing its colonial examinations, or even to dropping them altogether. The British government clearly thought otherwise, however, and for much of the twentieth century, as with the external system in general, the story overseas was one of expansion:

After 1900, British policy towards her colonies emphasised the need for alliance among the member colonies for economic and political reasons. . . The University of London's role was strengthened as the mother university of the British Empire.

(Namie 1989: 390)

As Omolewa has shown in his studies of the use and impact of the London external examinations in Nigeria, this arrangement suited both the colonial authorities and the local students. On the one hand 'London University's programs appeared fitted to the educational objectives of the Colonial Office to train a core of clerks, interpreters, and aides in government and private sectors of British territories' (Omolewa 1980: 659–60). This applied particularly strongly in countries where there was no indigenous higher education system, and often little in the way of good quality schools. Conversely, for the local population:

London University examinations became the determining factor in the assessment of individuals for jobs or social or political esteem. It became clear that success at the examinations brought considerable financial reward, social prestige and personal satisfaction to the Nigerian candidate. The examinations were therefore used to settle family rivalries, ethnic competition, and to achieve personal glory and dreams.

(Omolewa 1976: 351)

Before the Second World War it was estimated that:

About a tenth of them [University of London external students] were resident overseas, with Ceylon providing the largest proportion. In 1919 examinations were conducted at thirty overseas centres scattered throughout the Empire. From 1920, at the request of the Foreign Office, examinations were held widely throughout the rest of the world: at Jerusalem and Shanghai in that year, in 1922 in Tientsin, in 1923 at Baghdad and Istanbul, and subsequently in Alexandria, Bangkok, Isfahan, Buenos Aires, Athens, Jedda, Peking, Cairo and elsewhere. . . By 1937, there were seventy-nine overseas centres for London degree and matriculation examinations, dealing with a total of 4908 candidates.

(Harte 1986: 238)

Between 1900 and 1939, University of London examinations were held in 43 colonies and 14 other countries at various times; as well as on board one of the Navy's ships and, during the First World War, in a number of

German prisoner-of-war camps. Over this period, the examinations attracted a total of 42,601 overseas candidates, of whom 13,859 (33 per cent) passed. The majority, 9,430 (68 per cent) of the successful candidates came from just one colony, Ceylon, with the next largest contribution, 486 (4 per cent) coming from Jamaica (Namie 1989: 429–39). The University developed a particularly close relationship with the University College of Ceylon during the first half of the century, which continued to prepare students for London external examinations up until 1968, though it started its own degrees in 1942.

Unlike in the nineteenth century, nearly all of the University's examinations could now be taken, subject to demand and the availability of suitable supervision, at overseas centres. Not only that, but the University also demonstrated an increasing willingness to adapt its procedures, allowing for changes in syllabuses so as to reflect better local conditions and interests:

> By the 1920s, most of the requests for change in the colonial examinations were accepted by the Senate. For example, oriental languages such as Sinhalese, Swahili, Yoruba, Zuru and Tamil were accepted for Matriculation. Tamil, Sanskrit, Pali and Sinhalese were also accepted for Intermediate and BA. Early Indian History was set up for Intermediate Arts. Further, the examinations requiring practical examinations or viva voce, which colonial students, except in Ceylon, were not allowed to take, were granted in several places by setting an additional paper. For example, Botany, Chemistry, Physics and Zoology for science, and French and English for the MA, were arranged to be held in South Africa, Jamaica, Sydney and Canada.
>
> (Namie 1989: 122)

These practices were later to be considerably extended.

Towards the end of the Second World War, two Commissions and one Committee were established to make recommendations as to the development of higher education in the then British colonies (Colonial Office 1945a, 1945b, 1945c). They recommended the creation of an Inter-University Council for Higher Education in the Colonies. This would work as a cooperative association between the universities of Britain and the colonies, so as to foster the rapid development of colonial university colleges to independent university status. While this development was couched in terms of general inter-university collaboration, involving staff visits, exchanges and secondments, the commissions saw the University of London external system as playing a key central role.

A number of other British universities were also to be involved to a lesser extent. These included, most notably, the University of Durham, which had had, since the 1870s, a small-scale external relationship with both Codrington College in Barbados and Fourah Bay College in Sierra Leone (Whiting 1932). Durham University also offered, until recently, an external degree in music.

The University of London agreed to take on this new role, and duly entered into schemes of special relations with eight institutions in Africa and the Caribbean:

The essence of the special relationship is that it is personal. It is not a uniform scheme but is developed separately for each college. The college works out in consultation with the University of London the arrangements which best suit its local conditions. For example, if the stage of secondary school development makes it desirable in the interests of the schools and of the college to adopt a minimum entrance requirement different from that which is possible in the United Kingdom, the college can agree with the University a modified admission scheme. A lower entrance requirement has the corollary that the length of the degree course is extended by at least a year. Similarly, the content of the courses has been altered to take advantage of local opportunities and conditions. The college staff can work out with the appropriate board of studies in the University changes in the subject syllabus. . . An equally important feature of special relationship has been that members of the staffs of the colleges can take part in the setting and marking of examinations for their own students.

(Inter-University Council for Higher Education Overseas 1955: 5–6)

These partnership arrangements lasted altogether for 24 years, from 1947 until 1970, when the last of the university colleges involved attained independent status, and produced 7,000 London graduates (Adams 1947, 1950; Carr-Saunders 1961; Maxwell 1980; Pattison 1984). From reading the accounts of the work involved, it is clear that it was both demanding and enervating:

London did more than sponsor the university colleges; it took them into partnership. The University naturally retained control of its degrees, but teachers in the colleges had most of the privileges of teachers in the University's constituent schools: they could suggest syllabuses, were appointed University examiners and could register for higher degrees even if they were not London graduates. They learned how to manage the academic affairs of their own universities by participating in the affairs of an established university. The partnerships benefited both parties.

(Pattison 1984: 167)

After 1970 the overworked University seemed to lose interest for a while in its overseas role. Overseas registrations for the external degree were actually stopped in 1977, but then re-started again in 1983. Forms of partnership are now once again under consideration to help support the substantial numbers of external students resident overseas, who currently account for about half of the total registrations (see Table 6.5). In 1984, the University of London itself began to run vacation courses for its external degrees overseas, initially in Malaysia, something it had never done before. More direct linkages with overseas institutions are a strong future possibility.

A twenty-first century open university?

As the last two chapters have made clear, the University of London external system has undergone a great deal of change during the twentieth century. The numbers of students studying for its qualifications grew steadily up until the Second World War, then increased rapidly with the expansion in demand for higher education in the post-war period. Registrations subsequently declined during the 1970s and 1980s as the University sought to cut back its involvement in external work, handing this over, wherever possible, to other, better resourced, institutions such as the CNAA, the Open University and the newly established or independent universities at home and overseas.

Over this period, the nature of the work undertaken by the University of London external system has also changed, as it has endeavoured to become more closely involved in supporting its students, and engaged in various forms of partnership with institutions teaching for its qualifications. At the same time, of course, the context within which these developments were taking place was also changing; as, for example, the boundary between secondary and higher education shifted to become fixed (at least for the moment) in its present position, and as public concern over standards and comparability became more pronounced.

The last decade has witnessed further changes as the revived external system has sought a new role for itself, and, in doing so, has again raised the questions of external student support and institutional linkages. The external system now sees its academic profile as focusing on the subjects of law, economics and management, arts and languages, divinity, agrarian development, education and health studies (ULCESM 14 January 1986: 4).

In addition to maintaining and updating the existing syllabuses in what is by far its most popular subject area, law, as well as in divinity and a wide range of European, Asian and African languages and literatures (these constituting an impressive imperial legacy), many new qualifications have been introduced. Syllabuses for what is presently the second most popular qualification, the BSc(Econ) degree, were revised again in the mid-1980s, with named study routes offered in accounting, banking, trade and industry, geography, government and politics, management studies, and sociology, as well as economics itself.

The last few years have also witnessed the introduction or consideration of new first degrees in Chinese, combined studies, English and biblical studies, history, Japanese, Jewish history and nursing. There has been even more development at postgraduate level, with new syllabuses created or under discussion in subjects as diverse as audiology, commonwealth studies, linguistics and nuclear medicine.

The external system's current strategy appears to be twofold. On the one hand, it is focusing attention on the private student, who currently has little support, offering through its independent guided study scheme a basic but flexible means of guidance. On the other hand, the external system is becoming involved in the development in collaboration with other institutions, where the market will bear the costs, of complete new distance education courses.

To date, the latter have all been at postgraduate level and in professional areas. They include courses in occupational psychology and organizational behaviour, developed with Birkbeck College, in financial economics with the School of Oriental and African Studies, in agricultural development and environmental management with Wye College, and in distance education itself with the Institute of Education and the International Extension College. Some of these courses, like those in agricultural development, have been specifically aimed at the overseas student market (Bryson and Hakimian 1992; Teshome 1990), others at the home market, others at a mixture of the two.

If the twentieth century has seen the University of London external system become less open in some ways – for example, in the development of entrance requirements – it has remained just as open in others, and is reopening or becoming yet more open in still other ways. Once again, students can study wherever they want in the world, and they are essentially free to determine the time, pace and method of their studies. Other than the need to satisfy the University's general entrance requirements, which gives special consideration to mature students, and to be able to communicate in English, few restrictions are placed on who can register and study. And, through its recent increase in involvement in directly supporting its own students, the University has effectively added to the choices available to students in arranging their learning.

Though the future of the federal University of London remains in some doubt – as it has ever since its creation in 1836! – the University of London external system seems increasingly well placed to develop, and redevelop, its role in the years to come as a twenty-first century open university.

8

Contemporary Models of Distance Education and Open Learning

Traditions, generations and typologies

As we argued in Chapter 1, the current British understanding of distance education and open learning has been largely constrained by one prominent example: that of the Open University. Its example has been regularly compared, especially by those working for the Open University, with older established forms of correspondence education, and has been argued to be both technologically and educationally superior. The British Open University has also served as an inspiration for educators and politicians in many other countries, where its example has been updated and modified to suit local circumstances. Indeed, in any estimation the Open University idea must rank as one of the major British intellectual exports of the last two decades; much as the University of London model was in the late nineteenth century and in the period immediately following the Second World War. Within the United Kingdom, the Open University has been one of the major stimuli to the recent development of open learning, and its application to all levels and types of education and training.

Amid all of this developmental activity, the experience and lessons of the earlier (and continuing) British examples of open universities seem to have been ignored or forgotten. Thus, the University of London was neither consulted during, nor involved in, the ferocious planning activity which led up to the launch of the Open University. Since then there has only been patchy contact and strictly limited collaboration between the two organizations. While the University of London external system and the Open University have both had a massive effect and influence upon the development of education in Britain and overseas, they might just as well have been on different planets (rather than based about 50 miles apart) so far as their relations with each other over the last 20 years have been concerned.

These kinds of attitudes are, in many ways, very British, though perhaps especially English. Most other western developed countries have not experienced the peculiar elitism that developed in British higher education during the twentieth century, peaking between the 1950s and 1970s (see

Chapter 9). In those countries, the creation of a national and monolithic Open University would have seemed neither necessary, nor, if it had nevertheless been created, so odd, since a broader appreciation of alternative forms of distance or open education had been maintained. This wider understanding can be seen in the writings of researchers and practitioners from, for example, Australia, Canada, Sweden and the United States of America; while it is largely absent from British writing, much of which has been narrowly focused and distorted by the recency and visibility of the Open University.

The international academic debate on the nature of distance education and open learning (see also Chapter 1) has produced two complementary approaches to the study, classification and understanding of contemporary models of provision and practice: generations and typologies. While the former approach has been applied chiefly to the analysis of distance education systems, the latter has been used more generally.

The generational approach is at least implicitly historical, but it also embodies strong notions of progression or improvement. At its simplest, only two generations are recognized, the first being correspondence tuition, and the second involving the use of broadcasts as well as print, as at the Open University (Kaye and Rumble 1991). Seen from a technological point of view, a third generation, involving the use of computers in communication, teaching and learning, may then be added (Garrison 1985; Mason and Kaye 1989; Nipper 1989). Alternatively, the third generation can be interpreted from the student's perspective as resulting in increased learner choice and power (Kaufman 1989).

Some writers have gone so far as to recognize a fourth generation delivery system, seeing it as defined by the integration of personalized systems of instruction, computer-assisted learning and computer conferencing (Lauzon and Moore 1989). Scales has developed a more complicated, technologically based classification – part generation, part typology – to categorize practice in British Columbia. He recognizes six types of distance education, ranged along a continuum between 'provision of support' and 'need for self sufficiency' (Scales 1983).

The typology approach, by contrast, is essentially cross-sectional and timebound. As with generations, however, more or less complex classifications have been suggested. Kaye (1988), for example, reports the simple threefold typology of distance education institutions used by the International Centre for Distance Learning at the Open University:

1. Institutions set up exclusively to provide distance education.
2. Dual mode institutions offering both distance and face-to-face education in a range of subjects.
3. Those institutions which provide a few distance education courses alongside their predominantly face-to-face provision.

El-Bushra, Keegan, Valley, and Verduin and Clark have all produced rather more complicated, but somewhat similar, classifications involving five or six institutional types (Valley 1972; Keegan and Rumble 1982; Verduin and Clark 1991). The following eightfold typology of contemporary models of distance education and open learning has been produced by comparing and combining their categorizations:

1. Independent correspondence colleges (for example, the National Extension College, the Rapid Results College), offering print-based courses through the post.
2. Independent distance teaching institutions (for example, the Open University of the United Kingdom, Athabasca University in Canada), offering courses using a variety of media: print, audio and video tapes, broadcasts, telephone and computer conferencing, etc.
3. Dual mode institutions (for example, many Australian universities), offering both distance and face-to-face instruction in a range of subjects.
4. Correspondence/external/independent study/open learning departments or units within institutions focusing on face-to-face instruction (for example, the distance courses in business administration offered by Warwick University, Cranfield Institute of Technology and others; the School for Independent Study at the University of East London).
5. Institutions which offer distance education or open learning through consortia (for example, the recently launched Commonwealth of Learning and Open Polytechnic, the former University of Mid-America, the National Distance Centre in Ireland (Curran 1992)).
6. Examining/validating/accrediting bodies which also offer some teaching support (for example, university-without-walls programmes in the United States, the arrangements for independent guided study recently introduced by the University of London external degree system).
7. Examining/validating/accrediting bodies which do not offer any teaching support (for example, the University of London external degree system as it was until recently, and arguably also the recently defunct Council for National Academic Awards).
8. Distance/independent/open/self-directed learning, with the individual student using such materials as are available or desired, whether these have been designed for learning or not, and without any support from an institution (that is, private study).

As the examples given indicate, all but one of the eight types identified are currently to be found in the United Kingdom. It does seem significant that the missing type is the dual mode institution, since this exemplifies the fairly rigid organizational separation in Britain between distance and open learning and other, supposedly more conventional, forms of practice.

The strategy adopted in this chapter will combine elements of the generational and typological approaches, but with the major focus placed upon the models of distance education and open learning to be found in Britain today. As we have indicated, from a modern British perspective the impact and experience of the Open University inevitably looms large.

Hence the chapter will first briefly review the models which date from before the establishment of the Open University, then consider the Open University itself and its wider influence, and conclude with an examination of the models which have been developed since the advent of the Open University under the banner of open learning.

Pre-Open University models: correspondence study

Three of the models for British open universities which have been analysed in the preceding chapters are still extant in some form.

The nineteenth century extension movement, described in Chapter 2, became subsumed within universities' extra-mural provision, and is represented today in the activities of university departments of adult and continuing education. These departments continue to offer a range of liberal adult education courses on an open access basis to hundreds of thousands of students each year, providing one alternative means of progression, albeit for a small minority, into higher education. Though, for much of the twentieth century, their activities have remained marginal to the work of the universities as a whole (Lowe 1970; Legge 1982; Marriott 1984), their role is again becoming more prominent with the growth of part-time certificated forms of provision, and with the impetus provided by current policies for substantially expanding access to and participation in higher education (Tight 1990).

A second long-established model, the University of London external system, is also undergoing something of a rebirth. As a strictly examining body, it had preserved a hands-off relationship with the providers of correspondence education throughout its history, with the exception of the limited provision organized by the University itself. As indicated in Chapters 6 and 7, however, the London external system is now in the process of expanding and enhancing its role through the development of a flexible scheme of independent guided study designed to support the private student.

The third model is that provided by the correspondence colleges themselves. These grew up in the shadow of the University of London and other examining bodies in the late nineteenth and early twentieth centuries. They quite naturally and rapidly diversified their provision wherever possible to offer support for a whole range of school, university and professional examinations.

Their history has been little recorded or studied, but has been anything but straightforward. Many correspondence colleges have gone out of business after relatively short periods, and others have been bought out or have amalgamated in order to survive. To take a not untypical example, no trace now exists of the Royal Irish Correspondence College, based in Halifax, which advertised itself as offering courses for the Royal University of Ireland examinations in 1907 (Elliott 1973: 88). Nevertheless, there are a few extant correspondence colleges which can trace their roots back for nearly a century or more – for example, the National Extension College (which took over the University Correspondence College) and Wolsey Hall.

It is rather shaming to note that the last major study (indeed, one of the only major empirical studies) of correspondence education in Britain dates back over 20 years (Glatter *et al.* 1971); though this was followed up by a series of related studies in the 1970s (Harris 1972, 1975; Harris and Williams 1977). Glatter and his colleagues carried out extensive question- naire surveys of current and former students working for qualifications in commerce, comparing those studying for professional secretarial, banking and accounting qualifications with those aiming for A levels and for the London external BSc(Econ) degree. They were particularly concerned to find out more regarding the circumstances, study methods, achievements and costs of correspondence students. Extensive comparisons were also made with practices in a series of eastern and western European countries.

At the time of their study, Glatter and his colleagues estimated that there were at least 100,000 correspondence students in Britain, about 75,000 of whom were studying for advanced (that is to say, degree level) qualifi- cations. They concluded, rather depressingly, that 'on the whole, examin- ing bodies and professional associations under whose aegis the students are preparing for qualifications show little, if any, practical concern with the manner and efficacy of preparation and tuition.' (Glatter *et al.* 1971: 115).

The only significant and more recent comparative study of British correspondence education, of which we are aware, was based on data collected during a 1981 national survey of adult participation in all forms of education (Woodley 1986; Woodley *et al.* 1987). Woodley used these data to compare Open University undergraduate and associate students with those studying with the National Extension College (NEC), the National Association of Local Government Officers (NALGO) and two other large commercial correspondence providers. His major conclusion concerned the great variability – in terms of demographic characteristics, motivation, and social and educational mobility – both between and within these providers' client groups.

So far as the individual correspondence colleges are concerned, the most studied, indeed the only one that has been publicly studied in any depth, has undoubtedly been the NEC. Its prominence is partly due, no doubt, to its non-profit making status, but also relates to the pioneering role it has played over the years (Freeman 1983; Morpeth 1988; Richardson 1988). From its foundation in 1963 as an experimental body, the NEC has sought to offer a range of courses and support services from basic education up to degree level.

As well as providing straightforward correspondence courses, the NEC has developed the use of broadcast media, in which its early experiments were to have a considerable influence on the Open University. Individual student/tutor support schemes have also been provided in some cases, as in the preparation of students for London external degree examinations. More recently, the NEC has created a flexible means for collaborating with local further education colleges through its 'flexistudy' method (which will be discussed in more detail later in this chapter). However, with few permanent full-time staff and a large body of part-timers supporting a shifting population of thousands of students, the NEC's survival and future has always been uncertain (Jenkins and Perraton 1980).

Correspondence education, thinly disguised in some cases under the label of distance education, remains a vibrant and valid model in late twentieth century Britain. This is clearly demonstrated by the rapid expansion of provision using this mode for Master of Business Administration (MBA) qualifications (Northcott 1986; Asch and Smith 1988). University and polytechnic business schools offering the MBA degree – for example, Brunel, Cranfield, Strathclyde, Warwick and the Open University itself – have moved quickly to provide correspondence courses in what has been a lucrative and expanding, if increasingly competitive, market. In some cases, considerable use has been made of the expertise of established correspondence colleges: thus Warwick's distance MBA was originally developed in association with Wolsey Hall.

Many professions – notably accounting, banking, estate management, insurance and law – continue to rely heavily on correspondence education, both for initial training and, increasingly, for professional updating. In recent years, some of the professional bodies concerned have become more closely involved in this process, either by directly providing correspondence (and other) courses, or by collaborating with one or other of the private colleges.

The Open University

The origins, characteristics and development of the Open University of the United Kingdom have been widely studied, publicized and reported. They will not, therefore, be described here in the same detail as the other, generally less familiar, systems dealt with in this book.

The Open University was, and in many respects remains, a child of the 1960s. It had its origins in the coming together at that time of related political and educational developments. On the one hand, there was the desire and the commitment of the then leader of the Labour Party, Harold Wilson, and one of his senior colleagues, Jennie Lee, to introduce a major egalitarian innovation into what had become a narrowly elitist educational system, and thereby provide a stimulus to economic and technological development. And, on the other hand, there was the impetus produced by the expansion of adult education, the desire to develop a system for supporting London external degree students, and the excitement generated by a series of educational experiments using radio and television (Hoult 1975; Sherow and Wedemeyer 1990).

After the Labour Party came to power in the 1964 general election, a University of the Air Advisory Committee, chaired by Jennie Lee, was duly established. This recommended the adoption of a teaching system which would make extensive use of primetime broadcast television, the provision of a general degree curriculum in arts, engineering, science and social science, and a focus on home-based 'second chance' students, with no formal entrance requirements to be imposed. As the ensuing White Paper in 1966 made clear, much stress was to be placed on the comparability and parity of esteem which the new institution would enjoy with existing universities:

> The Government believe that by an imaginative use of new teaching techniques and teacher/student relationships, an open university providing degree courses as rigorous and demanding as those in existing universities can be established. . . The presentation of courses will variously involve a combination of television, radio, correspondence courses, programmed instruction, tutorials and practicals, short residential courses, and study and discussions at community viewing or study centres.
>
> (Secretary of State for Education and Science 1966: 3, 5–6)

Despite widespread, if often narrow-minded, opposition from educators, commentators and other political parties, a Planning Committee was set up in 1967 for what had by then become known as the Open University. This committee reported in 1969, recommending the establishment of an institution which would be structured much on the lines of other recently created universities, but which would differ from them in a number of ways. The Open University would focus its attention on students who had been 'precluded from achieving their aims through an existing institution of higher education'. It would use 'a fully integrated teaching system' to deliver courses at a distance through print, broadcasting and part-time tuition. And it would provide 'a broadly-based higher education' rather than specialist degrees (Open University Planning Committee 1969: 5, 7, 16).

With an eye on the potential market, the Planning Committee recommended that attention be given to the provision of courses for practising teachers. It also recommended a course structure based firmly around the regular submission of written assignments, and a teaching schedule based on the calendar rather than the academic year. Yet, despite some rather half-hearted attempts at market research – which included the suggestion that about 100,000 adults might wish to study with the institution – little serious attention was given to either demand or costs, both of which were massively underestimated, or to how potential students might best be prepared for entry.

On this basis, and at breakneck speed, the Open University went ahead, receiving its Royal Charter in May 1969 and beginning to enrol students scarcely more than six months later for a January 1971 start. The whole gamble might have been aborted almost immediately, however, when the Conservative Party, who had opposed the report of the Planning Committee, unexpectedly defeated the Labour Party in the 1970 general election. But the new Secretary of State for Education and Science, Margaret Thatcher, was persuaded to give the project her blessing, and from then on the Open University never looked back.

The early annual reports produced by the first vice-chancellor, Walter Perry, together with his later writings, indicate how the broad framework provided by the Planning Committee was quickly translated into the rigid organizational structure that has served the Open University to this day (Open University 1972, 1973a, 1973b; Perry 1976). All first degrees were to be for the Bachelor of Arts (BA) qualification, and were to be constructed in four levels from foundation upwards. Degrees were to consist of the equivalent of either 10 or 12 full course credits, for pass or honours qualifications respectively. The Scottish influence was clearly apparent here, as it had been at the foundation of the University of London and in the creation of the nineteenth century English civic universities.

The Open University's courses were developed by course teams, comprising a mixture of academics, broadcasters, editors, educational technologists and specialist external consultants. The amount of time and effort involved in the preparation of distance education courses had, however, again been seriously underestimated. One result was that many more permanent full-time staff came to be employed than had originally been envisaged. With a central base in the 'new city' of Milton Keynes, a dense regional network of study centres, counselling and tutorial services was quickly established throughout the United Kingdom. Residential summer schools were organized on a range of university campuses for all foundation, and some higher level, courses.

In its first year of operation, 130,000 enquiries and 43,000 applications were received; 24,191 students were provisionally registered and 19,581 finally registered, 75 per cent of whom obtained course credits. 'The big demand . . . came from the middle class, from the school teachers and from the professional groups.' (Open University 1972: 77). Compared with the general adult population, the Open University's students were already well educated: many of them were looking for a 'second bite' rather than a 'second chance'.

Throughout its history, demand for the Open University's courses has consistently and substantially outstripped the numbers of places available, as determined on an annual basis by the government. By 1990, the latest year for which statistics have been published, the number of undergraduates registered had built up to 72,622, of whom 17,496 were newly registered that year. In addition, there were 15,858 short course, 11,574 associate (doing single undergraduate courses) and 4,191 postgraduate students registered, and 62,174 free-standing learning packs were sold. By then teachers only accounted for 7 per cent of the new undergraduate intake, as compared with 40 per cent in 1971. Just over 8,000 Open

University students were awarded a degree in 1990; they would typically have been studying for several years. Graduation rates are falling: the indications are that less than half of the current enrolment will eventually achieve a degree qualification, though most will gain some credits (Open University 1992a).

The existing general analyses of the Open University have nearly all been produced by current or former members of its staff (a category into which both of the authors of this book also fall). These analyses almost invariably argue that the establishment of the Open University was a major innovation, that it substantially increased the availability of higher education opportunities in the United Kingdom, and that it had a considerable influence on other educational providers both at home and abroad (for example, Tunstall 1974; Perry 1976; Rumble 1982; Harry 1990). And it has to be conceded that there is a lot of justice in these assessments.

The Open University did popularize methods of course preparation and production based upon the cooperative division of labour among specialists in a course team, with their work timetabled within a highly planned manufacturing and publishing process (Lewis 1971, 1973). It has made considerable use of a developing range of educational technologies, including home experiment kits, computer-marked assignments, and audio and video tapes (Bates 1984). Broadcasts were never at the core of the educational process as had been envisaged, however, with print remaining as the essential and central course component.

The Open University's course materials and methods have been widely used and copied in other higher education institutions, though with little direct benefit to the Open University itself (Rogers 1983, 1984; Lee and Bibby 1987; Thorpe and Grugeon 1987). And it has provided a model of what could be achieved by a well resourced distance education institution, which has been adapted and developed in many countries throughout the world – for example, the Netherlands, Pakistan, Spain, Venezuela – often with the direct assistance of Open University staff (Rumble and Harry 1982).

The Open University has recruited large numbers of students during the last 20 years, far more than any other British university. Most of them would probably not have been able to experience higher education otherwise, with a large minority coming from relatively poor educational backgrounds (McIntosh *et al.* 1976, 1980). Yet, in doing so, it contributed to an escalation in qualification expectations, effectively closing off certain occupations, most notably teaching, to the non-graduate (Harris 1987). And, though it has been argued that many of the Open University's students have come from working class backgrounds, defined in terms of their father's occupations, the great majority had, like other higher education students, attained middle class status by the time they began studying:

whereas 39% of Open University students have fathers whose occupations were 'middle-class', this increased to 90% of students when their present occupations were considered. Therefore, while the Open University is undoubtedly used as a vehicle for enhancing upward social mobility, it is obvious that its students have already displayed a considerable degree of upward mobility by the time they enrol on their course of study.

> (Whitburn *et al.* 1976: 113–14; quoting figures from McIntosh
> 1974: 61)

Despite the substantial initial upfront costs involved in the preparation and production of distance education materials, the economics of the Open University have compared well – whether measured in terms of student input or graduate output – with those of other British universities, largely because of its mass student market (Wagner 1972, 1977, 1982; Laidlaw and Layard 1974). Comparisons with other providers of part-time forms of higher education have been less flattering, however, though much less visible (Smith and Saunders 1989; Rumble 1992).

This generally upbeat view of the Open University's success over the last 20 years has been shared by many, probably most, external commentators. The early criticisms centring on standards and validity have been largely silenced by the sheer numbers of students recruited, by exposure to the quality of the course materials produced, and, in thousands of cases, by part-time involvement as tutors, examiners and writers in the Open University's teaching process. It would not be easy to find an educator or a politician in Britain today who had never known one of its employees or students closely: many will have been employees or students themselves. In these circumstances, it is little wonder that the Open University's position and role has remained relatively unchallenged.

Two respected foreign commentators, examining the experience of the Open University alongside a series of other attempted higher education reforms in Europe, judged that:

> the Open University has succeeded to a remarkable degree. Approximately 20,000 new students have been admitted annually since 1971 – about a third lacking normal university [entrance] qualifications. . .
> The evidence to date suggests that about 50 per cent will obtain degrees in three to seven years, a figure comparable to that of American state universities but below that of more restrictive British institutions. Academic staff and teaching are probably as good as any found in Britain outside Oxbridge, and the OU degree is increasingly being regarded by employers as equivalent to that of conventional universities. The Open University has served as a model for the design of institutions in at least a dozen countries as diverse as Venezuela, Pakistan and Iran. Virtually the only criticism concerns the modest percentage of working-class students, but even here the OU's performance has been slightly better than that of traditional British universities.
>
> (Cerych and Sabatier 1985: 27–8)

Yet there are significant criticisms to be made and concerns to be addressed if the Open University is to continue to flourish. As an educational institution, it does still appear to be stuck firmly in the 1960s (though it is arguable that one or two others have yet to emerge fully from the nineteenth century). It still has something of an inferiority complex, continually feeling the need to stress the comparability of its products and status to that of the other universities. It remains committed to a heavily structured programme of first degree courses, offering a restricted range of subjects and options for general qualifications.

Despite all the claims which have been made for the advance of distance education over mere correspondence courses, the Open University's teaching and learning process remains firmly based on the printed text. The Open University has, in sharp contrast to the University of London external degree system, maintained a monopoly over the tuition of its students, one result of which has been that tutors of its less popular courses have had to cover vast areas of the country (see also Chapter 9). And the University's academic base, production methods and high quality course materials remain premised on, and can only be justified and supported by, mass recruitment.

In short, the Open University, successful as it undoubtedly has been in its own terms, is stuck with a particular model of distance education and open learning. It has been an innovation, but a highly constrained one; it may have deviated from the post-war British ideology of higher education in some respects, but it has slavishly mimicked the other elements:

> From this point of view, the significant point about the Open University is not its practice of open access or its use of distance teaching but its retention of the honours degree pattern and the three-hour unseen written examination.
>
> (Tight 1989b: 93)

Innovation is, of course, far from easy and inevitably constrained by circumstances. It would have been unreasonable, therefore, to have expected a greater move away from the then conventional patterns at the time when the Open University was established. Yet, it has been disappointing to observe how little the University has developed from its original structure, and to note how restrictive this has become.

It is reassuring, then, to see that some senior staff at the Open University are beginning to appreciate the competitive vulnerability of their position in the market (Rumble 1992). This has become particularly apparent as alternative, cheaper and more flexible models of distance education and open learning have been developed; and as conventional institutions have increasingly moved into the market sector which had hitherto been occupied in the United Kingdom by the Open University alone.

The Open University's latest strategic plan sees its future as a European, English language, distance teaching institution, with greatly expanded student numbers (notably at postgraduate level), and a subject base broadened to include both modern languages and more vocationally oriented provision (Open University 1992b).

Post-Open University models: open learning

The naming and establishment of the Open University was in itself, of course, a major stimulus for the subsequent development of open learning. In the words of its first chancellor, Geoffrey Crowther, the Open University's basic philosophy was to be 'open as to people, as to places, as to methods and as to ideas' (Open University 1992b: 5). While the development of this philosophy was, as we have argued, somewhat restricted in practice, it did provide many of those associated with the new institution with both the opportunity and the excuse to set out what purported to be a new educational ideology (see for example, Lewis and Spencer 1986; Thorpe and Grugeon 1987; Paine 1988; see also Chapter 1). In this activity they were given considerable assistance by those who were simultaneously trying to make British further education more flexible, student-centred and adult-oriented (see for example, Davies 1977, Scottish Education Department 1982; Further Education Unit 1983; Birch and Latham 1984; Bagley and Challis 1985).

It was realized from the start by at least some of those involved in these developments that:

> Open learning is an imprecise phrase to which a range of meanings can be, and is, attached. It eludes definition. But as an inscription to be carried in procession on a banner, gathering adherents and enthusiasms, it has great potential. For its very imprecision enables it to accommodate many different ideas and aims.
>
> (Mackenzie *et al.* 1975: 15)

Indeed, as suggested in Chapter 1, open learning is a much broader concept than distance education, and can equally well be applied outside distance education as within it. As such, it is perhaps an ideal organizing concept for continuing education (Tight 1988c, 1989b).

The slipperiness of the terminology has been made manifest during the 1980s, as open learning has been adopted by both industry and government as a cost-effective substitute for more conventional forms of training: 'ideas originating in the quite different context of opening up access for adults to higher education have been imported into training for teenagers in work-related skills.' (Bynner 1992: 105; see also McNay 1988). At the present time in Britain, open learning is very much a contested concept.

One, perhaps the, classic example of open learning as originally conceived was the development of 'flexistudy' by the National Extension College in conjunction with local further education colleges during the late 1970s (Barnet College of Further Education 1980; Sacks 1980; NEC 1981). Flexistudy is in essence a mixed-mode form of provision, embodying varied elements of distance and face-to-face education. The NEC's role was to produce the distance elements: packages of course materials to support study in a range of subjects and at a variety of levels. These materials would then be used in dual settings; both by the individual student when studying alone at home or at work, and by them when they made occasional visits to their local college for tutorials or group sessions.

The students were recruited by the colleges involved, not by the NEC. They could be recruited at any time of the year, and allowed to learn at their own pace. With the course materials being produced nationally, minority subjects could be accommodated. Flexistudy suited both the colleges and the NEC. The colleges were provided with a flexible mechanism, and with high quality materials, for supporting a wide range of local study needs. The NEC was removed from the administrative chores of direct national recruitment, and was able to give effective local support to correspondence students much more cheaply than the Open University could: 'the Flexistudy model is not simply an alternative model for running a correspondence college. It is a means of creating a number of separate, local, correspondence colleges' (Freeman 1982: 164).

The idea of open learning – open not just in terms of time, place and pace, but also in many cases in terms of entrance requirements, student backgrounds and learning methodologies – was taken up and exploited within the formal education system during the 1980s. Three examples, none of them directly connected with distance education, are of particular interest and will be briefly discussed here: the open college movement, independent learning and the assessment of prior learning.

The open college movement has brought together regional associations of educational providers – typically including both local further education colleges and institutions of higher education – to offer and accredit a coordinated programme of courses and support facilities for adults. A major aim of the movement has been to provide an adult alternative to A levels; designed to enable mature age access to higher education, qualification or employment opportunities. Starting with the Open College of the North West, based around Lancaster University and Lancashire Polytechnic (now the University of Central Lancashire), a range of open college models soon developed, placing different emphases on higher education, accreditation and recruitment strategies (Davies and Robertson 1986).

By 1990, open college networks had been established in most of the major urban districts in England and Wales, and were under consideration in many other areas (Unit for the Development of Adult Continuing Education 1989). With the demise of the Council for National Academic Awards, the open colleges have also now inherited much of the impetus behind the more general access movement.

The second example, independent study, was largely devised by North East London Polytechnic (now the University of East London). Here methods were developed to enable individual students to study for qualifications independently, with the support of specialist staff, group sessions and the facilities of the institution. These processes had to meet the criteria and standards set by the accrediting body; initially the CNAA, later the institution itself. The individual student was responsible for determining their own curriculum, syllabus, study methods and assessment pattern, for getting these approved, and for scheduling and carrying out the work involved (compare with the independent guided study scheme recently introduced by the University of London external system: see Chapter 7).

Study led initially to the Diploma in Higher Education (DipHE), and was then extended to enable a whole first degree to be completed by independent study (Percy *et al.* 1980; Stephenson 1980; O'Reilly 1991). Though this approach has been subject to considerable criticism, it continues to offer a relatively open route to and through higher education for mature students, many of whom come from educational and social backgrounds not normally associated with such study.

The accreditation or assessment of prior learning, or of prior experiential learning – abbreviated as APL, APEL and various similar acronyms – has, by contrast with the other approaches explored so far, been imported directly from the United States. This approach starts from the recognition or assumption that many adults possess considerable knowledge, understanding or skills, often developed through work, social or voluntary activities, which has not been, but is worthy of, accreditation towards an appropriate qualification (Evans 1983, 1988, 1992).

The various methods involved in producing and assessing evidence of prior learning are now quite widely understood and accepted, but their implementation remains patchy, particularly in higher education. This resistance appears to be partly due to the competing interpretations of learning and experiential learning involved (Weil and McGill 1989), and partly to the association of APL with more mechanistic and vocational competency-based methods of assessment.

At the same time as these ideas and models were being selectively introduced into further and higher education institutions, an alternative conception of open learning – seen rather narrowly as one form of distance education – was being applied in a series of government-led and industry-supported initiatives intended to remedy perceived deficiencies in vocational training. Two of these initiatives have achieved particular prominence: the Open Tech and the Open College (the latter not to be confused with the open college movement).

The Open Tech initiative was introduced by the then Manpower Services Commission (MSC) in 1982, with the aim of widening access to training opportunities for those working at technician and supervisory levels (MSC 1982; Tolley 1983). Pump-priming funds were provided for a range of project-based, collaborative and developmental schemes, with numerous learning packages being produced as a result (NEC 1986). The Open Tech initiative was, however, short-lived, and many of the projects for which it provided funds quickly folded once that support was withdrawn. It can also be criticized on the grounds that many of the learning packages produced were used, without support and with limited success, by employers as a cheap form of training. Yet the Open Tech initiative did help to stimulate the development of effective open learning units within some companies and colleges, and had an influence on more general policy developments within youth training.

The Open College, which began teaching in 1987, was a much more ambitious revisiting of the same territory:

> The Open College is an initiative that brings together broadcasters, educationalists and industry to provide vocational education and training for a mass audience. The objective is to improve the UK's economic performance, using open learning to widen access to training in a range of skills necessary for the changing world of work. The college provides courses that range from basic education up to degree level, and additionally some post-degree professional updating. All are aimed at helping students to improve their vocational competence. Courses are available through a combination of broadcasting on radio and television, workbooks, video, audio cassettes, computer software where appropriate, and kits. Local support is provided by colleges, employers and other learning establishments in both the public and private sectors.
>
> (Innes 1988: 148)

It sounded very much like a lower level, but more vocationally oriented, Open University. And this was indeed the intention of those involved, many of whom had been recruited or seconded from the Open University itself.

Despite a massive publicity campaign and an extension of government funding, the survival and success of the Open College is far from assured. Its approach has also been changed quite dramatically from the original strategy. The local network of learner support centres has been heavily rationalized, the subject range covered has been cut back, and, most significantly, the focus has been shifted away from the individual student and towards a limited number of large corporate clients (Innes 1992).

One of the most recent British initiatives in the field of open learning, the Open Polytechnic (or Open Learning Foundation as it has now been renamed), has shifted attention back to the more general philosophy of open-ness and access. The Open Polytechnic's approach has similarities to flexistudy, as applied to higher education, and is likely to pose a considerable challenge to the Open University. The Open Polytechnic will commission and publish learning materials, which will then be used as an integral part of degree courses, particularly those offered by the polytechnics (recently renamed as universities), throughout the country.

The intention is to enable a rough balance between distance study and face-to-face contact, with the Open Polytechnic's learning materials used in combination with less intensive forms of classroom teaching. The students involved will be recruited directly by their local institutions, allowing a significant expansion in participation. Many students may thereby be involved in higher education who would not be able to commit themselves to a more intensive attendance pattern, but who are not attracted to the Open University because of the lack of opportunities it provides for face-to-face interaction (Fitzgerald 1988; Open Polytechnic 1992).

Future models

From this veritable ferment of developmental activity in the fields of distance education and open learning in the United Kingdom, and overseas, during the last 20 years, we may deduce a number of likely future trends with a reasonable degree of confidence.

First, while neither distance education, nor the much broader conception of open learning, have yet to penetrate or influence significantly the practices of the mainstream educational institutions – the established universities and schools – they promise or threaten to do so in the near future. This is likely to occur, if only through the enforced expansion of the mainstream, and will probably lead to the development of the first British dual mode institutions, offering both distance and face-to-face instruction in a range of subjects. In this way we could, in a sense, be seen to be returning to the more open pattern of provision evident in the second half of the nineteenth and early twentieth centuries.

Second, there are likely to be many more attempts made to bring together or synthesize elements or approaches within distance education, open learning, independent study, experiential learning, student-centred learning and/or whatever other organizing concepts are adopted (see for example, Kember and Murphy 1990). On balance, this is also likely to result in a greater opening-up of the learning process.

And, third, and somewhat in contradiction, we may anticipate the further development of concepts, models and ideas, and their adoption and application within institutions of higher education (Hodgson *et al.* 1987; Evans and Nation 1992), as the debate around these issues continues.

9

Exclusivity and Beyond: The Decline of Open-ness in the Twentieth Century

Closing the doors

To most British academics it would seem perverse to describe the twentieth century as anything but a period of immense progress. The number of universities has increased from a mere dozen or so to almost a hundred. Entrance requirements for students have in most subject areas become ever more demanding while, most important of all perhaps, the commitment of academics to research is now on a scale beyond the wildest imaginings of those who inhabited academia in late Victorian and Edwardian times. It is very easy to forget, therefore, that such gains have been made at some cost, and that our society may have been damaged by making our universities more exclusive and demanding organizations.

At the beginning of the twentieth century, the British government was engaged in the difficult process of pressing British academics to emulate their counterparts in Germany and North America. In May 1901, Arthur Balfour, soon to become prime minister, thanking Andrew Carnegie for a new grant to the Scottish universities, expressed himself:

> amazed and almost ashamed at the indifference with which the British public has acquiesced in the wholly inadequate provision which we make for scientific training and research and this not merely in the Scotch [*sic*] universities but at Oxford, Cambridge and other great seats of learning.
>
> (Simpson 1983: 105)

Outside the field of medicine, what would now be seen as respectable university research was restricted to small pockets, presided over by enthusiastic professors often of German extraction. The modern PhD was still unknown in Britain, and it had, very tentatively, to establish itself here in the inter-war years during the course of what Simpson has described as 'a century of struggle for post-graduate education'.

Only in the immediate post-Second World War years would research, as we now know it, become a major concern of those university departments, most probably a majority, that had hitherto neglected or even despised it.

Two Newcastle lecturers have graphically described how research arrived in their own department, amid much mistrust and controversy, during the 1940s (Tyson and Tuck 1971). Their experiences were, no doubt, duplicated in a host of other establishments, including some of the faculties of Oxford and Cambridge.

This was in great contrast to the then current practice in America, where, at the prestigious University of Michigan at Ann Arbor, for example, they had long abandoned the style of 'petty colleges obedient to deteriorated traditions of English methods' and 'developed training . . . ideals and methods largely from Germany' (Hofstadter and Hardy 1952: 62). From as early as the 1860s, the growth of graduate schools in America began to make advanced work a prerequisite for the promotion and tenure of academics (Johanningmeier 1980). In the United Kingdom, however, a university career in the first part of the twentieth century could still be, and often was, based on success in undergraduate examinations.

The early years of the twentieth century were also notable for the abolition of the 'mere' examination boards that had hitherto constituted the University of London and the Royal University of Ireland. 'Teaching' universities were to be established in their place, which not only examined their registered students, but also insisted that such students should undergo face-to-face tuition in the classrooms of the university's constituent colleges.

There can be little doubt that this was in part a success for academic vested interests. In Dublin, Belfast, London and other British cities in the 1890s, face-to-face university institutions were not doing particularly well in beating off their rivals, the correspondence colleges and the crammers, many of whose students (as we have seen in Chapters 3 and 4) were achieving far greater examination success. Thus, the August 1890 issue of the *Journal of Education* reported, that of 849 successful candidates in the London matriculation examination, a 'bare half dozen had been educated at King's and University College – about a twentieth of those prepared by the University Correspondence College.' This brought a modest rejoinder from the correspondence college itself (in April 1891), which pointed out that the report had been somewhat exaggerated, and that in fact they had produced not one in four but only one in seven of the successful matriculation candidates. However, they were able to add that 'the proportion [was] considerably higher at other [higher level] exams'.

Table 4.2 indicates the unsuccessful fight being waged by Queen's College, Belfast against its rivals. Such university colleges would naturally welcome any organizational change which forced students into their own classrooms. No doubt they also believed that the experience they offered was superior, offering gifts and developing skills beyond examination success, but they needed to achieve a local monopoly of teaching if their future was to be guaranteed.

However, disgruntled college principals were never the sole advocates of change. Not only in Ireland, but throughout the United Kingdom as then constituted, universities were increasingly being seen not just as useful instructors but as the guardians of the spiritual and intellectual well-being of the nation. The universities were also in the process of becoming what they now are, but had never been before, the main organizers and stimulators of the country's scientific and cultural life. Many of the giants of earlier generations, such as Davy and Faraday, had made their careers without benefit of university experience. That would become more and more difficult in a twentieth century increasingly concerned to have its scientists formally certificated, while the worth of a great writer would be judged by their earning a place in the university curriculum.

The growing emphasis on research and the new sense of national mission produced also a gradual growth of ambition among the more able and ambitious undergraduates. An increasing number were to attempt honours as the twentieth century wore on, and, although it would not become the norm until after the Second World War – and, even then, would not become the universal aim in Scotland or Ireland – the organization of honours courses became more and more important (Bell 1965).

The raising of degree standards was also linked to the increased academic emphasis of the English public and grammar schools and, indeed, of the secondary sector generally. As they developed in the late nineteenth century, the schools saw the possibility of taking over some of the university's tasks. At that time (see Chapters 3 and 4) many schools successfully entered candidates for degree examinations. They also took over from the universities the task of preparing an even larger group of students for matriculation and other entrance examinations. Later pressures, coming both from the schools and from the universities, resulted, by the 1950s, in large portions of the first and second year undergraduate courses passing into the school domain (Curtis 1962; Kingdon 1991; see also Chapter 6). With university entry now delayed until students were 18- or 19-years-old, it became easier for undergraduates to proceed immediately to honours study.

The raising of undergraduate standards was further encouraged in the inter-war period by the blossoming of organizations designed to develop individual academic subject areas. The British Psychological Society, for example, had been tiny before the First World War. Founded in 1901 on the wave of the new interest in research, by 1904 it had only ten paid up members, and the entire membership used to meet for dinner and discussion in a London restaurant. By 1920, as a result of the development of the subject during the First World War, the number of members had increased by 500 per cent, and a number of universities were developing departments to serve the psychologists' high level training needs (Hearnshaw 1964; Bell 1986).

The training of psychologists, like many of the other new professionals, involved practical work in a laboratory, something most easily provided in a face-to-face college. The development of such professions served, therefore, to reinforce the Newmanian desire for a 'traditional' direct interaction between teacher and student, and helped to discredit both distance methods of teaching and isolated private study. With a renewed emphasis placed on the university's role as an Alma Mater, not only organizing their students' studies but also serving as a focus for their lives, a degree course was no longer to be seen as a commodity to be purchased at will from the most convenient provider.

All of these developments were to move the British and Irish universities further and further away from the more open world of the nineteenth century, when those enrolling for courses had no need ever to meet any university teacher face-to-face; a time when perfectly serious students, both in Scotland and elsewhere, could dip in and out of the curriculum without ever seeking the full degree. The commercial concerns and compromises of so many nineteenth century professors and tutors would gradually become discredited. It would no longer be possible, for example, for Durham to cut the length of its BA course to two years in order to undercut its distinguished southern rivals, or for professors in Edinburgh and Manchester actively to compete for students with the local schools (see Chapter 2). The new guardians of the nation's value system could no longer behave like academic shopkeepers.

Those academics intent on pursuing the new teaching ideals might not as yet spend much time on research, but they did not actively oppose its presence in the university as Newman himself had done (Newman 1859). Those who were concerned to produce a new generation of technical experts, or to emulate German and American models of research, were to be made increasingly free to do so by the bequests of industrial magnates like Carnegie, by the increasing government grants – distributed from 1919 onwards through the University Grants Committee (Shinn 1986) – and by the development of a national system of fixed academic salaries.

By the early 1950s a dominant notion had emerged of the 'normal' British university, and this increasingly influenced both academic and government decision-making (Tight 1989a). At its heart was a set of assumptions about Oxford and Cambridge that were not always justified, but were certainly potent. These included the ideals of ancientness and international recruitment, two qualities sometimes beyond a university's reach. Of more general application were the expectations that a university's:

> students . . . should be carefully selected . . . those who enter should be offered (to use a Victorian distinction) 'education' and not merely 'training'. This end necessitates . . . a small scale residential community affording close contact of teachers with taught in a shared domestic life.
>
> (Halsey and Trow 1971: 67)

Other elements of the 'normal' university were derived from America, or from the much firmer continental tradition brought directly to Britain by the many distinguished Jewish scholars who had arrived as refugees. Their presence, influence and industriousness helped to give an air of deceptive reality to British academia's new claims about their 'traditional' concern with research.

With the greater post-war government funding of individual students, first those demobilized from the armed forces and then school leavers, the criteria outlined by Halsey and Trow became easier to satisfy. Students could now be expected to pay for places in halls of residence, which began to mushroom even in Scotland, where the taboo on monkish practices had long since been swept away by the new academic fashions. Alongside residence came the widespread development of new systems of pastoral care, designed to make all universities more like an ideal Oxford college.

Both from an egalitarian point of view, and so as to satisfy the *amour propre* of academics, it then seemed desirable that the university world should become as homogeneous as possible. Universities' expectations of students, and the standards of their degrees, were to be held common throughout the system. These attitudes would have surprised not only the Victorians, but also those in other countries, such as the United States and France, who continued, even in the twentieth century, to see some merit in the maintenance of a varied set of higher education institutions, which were not all intended to be as impressive and exclusive as each other.

In 1900 such a varied, if smaller, set of institutions still existed in the United Kingdom. Alongside the two ancient English institutions were four equally ancient Scottish establishments, still asserting a different and more popular tradition. In Ireland the Royal University offered a very open and cheap alternative to a Trinity College intent on emphasizing its Oxbridge antecedents, though its entrance requirements were still low. In Wales, the new national university was much influenced by fashionable American models of organization (it was, for example, the first British university to award an MA degree on the basis of research (Bell 1965)), but it retained strong links with its distinctive working-class and chapel origins, and with the non-instrumental aims of the university extension movement (Marriott 1981).

In England a growing array of higher education institutions had come into existence, ranging from the new teaching university in London, with many students living at home or in the wider community, to the highly residential collegiate style of Durham. In Birmingham an independent university had just been established that saw itself as fulfilling the functions of the American land-grant colleges, servicing local industry and encouraging general local adult education as well as providing the latest scientific courses (Armytage 1955). In the northern English cities, Scottish-style institutions ambitiously embarked on many projects, but were increasingly dependent on the income to be derived from teacher-trainees attending their government-financed Day Training Colleges.

And both London and St Andrews universities were providing extensive opportunities for students to study for qualifications at a distance, both within the United Kingdom and overseas.

Such a set of institutions, had it been developed in a different way, might well have provided the inhabitants of late twentieth century Britain and Ireland with a remarkable variety of opportunities for higher study. Instead the ideal of a homogeneous university sector in the imagined Oxbridge style became so powerful that, by the 1960s, the state had to create its own sector of higher education through the polytechnics. These were intended to accommodate not only the worthwhile degree candidates that the universities now rejected, but also those interested in more practical forms of study that the universities were no longer keen to develop.

The universities had seized the opportunity to pursue a hitherto unattainable ideal. They closed their doors and sought perfection. Expectations increased as entry to the academic community was more and more restricted to an elite. Tasks thought unworthy of that elite were increasingly shed, regardless of what the eventual reaction might be from a parliament and public apparently quite willing, at least for a time, to leave the universities' agenda to themselves.

Behind closed doors

By the end of the 1970s, it was considered impolite, even threatening, to suggest that there was any variation in standards between institutions. A university was a university, and a degree was a degree, and worthy of common respect. Any differences between institutions were to be discerned only in terms of particular success at certain subject specialisms, or of idiosyncratic curricular arrangements such as the foundation years at Stirling and Keele.

There were a handful of unusual institutions, like Birkbeck College and the new Open University (not to mention the polytechnics), but their distinctiveness was limited and largely contained within those institutions. For the 'normal' undergraduate, entering university straight from school and studying full-time, an impressively standardized system was waiting. Its homogeneity was institutionalized in 1961 with the creation of the Universities Central Council for Admissions (UCCA), a single clearing house for university applications.

But the modern British universities, caught up in their pursuit of excellence, had lost sight of some of the other characteristics of their overseas role models. Finding themselves able for the first time to pick and choose their students, they forgot how most of the North American institutions they were so keen on emulating had basic entrance requirements that were far less demanding. Those same prestigious institutions that produced so many influential publications, turned out so many hundreds of well-trained PhDs, and were regularly chosen to handle billion dollar commercial and defence contracts, were usually also quite happy – as the British universities had once been – to keep their doors open to those middle-range students now so often falling foul of British entrance requirements. They were even able to welcome those with mediocre high school records, who had no desire to become academics or even high level professionals, but were simply seeking the social experience of 'college' (Boyer 1987).

Woodward and Broder (1992) have noted how former Vice-President Quayle, for example, failed to get high school grades good enough to assure him a place at the university attended by his father and grandfather. He was nevertheless admitted as a 'legacy' student, and managed eventually to graduate from law school. Indeed his academic career recalls the experience of many well-known but academically undistinguished British figures, who took advantage of the continued open-ness of universities in the years between the wars. It provides a salutary reminder also that without the finance that such apparently unpromising but affluent students provide, both as undergraduate fee-payers and later as 'alumni', many American graduate schools could not continue to exist. Not only the American university system, but American society in general, has depended on the continuation of this ready availability of college places to satisfy the aspirations and needs of individuals and to provide that supply of well-educated middle management that has been seen as the key to American post-war economic success (Servan-Schreiber 1969).

Because such an open system exists, a far higher proportion of American citizens are able to participate in some form of convenient higher education, whether full-time or part-time, face-to-face or at a distance. While much of that education takes place at a relatively low level when compared with current British norms, it does nevertheless, ensure a far greater access to advanced academic work than would be usual in Britain (Grant 1973).

With hindsight, it seems remarkable that the British universities were able to increase their entrance requirements during the 1950s and 1960s with very little public challenge. No doubt the disgruntled parents of those unsuccessful applicants who on earlier criteria would have had little difficulty in finding a university place, were too shamefaced to draw public attention to their children's 'failure'. Perhaps also, after the general privations of the 1940s, British people were already too well conditioned to raise questions about the rationing of any commodity deemed by its supplier to be scarce. Even egalitarians fighting for the abolition of what they saw as invalid and socially divisive selection for secondary schools, showed remarkably little interest in challenging the ever more rigorous screening of university candidates. While some drew attention to what they felt were the unacceptable advantages enjoyed by the pupils of certain independent schools when satisfying the entrance requirements of Oxford and Cambridge colleges, they rarely if ever challenged the need for such rigorous selection in itself (see for example, Benn and Simon 1970).

The obvious parallel with the eleven plus examination and the privileges of the grammar school child was seldom noticed. Those who advocated the creation of comprehensive universities (for example, Pedley 1977) were not taken seriously, not least because the creation of enough places within the post-war ideal university pattern was clearly a financial impossibility. It seemed better in the circumstances to leave the management of such things to the universities themselves. Only occasionally was the notion that the new rigorous entrance requirements were neither traditional or essential put forward (Peterson 1961).

In fact, Pedley's plans for the comprehensive university were quite sophisticated. He did not suggest that there should be open access to the same kind of university experience for everyone, least of all to the elitist experience then in vogue. Instead, in tones that might have fitted Newman, he expressed the belief that in:

> existing colleges, whether their base be primarily technological or artistic or agricultural or pedagogic, there are precious human and educational resources which are bound up in that community and which would be lost if the identity of the college *as a community* were destroyed.
>
> (Pedley 1977: 84; original emphasis)

He proposed that all the post-secondary educational establishments in a particular area should be brought together in a loose federation (somewhat similar, perhaps, to the historic University of London pattern). Such an idea was unlikely, however, to interest a university sector confident that its component institutions' rights to exclusivity were generally accepted.

Unfortunately even the Robbins Report (Committee on Higher Education 1963), with its liberal advocacy of a guaranteed university place for everyone suitably qualified, left the question of what constituted suitability largely in the hands of an increasingly exclusive university world. There was little support for those who suggested that Britain should follow the pattern of many European countries by establishing basic entrance requirements and then seeking to provide higher education places for all those who managed to achieve them. Instead each university department remained free to establish its own criteria of acceptability, based all too often not on objective standards but on the current resources available and the extent of public demand.

Thus, the predominantly female candidates for courses in the most popular modern languages found themselves being judged in far more severe terms than the largely male candidates for some of the less popular forms of engineering. Conversely, levels of school attainment deemed essential in the 1970s were often abandoned in the less affluent 1980s in order to accommodate students from overseas, who were obliged to pay considerably greater fees than their British counterparts. There was little sign of any desire to define the real nature of that general aptitude for university study the existence of which was so often assumed in the rhetoric of official pronouncements.

Even the polytechnics, intended by government to relieve the pressures created by university exclusivity, were in many cases themselves to become just as rigorous in their entrance requirements (Pratt and Burgess 1974). Increasingly, they came to compete with the universities for the same students and the same academic prestige. They did so on such a scale and with such success that they were readily accepted into the university world in 1992 with hardly a murmur of disapproval from the guardians of standards.

The true nature of open-ness

From the beginning of the 1970s there was, of course, to be one major exception to the increasingly homogeneous pattern of British university education. The Open University chose to oppose exclusivity by having no entrance requirements at all, and thus posed a challenge to much that the post-war university stood for. Yet, in a quite remarkable manner, it was to be quickly accepted, and it met with little continuing opposition from the rest of the university world (see Chapter 8). In essence, the academic community was able to isolate the Open University, regarding it as a special case whose rejection of selection could have no significance for undergraduate studies in general.

The Open University's world seemed and seems a separate world. It has no relevance to the normal forecasting of higher education needs, with educational economists and demographers regularly feeling able to exclude its statistics from their work, and to confine mention of it to brief footnotes. In Scotland the Open University teaches more undergraduates than all but four of the other universities, yet a committee which fervently advocated the establishment of a separate funding body for Scottish higher education in 1985 was happy that the Open University in Scotland should continue to be controlled from its English headquarters at Milton Keynes (Scottish Tertiary Education Advisory Council 1985; Bell 1986).

Such detached tolerance is understandable. Even though the creation of the Open University represented a considerable return to open-ness in British higher education, its understandable commitment not to sell its students short, and to prove itself part of the 'real' university world, meant that it could never make too direct a challenge to that world's post-war assumptions. Thus, in order to remain respectable in the eyes of its peers, the new university's courses have had to adopt an approach and a language which sometimes involves just as many assumptions about previous academic experience as do the entrance requirements of other universities.

Not surprisingly, a significant number of Open University students with poor educational backgrounds (as judged by conventional criteria) fall by the wayside. This is a straightforward function of the desire to maintain standards and to keep outside respect for the Open University degree. As Chapters 3, 4 and 5 make clear, a large number of candidates for the examinations of the University of London, the Royal University of Ireland and for the St Andrews LLA also failed (see Tables 3.6 and 5.1).

This eventuality is made even more likely today, however, by the absence in the Open University of any system of initial examinations, such as existed for students wishing to enter the London and Royal University degree structures. There is no equivalent either to the preliminary classes run by professors in Scotland in the days of unrestricted entry there, courses meant not as the first hurdle of the race but as a general induction for those without adequate secondary experience into the language and ways of higher education.

Some such arrangement is probably essential in any university that is completely open in its entrance procedures, and, though their establishment has often been considered by Open University committees, the running of preliminary courses has up to now been seen to lie outside the duties of a 'real' university. They have been viewed as a business far more appropriate to Britain's institutions of further education, not all of which, unfortunately, have had either the funding or the inclination to provide them.

The task of providing full open-ness and real opportunities for the academically inexperienced in the exclusive university world of late twentieth century Britain clearly involves more than merely getting rid of entrance requirements. It is also important to give such students time to grasp a concept or a chain of reasoning, to move at their own pace and to undertake their studies at their own best moments. Unfortunately, for administrative and resource reasons, this is not always possible in a highly integrated system with a nationally determined timetable. All the Open University's undergraduate study must take place between February and October, and, while failure is not final, having a second chance involves paying the quite considerable fees a second time. Very often the student facing academic difficulties is also among the least affluent.

The financial position of most part-time students in Britain is a hard one, given the absence of mandatory grants. Certainly the burdens are greater than in Victorian times when universities' administrative procedures and support services were considerably simpler and cheaper to run. The financial challenge was a relatively small one for a Royal University of Ireland private student, paying a mere £1 a year, with no other compulsory expenditure than that on a trip to Dublin for the final examination. Contrast this with the challenge to an Open University student paying not only a large course fee but facing also perhaps the travel and incidental costs of a compulsory summer school. While the Victorian distance universities never presented their students with the rich materials and support systems of the Open University, there can be little doubt that, whatever their academic drawbacks by modern standards, they were far more open to those of limited means.

Moreover, there was a further open-ness. The Victorian students, though no doubt sometimes lacking the support and advice intended to flow from the more complex modern arrangements, were at least able to choose a tutor or learning system to suit their own taste and pocket. Neither London University, nor its St Andrews and Royal University equivalents, ever imposed a tutor on anyone, or demanded that monopoly on the teaching of their own courses which the Open University has until now felt compelled to demand (at least in its United Kingdom operations).

The Open University's decision to keep all of the teaching of its carefully prepared courses under its own control is understandable. To teach and examine one's own students has, in twentieth century Britain, come to seem so natural a characteristic of any 'real' university that the Open University, in its search for acceptability and respectability, would have been foolish to ignore it. Moreover, this monopoly has obviously had advantages in bringing the compilers and examiners of courses closer to the students. Yet, it has sometimes involved the allocation of students, especially those on low population courses, to tutors many miles away, often making direct personal contact expensive or impossible. Although people in remoter areas have gained and benefited from their studies, this has often been at far greater cost and inconvenience than might have been the case in late Victorian times.

The Open University is, of course, alive to such difficulties, and in July 1992 two regional directors, bearing in mind the planned expansion in student numbers, suggested a radical rethink on tutoring which would abandon the university's own close control of tutorial arrangements (*Open House*, July 1992). They proposed entering into new collaborative arrangements with other local providers of continuing education, with an Open University presence being established 'in every Further Education, Higher Education and adult education centre in the country as well as in village halls, community centres and even mosques.' The Open University would gain 'a greater overall presence, a mechanism for recruiting students . . . [and] local foundation level tuition and open days, weekends and evenings, in more supportive and friendly environments.'

Their views remain personal, but they have identified an agenda which recalls not merely the nationwide arrangements of the Victorian distance institutions, but also the comprehensive university proposals made in the 1970s by Pedley. Indeed, Pedley himself forecast some of the problems that a highly centralized Open University would face as its student body increased. He felt that greater collaboration with other bodies would:

> reduce the in-built handicap of being a relatively inflexible and primarily one-way system of communication in which the daily interaction of tutor and student, normal and invaluable in traditional colleges, university and adult education classes, cannot take place.
>
> (Pedley 1977: 101)

But the proximity of tutoring is not the only issue. The ability to choose a tutor from an array of possibilities is also an important element of open-ness. The Open University's students cannot be sure that they will be allocated a personally satisfactory set of tutors even if most of those tutors live just round the corner. In the more open situation of late Victorian Britain, university students were presented with a far richer choice. They could themselves decide to seek tuition from professional university teachers or, if they happened to be attending an academically ambitious establishment, they could stay on at school to study in the 'university class'. If their schooling had been limited or unsuccessful, and they felt the need of some remedial treatment, they could enlist at one of the cramming establishments or hire a personal tutor. Or they could save money by dispensing with tutors completely, doing all the necessary work at home or in the local public library.

Victorian university students could also choose to follow a correspondence course (now despised in many quarters, not least at the Open University itself). Their correspondence tutors might well be at a great distance, but they could still offer advice and criticism with great regularity, usually far more regularly than Open University finances now allow. Moreover, such advice and criticism could be rejected by the student, for the tutor was in no way part of the official university assessment mechanism. Unlike Open University tutors, they were not bound from the very beginning of the course to award marks that would eventually count in the overall course examination.

The freedom to choose one's own tutor, to study at one's own pace and in one's own manner, and with no obligation to anyone except the final examiner, were all a function of the more loose-knit Victorian system of higher education. It is perhaps unreasonable, therefore, to criticize the Open University too strongly for placing greater restrictions on its students' freedoms in a more complex, demanding and restrictive academic world. But we can at least ask ourselves whether any lessons can be learned for the future from the experiences and practices of the past.

Reopening the doors

It is tempting to see in recent educational 'innovations', such as those examined in Chapter 8, a return to at least some of the Victorian open-ness. The National Extension College's experiments with flexistudy, giving students freedom to select a local tutor and to work at their own pace, and the Open Polytechnic's decision to leave teaching to its component local institutions both recall some of the freedoms of the Victorian system. There is now, as we have just indicated, a real possibility that the Open University will begin authorizing other institutions to teach some of its courses. The reinvigoration of the University of London's external degree system, with the development of an independent guided study scheme and the launching of distance education courses at postgraduate level (discussed in Chapters 6 and 7), is also reopening higher educational opportunities in Britain and overseas.

At the same time, the growing interest in the transfer of credits earned within the degree structure of one institution to those of another, along with the modularization of university courses that is making such a process easier, promises greater freedom of choice for the student and also poses a constructive threat to the idea of each university being an inviolate and independent institution. Under related schemes, credits may be awarded for previous non-university learning or life experience. The fact that the Open University has now taken over a national responsibility for the coordination of such developments, from the disbanded Council for National Academic Awards, awakens the hope that such new ideas will be more readily incorporated into its own degree structures. But the way forward is not necessarily easy.

Despite its tolerance of the Open University's open entry policy, the rest of the university world was initially far more cautious about its multi-media approach to teaching. The links between television and entertainment were too close for many delicate academic stomachs in the early 1970s. Twenty years later, far grander forms of electronic technology dominate the 'real' university world. Far from being a pioneer in the use of microcomputers, the Open University has had to struggle imaginatively to adapt its distance teaching methods to incorporate what has become conventional in other universities. On the other hand, its television programmes are now taken seriously enough for them to be widely used in the classrooms of the face-to-face universities themselves. Indeed, they are sometimes taken more seriously there than by the Open University's students, who are often more intent on completing successfully their 'traditional' written assignments and examinations.

It is important, therefore, to remember that, amid all the technological development, the new commitment to more flexibly structured degree patterns and methods of facilitating learning, the minds of many students are still just as concentrated on examination success as were those of the late Victorians. Moreover, students still seek such success within an academic world which is not wholly wedded to the exciting new open-ness of credit transfer, modularization and the accreditation of prior learning. There is still a powerful body of influential academic opinion that seeks to defend standards which they believe were achieved by the very abandonment of Victorian and early twentieth century open-ness, and by the imposition of a safer exclusivity. There needs, they believe, to be constant vigilance against an enemy ever ready to pounce. While most people probably believe that the present standards of the universities are high ones, significantly higher than those of the 1930s or even the 1950s, some clearly do not. For example, Professor Lord Russell, writing to *The Independent* (3 August 1992), expressed the belief that: 'academics, often unconsciously, have lowered their requirements for work to what their students are able to do, so that an Upper Second in 1992 may involve less work than a Lower Second in 1984.'

In the light of such views, there is no reason to believe that a return to a greater open-ness within higher education can be embarked on lightly, or that there will be a ready acceptance in the university world of a wider application of some of the recent developments described in the previous chapter. There are still many who find it difficult to believe that the opportunities now increasingly being offered to part-time and adult students in any way form a valid academic experience worthy of certification by a university. And it needs to be recognized that the real traditions of the British open universities, which disappeared as a consequence of the seller's market of the last 40 years, are not necessarily best revived by complex manipulations of the certification system.

Nor for most students is the abandonment of certification an option. As noted in Chapter 2, one branch of the Victorian extension movement, when faced by the increasingly elitist demands of the university establishment, chose to opt out of the search for certification and instead organize a tutorial system in which study was pursued for its own sake. Such activities, when well conducted, attracted many students but earned only limited academic respect. All too often they were and are seen as optional extras in the university's array of provision, something to be dispensed with when times are hard or to be converted into a vehicle for something more 'useful', such as professional updating, that will attract outside funding.

As Tough has demonstrated, in advanced western societies there is a far wider body of potential students for higher education than we have usually imagined. Such students are willing to arrange courses of study for themselves, and independently seek appropriate information and support from many agencies (Tough 1971). But these activities require considerable personal resource and initiative if they are to be successful and satisfying. They can also prove expensive for those involved. Even groups of enthusiastic students and tutors, as the well-supported Open College of the Arts founded by Michael Young in the mid-1980s soon discovered, cannot long survive nowadays without funding from either private or government patronage, or from the fees of students intent on some sort of certification.

It was the existence of just such a body of students, keen on degree-level study, that kept the Victorian open universities going, and that much later convinced government of the Open University's viability. The future of the more open tradition of British university life probably does not lie, therefore, in self-organization, in the complexities of module transfer, or in the conversion of experience into credits, useful as these may be. It probably lies rather in a development of an open university system or systems that will regain some of the simplicity of structure, adaptability and cheapness of their Victorian predecessors.

Clearly, we cannot return very readily to the more restricted curriculum of the last century. The Royal University of Ireland and the St Andrews LLA scheme, had they survived, would no doubt (like the University of London external system) long since have had to make profound changes in the content of their courses. Many modern students would not be willing, as many London external students still are, to receive a syllabus and brief study guidance at the beginning of the academic year, and then make their own arrangements to prepare for examination. Many would probably be happier with an open learning package to guide them through their work. Some might well prefer to hire a tutor.

But it should be possible to allow a wider range of agencies to undertake the preparation of students, and for those agencies to be widespread throughout the country, offering students a real choice to suit their own taste, pocket and previous experience. As universities themselves, under increasing financial pressure, begin to question some of the certainties of the last three decades in a rather more flexible way, there is now a chance for the open university systems of the future to develop in a more challenging and less cautious fashion.

It is important, however, that, if we are to develop sensible alternatives, they should be based on a truer interpretation of our universities' past, and on a fuller understanding of the line of well-tried open university traditions.

References

Adams, J. (1923) *Report of the Imperial Education Conference*. London, Imperial Education Conference.

Adams, W. (1947) 'Higher education in the British colonies', *Universities Quarterly*, 1, 145–53.

Adams, W. (1950) 'Colonial university education', *Universities Quarterly*, 4, 283–92.

Akenson, D. (1970) *The Irish University Experiment: The National System of Education in the Nineteenth Century*. London, Routledge and Kegan Paul.

Allchin, W. (1905) *An Account of the Reconstruction of the University of London*, 3 volumes. London, Lewis, Eyre and Spottiswoode.

Anderson, R. (1983) *Education and Opportunity in Victorian Scotland: Schools and Universities*. Oxford, Oxford University Press.

Armytage, W. (1955) *Civic Universities: Aspects of a British Tradition*. London, Benn.

Asch, D. and Smith, R. (1988) 'Management education and distance learning: a new model?', *Management Education and Development*, 19(2), 116–26.

Ashby, E. and Anderson, M. (1966) *Universities, British, Indian, African: A Study in the Ecology of Higher Education*. Harvard University Press.

Attwater, A. (1936) *Pembroke College, Cambridge: A Short History*. Cambridge University Press.

Bååth, J. (1981) 'On the nature of distance education', *Distance Education*, 2(2), 212–19.

Bagley, B. and Challis, B. (1985) *Inside Open Learning*. Coombe Lodge, Further Education Staff College.

Barnet College of Further Education (1980) *Flexi-study: A Manual for Local Colleges*. Cambridge, National Extension College.

Barnett, R. (1990) *The Idea of Higher Education*. Milton Keynes, Open University Press.

Bartle, G. (1976) *A History of Borough Road College*. Kettering, Dalkeith Press.

Bates, A. (ed.) (1984) *The Role of Technology in Distance Education*. London, Croom Helm.

Beaglehole, J. (1937) *The University of New Zealand: An Historical Study*. Auckland, Council for Educational Research.

Bell, R. (1965) *The MA Degree in the English Universities*, MEd thesis. Edinburgh University.

Bell, R. (1973) 'The growth of the modern university', in R. Bell and A. Youngson (eds) *Present and Future in Higher Education*. London, Tavistock.

Bell, R. (1986) *Educational Studies in the Scottish Universities, 1870–1970*, PhD thesis. Open University.

Bellot, H. (1929) *University College London, 1826–1926*. London, University of London Press.

Bellot, H. (1969) *The University of London: A History*. Bristol, privately printed (reprint of an extract from Volume 1 of the Victoria History of the County of Middlesex).

Benn, C. and Simon, B. (1970) *Half Way There: A Report on British Comprehensive School Reform*. London, McGraw Hill.

Birch, D. and Latham, J. (1984) *Managing Open Learning*. Coombe Lodge, Further Education Staff College.

Bittner, W. and Mallory, H. (1933) *University Teaching by Mail: A Survey of Correspondence Instruction*. New York, Macmillan.

Board of Education (1926) *Report of the Departmental Committee on the University of London*, Cmd 2612. London, HMSO.

Boot, R. and Hodgson, V. (1987) 'Open learning: meaning and experience', in V. Hodgson, S. Mann and R. Snell (eds) *Beyond Distance Teaching Towards Open Learning*. Milton Keynes, Open University Press.

Bowen, D. (1983) *Paul, Cardinal Cullen and the Shaping of Modern Irish Catholicism*. Dublin, Gill and Macmillan.

Boyer, E. (1987) *College: The Undergraduate Experience in America*. New York, Harper and Row.

Bremner, C. (1897) *The Education of Girls and Women in Great Britain*. London, Swan Sonnenschein.

Brook, F. (1958) *The University of London 1820–1860, with Special Reference to its Influence on the Development of Higher Education*. PhD thesis. University of London.

Brubacher, J. (1978) *The Philosophy of Higher Education*. San Francisco, Jossey-Bass.

Bryant, M. (1986) *The London Experience of Secondary Education*. London, Athlone Press.

Bryson, J. and Hakimian, H. (1992) 'The Wye College external programme and third world agriculture', in G. Rumble and J. Olivera (eds) *Vocational Education at a Distance*. London, Kogan Page.

Burgess, T. and Pratt, J. (1970) *Policy and Practice: The Colleges of Advanced Technology*. London, Allen Lane, Penguin Press.

Burns, C. (1924) *A Short History of Birkbeck College*. London, University of London Press.

Bynner, J. (1992) 'The rise of open learning: a UK approach to work-related education and training', *International Journal of Lifelong Education*, 11(2), 103–14.

Cant, R. (1970) *The University of St Andrews: A Short History*. Edinburgh, Scottish Academic Press.

Carr-Saunders, A. (1961) *New Universities Overseas*. London, George Allen and Unwin.

Cerych, L. and Sabatier, P. (1985) *Great Expectations and Mixed Performance: The Implementation of Higher Education Reforms in Europe*. Stoke-on-Trent, Trentham Books.

Charlton, H. (1951) *Portrait of a University 1851–1951: To Commemorate the Centenary of Manchester University*. Manchester, Manchester University Press.

Clarke, A. (1953) *A History of Cheltenham Ladies' College, 1853–1953*. London, Faber.

Colonial Office (1945a) *Report of the Commission on Higher Education in the Colonies.* Cmd 6647. London, HMSO.

Colonial Office (1945b) *Report of the West Indies Committee of the Commission on Higher Education in the Colonies.* Cmd 6654. London, HMSO.

Colonial Office (1945c) *Report of the Commission on Higher Education in West Africa.* Cmd 6655. London, HMSO.

Committee of Enquiry into the Academic Validation of Degree Courses in Public Sector Higher Education (1985) *Report.* Cmnd 9501. London, HMSO.

Committee of Enquiry into the Governance of the University of London (1972) *Final Report.* London, University of London.

Committee on Higher Education (1963) *Report, Appendices and Evidence.* Cmnd 2154. London, HMSO.

Cotgrove, S. (1958) *Technical Education and Social Change.* London, George Allen and Unwin.

Cottle, B. and Sherborne, J. (1951) *The Life of a University.* Bristol, Bristol University Press.

Cruickshank, M. (1970) *A History of the Training of Teachers in Scotland.* London, University of London Press.

Curran, C. (1992) 'Institutional models of distance education: a national cooperative programme', *Higher Education Management,* 4(1), 54–70.

Curtis, S. (1965) *History of Education in Great Britain.* London, University Tutorial Press (6th edn).

Davie, G. (1961) *The Democratic Intellect: Scotland and Her Universities in the Nineteenth Century.* Edinburgh, Edinburgh University Press.

Davies, D. and Robertson, D. (1986) 'Open college: towards a new view of adult education', *Adult Education,* 59(2), 106–14.

Davies, T. (1977) *Open Learning Systems for Mature Students.* London, Council for Educational Technology.

Donaldson, J. (1911) *Addresses Delivered in the University of St Andrews, 1886–1910.* St Andrews, St Andrews University.

Dudley-Edwards, O. (1987) *Eamonn de Valera.* Cardiff, GPC Books.

Duke, C. (1967) *The London External Degree and the English Part-time Degree Student.* Leeds, Leeds University Press.

Dunsheath, P. and Miller, M. (1958) *Convocation in the University of London: The First Hundred Years.* London, Athlone Press.

Elliott, S. (1973) *Tuition by Correspondence: A Study of Growth in Britain, Principally During the Period 1870 to 1914,* MEd thesis. Leicester, University of Leicester.

Elliott, S. (1989) *University First Degrees by Part-time Evening Study in England and Wales: An Examination of Opportunity and Attitudes During Two Centuries,* PhD thesis. University of Birmingham.

Ellman, R. (1959) *James Joyce.* New York, Oxford University Press.

Erdos, R. (1967) *Teaching by Correspondence.* London, Longmans/UNESCO.

Evans, F. (1969) *Borough Polytechnic 1892–1969.* London, Borough Polytechnic.

Evans, N. (1983) *Curriculum Opportunity: A Map of Experiential Learning in Entry Requirements to Higher and Further Education Award Bearing Courses.* London, Further Education Unit.

Evans, N. (1988) *The Assessment of Prior Experiential Learning.* London, Council for National Academic Awards.

Evans, N. (1992) *Experiential Learning: Assessment and Accreditation.* London, Routledge.

Evans, T. and Nation, D. (1992) 'Theorising open and distance learning', *Open Learning*, 7(2), 3–13.

Faherty, J. (1976) *From Technical College to University: A Case Study of Brunel College*, MPhil thesis. Brunel University.

Fiddes, E. (1937) *Chapters in the History of Owens College and of Manchester University 1851–1914*. Manchester, Manchester University Press.

The First Book of Discipline (1560).

Fitzgerald, M. (1988) 'New developments in part-time provision', *Association for Part-time Higher Education Newsletter*, 2, 9–10.

Foden, F. (1989) *The Examiner: James Booth and the Origin of Common Examinations*. Leeds, University of Leeds Department of Adult and Continuing Education.

Freeman, R. (1982) 'Flexistudy', in J. Daniel, M. Stroud and J. Thompson (eds) *Learning at a Distance: A World Perspective*. Athabasca, Athabasca University.

Freeman, R. (1983) 'The National Extension College', in M. Tight (ed.) *Educational Opportunities for Adults*. London, Croom Helm.

Further Education Unit (1983) *Flexible Learning Opportunities*. London, Further Education Unit.

Garrison, D. (1985) 'Three generations of technological innovations in distance education', *Distance Education*, 6(2), 235–41.

Garrison, D. (1989) *Understanding Distance Education: a framework for the future*. London, Routledge.

Garrison, D. and Baynton, M. (1989) 'Beyond independence in distance education', in M. Moore and G. Clark (eds) *Readings in Principles of Distance Education*. Pennsylvania State University, American Center for the Study of Distance Education.

Garrison, D. and Shale, D. (1990) 'Tilting at windmills? Destroying mythology in distance education'. *International Council for Distance Education Bulletin*, 24, 42–6.

Glatter, R., Wedell, E., Harris, W. and Subramanian, S. (1971) *Study by Correspondence: An Enquiry into Correspondence Study for Examinations for Degrees and Other Advanced Qualifications*. London, Longman.

Godwin, G. (1939) *Queen Mary College: An Adventure in Education*. London, Queen Mary College.

Gosden, P. and Taylor, A. (eds) (1975) *Studies in the History of a University 1874–1974*. Leeds, Arnold.

Grant, N. (1973) 'The structure of higher education: some international comparisons', in R. Bell and A. Youngson (eds) *Present and Future in Higher Education*. London, Tavistock Press.

Gresham University Commission (1894) *The Report of the Commissioners Appointed to Consider the Draft Charter for the Proposed Gresham University in London, together with dissentient and other notes*. C 7259 and 7425. London, HMSO.

Halsey, A. and Trow, M. (1971) *The British Academics*. London, Faber and Faber.

Harris, D. (1987) *Openness and Closure in Distance Education*. London, Falmer Press.

Harris, W. (1972) *Home Study Students*. Manchester, University of Manchester Department of Adult Education.

Harris, W. (1975) *The Distance Tutor: Education by Correspondence*. Manchester, University of Manchester Department of Adult Education.

Harris, W. and Williams, J. (1977) *A Handbook on Distance Education*. Manchester, University of Manchester Department of Adult and Higher Education.

Harry, K. (1990) 'The Open University, United Kingdom', in B. Koul and J.

Jenkins (eds) *Distance Education: A Spectrum of Case Studies.* London, Kogan Page.

Harte, N. (1986) *The University of London 1836–1986: An Illustrated History.* London, Athlone Press.

Harte, N. and North, J. (1991) *The World of UCL 1828–1990.* London, University College London.

Hayek, F. (1946) 'The London School of Economics 1895–1945'. *Economica*, 13, 1–31.

Hearnshaw, F. (1929) *The Centenary History of King's College London, 1828–1928.* London, Harrap.

Hearnshaw, L. (1964) *A Short History of British Psychology.* London, Methuen.

Hodgson, V., Mann, S. and Snell, R. (1987) *Beyond Distance Teaching Towards Open Learning.* Milton Keynes, Open University Press.

Hofstadter, R. and Hardy, C. (1952) *The Development and Scope of Higher Education in the United States.* New York, Columbia University Press.

Holmberg, B. (1983) 'Guided didactic conversation in distance education', in D. Sewart, D. Keegan and B. Holmberg (eds) *Distance Education: International Perspectives.* London, Croom Helm.

Holmberg, B. (1986a) *Growth and Structure of Distance Education.* London, Croom Helm.

Holmberg, B. (1986b) 'A discipline of distance education', *Journal of Distance Education*, 1(1), 25–40.

Houle, C. (1974) *The External Degree.* San Francisco, Jossey-Bass.

Hoult, D. (1975) *The Open University: Its Origins and Establishment*, MEd thesis. Hull, University of Hull.

Huddersfield Technical College (1905) *Annual Report.* Huddersfield, Huddersfield Technical College.

Humberstone, T. (1926) *University Reform in London.* London, George Allen and Unwin.

Innes, S. (1988) 'The Open College: a personal view', in N. Paine (ed.) *Open Learning in Transition: An Agenda For Action.* Cambridge, National Extension College.

Innes, S. (1992) 'The British Open College: a flexible response', in G. Rumble and J. Olivera (eds) *Vocational Education at a Distance.* London, Kogan Page.

Inter-University Council for Higher Education Overseas (1955) *Inter-University Council for Higher Education Overseas 1946–54.* Cmd 9515. London, HMSO.

Irish Universities Commission (1902) *First Evidence.* Cmnd 826. Dublin, HMSO.

Irish Universities Commission (1903) *Final Report.* Cmnd 1483. Dublin, HMSO.

Jenkins, J. and Perraton, H. (1980) *The Invisible College: NEC 1963–1979.* Cambridge, International Extension College.

Johanningmeier, E. (1980) 'American educational research: the application and misapplication of psychology to education', in J. Smith and D. Hamilton (eds) *The Meritocratic Intellect.* Aberdeen, Aberdeen University Press.

Jones, D. (1988) *The Origins of Civic Universities: Manchester, Leeds and Liverpool.* London, Routledge.

Jordan, A. (1990) *Margaret Byers: Pioneer of Women's Education and Founder of Victoria College, Belfast.* Belfast, Queen's University Institute of Irish Studies.

Kaufman, D. (1989) 'Third generation course design in distance education', in R. Sweet (ed.) *Post-secondary Distance Education in Canada.* Athabasca, Canadian Society for Studies in Education.

Kaye, A. (1988) 'Distance education: the state of the art', *Prospects*, 18(1), 43–54.

Kaye, A. and Rumble, G. (eds) (1981) *Distance Teaching for Higher and Adult Education.* Beckenham, Croom Helm.

Kaye, A. and Rumble, G. (1991) 'Open universities: a comparative approach', *Prospects,* 21(2), 214–26.

Keegan, D. (1980) 'On defining distance education', *Distance Education,* 1(1), 13–36.

Keegan, D. (1986) *The Foundations of Distance Education.* Beckenham, Croom Helm.

Keegan, D. (1989) 'Problems in defining the field of distance education', in M. Moore and G. Clark (eds) *Readings in Principles of Distance Education.* American Center for the Study of Distance Education, Pennsylvania State University.

Keegan, D. and Rumble, G. (1982) 'Distance teaching at university level', in G. Rumble and K. Harry (eds) *The Distance Teaching Universities.* London, Croom Helm.

Kember, D, and Murphy, D, (1990) 'A synthesis of open, distance and student centred learning', *Open Learning,* 5(2), 3–8.

Kingdon, M. (1991) *The Reform of Advanced Level.* London, Hodder and Stoughton.

Knight, W. (1887) *The Higher Education of Women, with special reference to the St Andrews University LLA Title and Diploma.* Edinburgh, Blackwood.

Laidlaw, B. and Layard, R. (1974) 'Traditional versus Open University teaching methods: a cost comparison', *Higher Education,* 3, 439–68.

Lancaster, O. (1967) *With an Eye to the Future.* London, John Murray.

Lane, M. (1975) *Design for Degrees: New Degree Courses Under the CNAA 1964–1974.* London, Macmillan.

Laurance, D. (1969) *The College of Estate Management 1919–1969.* London, College of Estate Management.

Laurie, S. (1901) *The Training of Teachers and Methods of Instruction.* Cambridge, Cambridge University Press.

Lauzon, A. and Moore, G. (1989) 'A fourth generation distance education system: integrating computer-assisted learning and computer conferencing', *American Journal of Distance Education,* 3(1), 38–49.

Laws, S. (1946) *Northampton Polytechnic, London EC1, 1896–1946.* London, Northampton Polytechnic.

Lee, B. and Bibby, J. (1987) *The Feasibility of Adapting Open University Materials for Use in Polytechnics and Similar Institutions.* London, Council for National Academic Awards.

Legge, D. (1982) *The Education of Adults in Britain.* Milton Keynes, Open University Press.

Lewis, B. (1971) 'Course production at the Open University', *British Journal of Educational Technology,* 2, 4–13, 111–23, 189–204; 3, 108–28.

Lewis, B. (1973) 'Educational technology at the Open University: an approach to the problem of quality', *British Journal of Educational Technology,* 4, 188–204.

Lewis, R. (1986) 'What is open learning?', *Open Learning,* 1(2), 5–10.

Lewis, R. (1990) 'Open learning and the misuse of language: a response to Greville Rumble', *Open Learning,* 5(1), 3–8.

Lewis, R. and Spencer, D. (1986) *What is Open Learning?* London, Council for Educational Technology.

Locke, M. (1978) *Traditions and Controls in the Making of a Polytechnic: Woolwich Polytechnic 1890–1970.* Woolwich, Thames Polytechnic.

Lowe, J. (1970) *Adult Education in England and Wales: A Critical Survey.* London, Michael Joseph.

Lowe, R. (1988) *Education in the Postwar Years: A Social History.* London, Routledge.

Lumsden, L. (1911) 'The university education of women at St Andrews', in *Votiva Tabella: a memorial notice of St Andrews University*. St Andrews, St Andrews University.

McDowell, R. and Webb, D. (1982) *Trinity College, Dublin, 1592-1952: An Academic History*. Cambridge, Cambridge University Press.

McIntosh, N. (1974) 'The OU student', in J. Tunstall (ed.) *The Open University Opens*. London, Routledge and Kegan Paul.

McIntosh, N., Calder, J. and Swift, B. (1976) *A Degree of Difference: A Study of the First Year's Intake of Students to the Open University of the United Kingdom*. Guildford, Society for Research into Higher Education.

McIntosh, N., Woodley, A. and Morrison, V. (1980) 'Student demand and progress at the Open University: the first eight years', *Distance Education*, 1(1), 37–60.

MacKenzie, N., Postgate, R. and Scupham, J. (1975) *Open Learning: systems and problems in post-secondary education*. Paris, UNESCO.

MacKenzie, O., Christensen, E. and Rigby, P. (1968) *Correspondence Instruction in the United States*. New York, McGraw Hill.

McNay, I. (1988) 'Open learning: a jarring note', in N. Paine (ed.) *Open Learning in Transition: An Agenda for Action*. Cambridge, National Extension College.

McPherson, A (1973). 'Selections and survivals: a sociology of the ancient Scottish universities', in R. Brown (ed.) *Knowledge, Education and Cultural Change*. London, Tavistock.

Manpower Services Commission (1982) *An 'Open Tech' Programme: response to the consultation*. Sheffield, Manpower Services Commission.

Mansbridge, A. (1913) *University Tutorial Classes: A Study in the Development of Higher Education Among Working Men and Women*. London, Longmans Green.

Marriott, S. (1981) *A Backstairs to a Degree: Demands for an Open University in Late Victorian England*. Leeds, University of Leeds Department of Adult and Continuing Education.

Marriott, S. (1984) *Extramural Empires: Service and Self-Interest in English University Adult Education 1873–1983*. Nottingham, University of Nottingham Department of Adult Education.

Mason, R. and Kaye, A. (eds.) (1989) *Mindweave: Communications, Computers and Distance Education*. Oxford, Pergamon Press.

Maxwell, I. (1980) *Universities in Partnership: The Inter-University Council and the Growth of Higher Education in Developing Countries 1946–70*. Edinburgh, Scottish Academic Press.

Meenan, J. (ed.) (1956) *Centenary History of the Literary and Historical Society of University College, Dublin, 1855–1955*. Tralee, Kerryman.

Ministry of Education (1956) *Technical Education*. Cmnd 9703. London, HMSO.

Ministry of Education, Scottish Education Department (1960) *Grants to Students*. Cmnd 1051. London, HMSO.

Montgomery, R. (1965) *Examinations: An Account of Their Evolution as Administrative Devices in England*. London, Longman.

Moody, T. (1957) 'Higher education', in *Ulster Since 1800*. London, British Broadcasting Corporation.

Moody, T. (1958) 'The Irish university question of the nineteenth century', *History*, 43, 148.

Moody, T. and Beckett, J. (1959) *Queen's, Belfast, 1845–1949: The History of a University*. London, Faber and Faber.

Moore, M. (1973) 'Toward a theory of independent learning and teaching', *Journal of Higher Education*, 44(12), 661–79.

Moore, M. (1977) 'A model of independent study', *Epistolo Didaktida*, 1, 6–40.

Moore, M. (1990) 'Recent contributions to the theory of distance education', *Open Learning*, 5(3), 10–15.

Morpeth, R. (1988) 'The National Extension College: present and future', *Open Learning*, 3(2), 34–6.

Namie, Y. (1989) *The Role of the University of London Colonial Examinations Between 1900 and 1939, with special reference to Mauritius, the Gold Coast and Ceylon*, PhD thesis. University of London.

National Extension College (1981) *Flexistudy: Some Questions Answered*. Cambridge, National Extension College.

National Extension College (1986) *Open Tech Directory*. Cambridge, National Extension College.

Newman, J. (1859) *On the Scope and Nature of University Education*. London, Dent (1915 edn).

Nipper, S. (1989) 'Third generation distance learning and computer conferencing', in R. Mason and A. Kaye (eds) *Mindweave: Communication, Computers and Distance Education*. Oxford, Pergamon Press.

Noffsinger, J. (1926) *Correspondence Schools, Lyceums and Chautauquas*. New York, Macmillan.

Northcott, P. (1986) 'Distance education for managers: an international perspective', *Open Learning*, 1(2), 33–41.

O'Connor, U. (1964) *Oliver St John Gogarty: A Poet and His Times*. London, Jonathan Cape.

Omolewa, M. (1976) 'London University's earliest examinations in Nigeria, 1887–1931'. *West African Journal of Education*, 20(2), 347–60.

Omolewa, M. (1980) 'The promotion of London University examinations in Nigeria, 1887–1951', *International Journal of African Historical Studies*, 13(4), 651–71.

Open Polytechnic (1992) *Open Polytechnic: Creating New Opportunities in Higher Education*. London, Open Polytechnic.

Open University (1972) *The Early Development of the Open University: Report of the Vice-Chancellor January 1969 – December 1970*. Milton Keynes, Open University.

Open University (1973a) *The First Teaching Year of the Open University: Report of the Vice-Chancellor 1971*. Milton Keynes, Open University.

Open University (1973b) *Report of the Vice-Chancellor to the Council 1972*. Milton Keynes, Open University.

Open University (1992a) *Open University Statistics 1990: Students, Staff and Finance*. Milton Keynes, Open University.

Open University (1992b) *Strategic Plan, 1992: Third Draft*. Milton Keynes, Open University.

Open University Planning Committee (1969) *Report to the Secretary of State for Education and Science*. London, HMSO.

O'Reilly, D. (1991) 'Developing opportunities for independent learners', *Open Learning*, 6(3), 3–13.

Paine, N. (ed.) (1988) *Open Learning in Transition: An Agenda for Action*. Cambridge, National Extension College.

Parton, H. (1979) *The University of New Zealand*. Auckland, Auckland University Press.

Patterson, A. (1962) *The University of Southampton: A Centenary History of the Evolution and Development of the University of Southampton, 1862–1962*. Southampton, University of Southampton.

Pattison, B. (1984) *Special Relations: The University of London and New Universities Overseas, 1947–1970*. London, University of London.

Paul, R. (1990) *Open Learning and Open Management: Leadership and Integrity in Distance Education*. London, Kogan Page.

Pearson, K. (1892) *The New University for London: A Guide to its History and a Criticism of its Defects*. London, Fisher Unwin.

Pedley, R. (1977) *Towards the Comprehensive University*. London, Macmillan.

Percy, K., Ramsden, P. and Lewin, J. (1980) *Independent Study: Two Examples from English Higher Education*. Guildford, Society for Research into Higher Education.

Perraton, H. (1987) 'Theories, generalisation and practice in distance education', *Open Learning*, 2(3), 3–12.

Perry, W. (1976) *Open University: A Personal Account by the First Vice-Chancellor*. Milton Keynes, Open University Press.

Peters, O. (1965) *Der Fernunterricht*. Weinheim, Julius Beltz.

Peters, O. (1983) 'Distance education and industrial production: a comparative interpretation in outline', in D. Sewart, D. Keegan and B. Holmberg (eds), *Distance Education: International Perspectives*. Beckenham, Croom Helm.

Peters, O. (1989) 'The iceberg has not melted: further reflections on the concept of industrialisation and distance teaching', *Open Learning*, 4(3), 3–8.

Peterson, A. (1961) 'The higher education of teachers', *Hibbert Journal*, 59, 146–53. London, Allen and Unwin.

Pittman, V. (1990) 'Correspondence study in the American university: a historiographic perspective', in M. Moore, P. Cookson, J. Donaldson, and B. Quigley (eds) *Contemporary Issues in American Distance Education*. Oxford, Pergamon Press.

Pratt, J. and Burgess, T. (1974) *Polytechnics: A Report*. London, Pitman Publishing.

Reader, W. (1966) *Professional Men: The Rise of the Professional Classes in Nineteenth Century England*. London, Weidenfeld and Nicolson.

Redgrave, M. (1983) *To My Mind's Eye: An Autobiography*. London, Weidenfeld and Nicolson.

Richardson, M. (1988) 'The National Extension College and the Open University: a comparison of two national institutions', in N. Paine (ed.) *Open Learning in Transition: An Agenda for Action*. Cambridge, National Extension College.

Rice, G. (1957) *The Royal University of Ireland, 1879–1909*, MA thesis. University College, Cork.

Robinson, E. (1968) *The New Polytechnics*. London, Cornmarket.

Rogers, W. (1983) 'Alternative uses of materials: research findings', *Teaching at a Distance*, 25, 58–68.

Rogers, W. (1984) 'Alternative uses of materials', *Teaching at a Distance*, 26, 49–54.

Roget, D. (1887) *An Introduction to Old French*. Oxford, Oxford University Press.

Rothblatt, S. (1968) *The Revolution of the Dons: Cambridge and Society in Victorian England*. London, Faber and Faber.

Rothblatt, S. (1987) 'Historical and comparative remarks on the federal principle in higher education'. *History of Education*, 16(3), 151–80.

Royal Commission on University Education in London (1913) *Final Report*. Cd 6717. London, HMSO.

Royal University of Ireland, *Calendar* (RUIC).

Royal University of Ireland, Senate, *Minutes* (RUISM).

Royal University of Ireland, Standing Committee, *Minutes* (RUISCM).

Rumble, G. (1982) *The Open University of the United Kingdom: An Evaluation of an Innovative Experience in the Democratisation of Higher Education*. Milton Keynes, Open University Distance Education Research Group.

Rumble, G. (1986) *The Planning and Management of Distance Education*. Beckenham, Croom Helm.

Rumble, G. (1989) '"Open learning", "distance learning", and the misuse of language', *Open Learning*, 4(2), 28–36.

Rumble, G. (1992) 'The competitive vulnerability of distance teaching universities', *Open Learning*, 7(2), 31–45.

Rumble, G. and Harry, K. (eds) (1982) *The Distance Teaching Universities*. Beckenham, Croom Helm.

Sacks, H. (1980) 'Flexistudy: an open learning system for further and adult education', *British Journal of Educational Technology*, 11(2), 85–95.

Scales, K. (1983) 'A typology applied to distance education in British Columbia', *Lifelong Learning*, 7(3), 14, 26–28.

Scottish Education Department (1982) *Distance No Object: Examples of Open Learning in Scotland*. Edinburgh, HMSO.

Scottish Tertiary Education Advisory Council (1985) *Future Strategy for Higher Education in Scotland*. Cmnd 9676. Edinburgh, HMSO.

Scottish Universities Commission (1893) *Evidence*. Cmnd 276. Edinburgh, HMSO.

Scrimgeour, R. (ed.) (1950) *The North London Collegiate School for Girls 1850–1950*. Oxford, University Press.

Secretary of State for Education and Science (1966) *A University of the Air*. Cmnd 2922. London, HMSO.

Servan-Schreiber, J. (1969) *The American Challenge*. Harmondsworth, Penguin.

Shale, D. (1990) 'Toward a reconceptualisation of distance education', in M. Moore, P. Cookson, J. Donaldson and B. Quigley (eds) *Contemporary Issues in American Distance Education*. Oxford, Pergamon.

Shale, D. and Garrison, D. (1990) 'Education and communication', in D. Garrison and D. Shale (eds) *Education at a Distance: From Issues to Practice*. Malabar, Florida, Robert Krieger.

Sherow, S. and Wedemeyer, C. (1990) 'Origins of distance education in the United States', in D. Garrison and D. Shale (eds) *Education at a Distance: From Issues to Practice*. Malabar, Florida, Robert Krieger.

Shinn, C. (1986) *Paying the Piper: The Development of the University Grants Committee 1919–46*. London, Falmer Press.

Silver, H. (1990) *A Higher Education: the Council for National Academic Awards and British Higher Education 1964–1989*. London, Falmer Press.

Simmons, J. (1958) *New University*. Leicester, Leicester University Press.

Simpson, R. (1983) *How the PhD came to Britain: A Century of Struggle for Postgraduate Education*. Guildford, Society for Research into Higher Education.

Smart, R. (1968) 'Literate ladies: a fifty year experiment', *St Andrews University Alumnus Chronicle*, 59, 21–31.

Smith, D. and Saunders, M. (1989) 'Costing part-time provision', *Open Learning*, 4(3), 28–34.

Smith, P. and Kelly, M. (eds) (1987) *Distance Education and the Mainstream: Convergence in Education*. London, Croom Helm.

Southey, R. and Southey, C. (1844) *The Life of Dr Andrew Bell*. London.

Sparrow, J. (1967) *Mark Pattison and the Idea of a University*. Cambridge, Cambridge University Press.

Stephenson, J. (1980) 'Higher Education: School for Independent Study', in T. Burgess and E. Adams (eds) *Outcomes of Education*. London, Macmillan.

Stewart, W. (1989) *Higher Education in Postwar Britain*. London, Macmillan.

Teachers of the Society of Jesus (1930) *A Page of Irish History: The Story of University College, Dublin*. Dublin, Talbot Press.

Teshome, A. (1990) 'Wye external programme: current practices and prospects for development'. *Distance Education*, 11(1), 161-72.

Thompson, F. (ed.) (1990a) *The University of London and the World of Learning, 1836–1986*. London, Hambledon Press.

Thompson, F. (1990b) 'The humanities', in F. Thompson (ed.) *The University of London and the World of Learning, 1836-1986*. London, Hambledon Press.

Thorpe, M. and Grugeon, D. (eds) (1987) *Open Learning for Adults*. Harlow, Longman.

Tierney, M. (ed.) (1954) *Struggle with Fortune: A Miscellany for the Centenary of the Catholic University of Ireland, 1854–1954*. Dublin, Browne and Nolan.

Tierney, M. (1980) *Eion MacNeill: Scholar and Man of Achievement*. Oxford, Clarendon Press.

Tight, M. (1987a) 'Mixing distance and face-to-face higher education', *Open Learning*, 2(1), 14–18.

Tight, M. (1987b) 'London University external developments', *Open Learning*, 2(2), 49–51.

Tight, M. (1988a) 'Distance education: discipline and service', *Journal of Distance Education*, 3(1), 81–4.

Tight, M. (1988b) 'Defining distance education', *International Council for Distance Education Bulletin*, 18, 56–60.

Tight, M. (1988c) 'Open learning for continuing education', *Open Learning*, 3(2), 23–6.

Tight, M. (1989a) 'The ideology of higher education', in O. Fulton (ed.) *Access and Institutional Change*. Milton Keynes, Open University Press.

Tight, M. (1989b) 'Open learning and continuing education', in P. Jarvis (ed.) *Britain: Policies and Practice in Continuing Education*. San Francisco, Jossey-Bass.

Tight, M. (1990) *Higher Education: A Part-Time Perspective*. Milton Keynes, Open University Press.

Tight, M. (1992) 'Reclaiming our traditions: part-time higher education in Britain', *Higher Education Review*, 24(2), 52–73.

Tolley, G. (1983) *The Open Tech: Why, What and How?* London, Association of Colleges for Further and Higher Education.

Tough, A. (1971) *The Adult's Learning Projects: A Fresh Approach to Theory and Practice in Adult Learning*. Toronto, Ontario Institute for Studies in Education.

Tunstall, J. (ed.) (1974) *The Open University Opens*. London, Routledge and Kegan Paul.

Tyson, J. and Tuck, J. (1971) *The Origins and Development of the Training of Teachers in the University of Newcastle upon Tyne*. Newcastle upon Tyne, University of Newcastle upon Tyne.

Unit for the Development of Adult Continuing Education (1989) *Open College Networks: Current Developments and Practice*. Leicester, UDACE.

University College, Dundee (1883) *The Opening Ceremony, Professor Stuart's Inaugural*

Address, and Description of the College Buildings. Dundee, University College Dundee.

University of Glasgow, Correspondence Course Committee, *Minutes.*

University of London (1966) *Reorganisation 1964–1966.* London, University of London.

University of London (1982) *Discussion Paper by the Vice-Chancellor on the Future of the London External System.* London, University of London.

University of London (1983) *The University's Policy for the External System.* London, University of London.

University of London, *Calendar* (ULC). Published annually from 1844.

University of London, *Minutes of Senate* (ULSM). Series begins 4/3/1837.

University of London, Advisory Service for External Students, *Annual Reports* (ULASESAR). Series begins in 1925.

University of London, Commerce Degree Bureau, *Annual Reports* (ULCDBAR). Series begins in 1923.

University of London, Committee for External Students (1987) *Independent Guided Study: Final Report.*

University of London, Committee for External Students (1988) *The Strategic Development Plan.*

University of London, Council for External Students (1910) *Report for Transmission to the Royal Commission on University Education in London.*

University of London, Council for External Students, *Minutes* (ULCESM). Series begins in 1900. Council later changes its name to Committee for External Students.

University of London Commission (1889) *Report of the Royal Commissioners Appointed to inquire whether any and what kind of University or Powers is or are required for the Advancement of Higher Education in London.* C 5709. London, HMSO.

University of St Andrews, LLA Committee, *Minutes* (USALLACM).

University of St Andrews, Local Examinations Committee, *Minutes* (USALECM).

University of St Andrews, Senate, *Minutes.*

Valley, J. (1972) 'External degree programs', in S. Gould and K. Cross (eds) *Explorations in Non-traditional Study.* San Francisco, Jossey-Bass.

Venables, P. (1978) *Higher Education Developments: The Technological Universities 1956–1976.* London, Faber.

Verduin, J. and Clark, T. (1991) *Distance Education: The Foundations of Effective Practice.* San Francisco, Jossey-Bass.

Wagner, L. (1972) 'The economics of the Open University', *Higher Education,* 1, 159–83.

Wagner, L. (1977) 'The economics of the Open University revisited', *Higher Education,* 6, 359–81.

Wagner, L. (1982) *The Economics of Educational Media.* London, Macmillan.

Walsh, W. (1897) *The Irish University Question.* Dublin, Gill.

Webb, S. (1904) *London Education.* London, Longmans Green.

Weil, S. and McGill, I. (eds) (1989) *Making Sense of Experiential Learning: Diversity in Theory and Practice.* Milton Keynes, Open University Press.

Whitburn, J., Mealing, M. and Cox, C. (1976) *People in Polytechnics: A Survey of Polytechnic Staff and Students 1972/3.* Guildford, Society for Research into Higher Education.

Whiting, C. (1932) *The University of Durham 1832–1932.* London, Sheldon Press.

Winstanley, D. (1940) *Early Victorian Cambridge*. Cambridge, Cambridge University Press.

Wood, A. (1953) *A History of the University College Nottingham 1881–1948*. Oxford, Blackwell.

Wood, E. (1965) *A History of the Polytechnic*. London, Macdonald.

Woodley, A. (1986) 'Distance students in the United Kingdom', *Open Learning*, 1(2), 11–13.

Woodley, A., Wagner, L., Slowey, M., Hamilton, M. and Fulton, O. (1987) *Choosing to Learn: Adults in Education*. Milton Keynes, Open University Press.

Woodward, R. and Broder, D. (1992) *The Man Who Would Be President Dan Quayle*. London, Sceptre.

Young, D. (1969) *St Andrews: Town and Gown, Royal and Ancient*. London, Cassell.

Index